MW01628416

NEW CHRISTIANITY FOR THE NEW SOUTH

NEW CHRISTIANITY FOR THE NEW SOUTH

William Louis Poteat and Liberal Religion in the Baptist South

PAUL A. SANCHEZ

Published by the University of South Carolina Press
Columbia, South Carolina 29208

uscpress.com

Printed in the United States of America

Library of Congress Cataloging-in-Publication Data
can be found at http://catalog.loc.gov/.

ISBN: 978-1-64336-631-9 (hardcover)
ISBN: 978-1-64336-686-9 (ebook)

To my beloved Sanchez Team

Contents

Preface

From the time that I began my doctoral program, I planned to write on Southern Baptists during the Civil War to explore the religious life of evangelicals under wartime conditions. When the record of primary sources proved thinner than expected, my supervisor, Greg Wills, asked if I were familiar with a Baptist figure named William Louis Poteat. I had heard the name but knew little about him or the religious movement that he helped lead in the early twentieth century. By the end of this initial conversation my curiosity was piqued. Although as an evangelical Christian I could hardly be a disinterested observer when studying the clash in American Protestantism between fundamentalists and liberals, I was intrigued by the questions that framed this story, both theological and historical, as I reflected on the spiritual and intellectual crisis many educated Americans faced in this period. With only a brief exploration of the topic, I became fascinated with Poteat and his place in the larger story of liberal Christianity in America. As my research progressed, I became absorbed by the Southern scene in which I sensed a connection between the growth of liberalism and the rise of the New South in the late nineteenth and early twentieth century. This connection proved to be a pivotal part of the narrative that emerged.

Examining social location in the New South provided insight into the transformation that took place in American religion with education and social class suggesting a powerful influence. Most scholars seemed to suggest that theological liberalism had been almost nonexistent in the South, especially among Baptists. However I found a surprising number of counterexamples as something resembling a movement became evident, which consequently provided even more ground to explore. I concluded that as social conditions emerged in the South that mirrored those taking root in the urbanizing North, analogous cultural and religious phenomena arose in southern towns and cities. I believe this work provides fresh insight into the story of religion in the South during the New South era.

It also furnishes a broader picture of liberal Protestantism in America by suggesting that theological liberalism was a national phenomenon, even as scholars, with some notable exceptions, have focused almost exclusively on the northern United States when studying this movement.

This project took me to archives across the southeastern United States. The Southern Baptist Historical Library and Archives hold an impressive collection, and Taffey Hall and her staff were exceptionally helpful. At Samford University's Harwell Goodwin Davis Library, Rachel Cohen and her staff were accommodating and resourceful. The staff at Furman University's James B. Duke Library Special Collections provided materials related to Edwin McNeill Poteat Sr. and the Poteat family. Jason Tomberlin and the staff at the University of North Carolina's Louis Round Wilson Library and Special Collections were exceptionally professional and provided a delightful environment for research. A visit to Southeastern Baptist Theological Seminary allowed me to walk the original campus of Wake Forest College, where William Louis Poteat was president. I stood in the building where Poteat conducted scientific experiments in his laboratory. Southeastern's librarian, Jason Fowler, discussed the history of Wake Forest and Poteat with me and provided insights for my research. Wake Forest University's Z. Smith Reynolds Library holds the William Louis Poteat collection. Rebecca Peterson May and her staff made the days that I spent there over two separate trips a pleasant experience. I made several visits to the James P. Boyce Library at the Southern Baptist Theological Seminary. Archivist Adam Winters was always helpful, and his personal knowledge of the field of study never ceased to impress me. I would like to thank the North Caroliniana Society for selecting me for the Archie K. Davis Fellowship, which provided a grant for my research.

I owe Greg Wills a great debt of gratitude for his guidance and mentorship during the original version of this project. His own interest and background in this area of research proved invaluable to me, as did his insights into the central questions that emerged from my research. Wills's personal knowledge of archival collections helped me considerably. I am also thankful to John Wilsey, who served on my dissertation committee and provided valuable insights after reading the manuscript and beforehand through several conversations. His interest in the history of ideas inspired me as I explored the late nineteenth and early twentieth centuries' intellectual currents and considered how the rise of theological liberalism was shaped by the conditions of one's social and cultural location. Stephen Wellum, a theologian, offered insights related to the key theological questions in my work. Ken Stewart provided meticulous feedback through notes and substantive engagement, especially related to Poteat's conservative opponents. Feedback from other scholars, as anonymous reviewers, revealed weaknesses in my work and helped clarify my argument. Much credit is due to these scholars. Any remaining deficiencies in this work are naturally mine alone.

Most important, I am thankful for the unwavering support of my family throughout my work, including through the process of revising this manuscript for publication. I could never have completed it without my wife's perpetual encouragement and support. And I am truly grateful for my children's patient understanding, as well as their honest curiosity about my work as a historian. I love them dearly. I hope watching me inspires them to value history and more important to learn from it.

Chapter One

A TRADITIONAL FAITH

William L. Poteat's upbringing in the rural South and within the spiritual atmosphere of a Southern Baptist church is hardly the background that one expects of a public champion of liberal theology. Poteat was a kindred spirit to contemporaries like Shailer Matthews, George Burman Foster, and William Newton Clarke. The story of Poteat's devotion to liberal Christianity challenges the common narrative about southern religion in the early twentieth century. The assumption of a uniformly conservative South has led most scholars to overlook the region when studying the rise of theological liberalism in America. As a result, liberalism has been considered almost exclusively a northern phenomenon rather than a national movement that impacted American Protestantism as a whole. The story of this southern educator and public intellectual offers a fresh counter-narrative. It suggests a greater level of complexity in southern religion and society by revealing a liberal movement in the South that paralleled the better-known story of American theological liberalism. Poteat's long tenure as professor of biology and president of North Carolina Baptists' Wake Forest College provided a strategic base from which to firmly establish a tradition of theological liberalism among Southern Baptists. His influence extended far beyond Wake Forest to other academic institutions, churches, and civic groups through his publications, academic lectures, speeches, and personal relationships. He was the most public and outspoken of Baptist liberals in the South in the first half of the twentieth century. And Poteat was not the only one but played a leading role in spreading liberalism among Baptists in North Carolina and the South. In alliance with several like-minded leaders, Poteat left an enduring legacy for the region's religious history.

At a young age however Poteat adopted the traditional Baptist faith of his family. Throughout his studies at Wake Forest College in the 1870s, he maintained traditional evangelical views, but a dramatic shift occurred when he began his career as a professor. This shift was precipitated by a confrontation with modern ideas that led him to question the truthfulness of the Bible, the relationship between science and religion, and ultimately the viability of Christianity in the modern age. Emerging from his crisis, Poteat embraced Darwinian evolution to explain the earth's biological origins and modified his religious views for a comprehensive redefinition of Christianity. But the relative ease of Poteat's shift seems unexpected in light of his background in a region and ecclesial denomination that have often been characterized as monolithically conservative in the late nineteenth and early twentieth century.

Poteat did more than embrace new views. He became a leading religious figure in the South and a public representative of a modernized Christianity. He aimed to revise Christianity for the cultured despisers of southern society, both real and imagined. Poteat was captivated by the drama of the modern age. The challenges raised in the nineteenth century led him, like many others, to feel uneasy about his faith. One of Poteat's colleagues in the Baptist Congress, an annual gathering of Baptist leaders from across the United States, summarized the challenges that educated evangelicals like Poteat faced: "We are living in an iconoclastic age. The very foundations of truth are being tested afresh." He argued that if religious tradition and dogma failed to pass the tests of modernity, they would be "torn to pieces."[1] Poteat felt the power of the challenges raised by modern currents of thought and the new sentiments of the age that made Christianity appear suspect. Poteat determined that the only hope of maintaining Christianity's relevance in the modern world was to remake Christianity into a truly modern religion.

Several works have explored Poteat's life and portions of his career, but none has been dedicated primarily to his thought and religious life. Two full-length works on Poteat have appeared since the 1960s. Historian Randal L. Hall's *William Louis Poteat: A Leader of the Progressive-Era South* was published in 2000, and Suzanne C. Linder's *William Louis Poteat: Prophet of Progress* was published in 1966. Both are traditional biographies and focused on the breadth of Poteat's life and career. Hall gave special attention to Poteat's work as an educator and activist in the Progressive-Era South. Linder approached Poteat through a decidedly congenial lens and depicted him as a noble crusader for social and cultural progress in North Carolina and the South. Willard B. Gatewood Jr.'s *Preachers, Pedagogues, & Politicians: The Evolutionary Controversy in North Carolina, 1920–1927* was published in 1966 and explored Poteat's role in North Carolina's evolution controversies in the 1920s. This book however centers on Poteat's thought and religious life with the goal of adding insight into the emergence and spread of theological liberalism among Baptists in the South. It explores the social and cultural setting of liberal religion in the South with the aim of illuminating the motivations and ideas that energized Poteat and his liberal contemporaries in the formative New South era. Taking into account a notable oversight of research on liberalism in the South, I argue that a southern wing of theological liberals emerged in the South in the early twentieth century connected to the cultural impulse and social transformation of the New South. Although closely resembling their northern counterparts theologically, southern liberals did not achieve the same level of dominance as their northern counterparts. However Poteat proved that outspoken liberals could thrive among Southern Baptists in the highest places of leadership and influence, and a relatively small but noteworthy number of them did so. This story reveals how a theological modernist became a Southern Baptist statesman in the early twentieth century.

RELIGIOUS BACKGROUND

Poteat grew up within a conventional evangelical family and a conservative church setting. His mother, Julia McNeill Poteat, came from a family of committed Baptists and was herself educated at a Baptist college in Oxford, North Carolina.[2] The early religious background of William Poteat's father James is uncertain, but shortly after he married Julia, James began attending the local Baptist church in Yanceyville, North Carolina. James and two of his sons from a previous marriage professed faith in Jesus Christ, were baptized in the summer of 1858, and became members of the church. In short order James became a clerk, deacon, and church trustee.[3] William Poteat was two years old when his father and half-brothers were baptized. From his early childhood he experienced a family that was committed to its local Baptist church and by every indication was a family that fully embodied a traditional Baptist faith. In addition to serving his local church, James assumed regional leadership in the local Baptist association and served on the executive committee and as moderator for annual meetings. In October 1866 he was appointed a trustee for North Carolina Baptists' Wake Forest College, which had reopened in January 1866 after its closure during the Civil War.[4]

William Poteat followed his father's example of denominational leadership, but the path that he took distanced him from his background in notable ways. The faith that characterized William Poteat's public career seemed to represent the New South as much as his father's symbolized the Old. The New South vision of progress did not dismiss southern tradition entirely, but neither did it look to the past for its driving impulse. Poteat eventually found enlightenment in a new arena of higher education that looked northward and across the Atlantic to follow the astonishing advances of modern science, along with revolutionary modes of thought that captivated many thoughtful men and women in this era. But from his childhood and early years of adulthood, Poteat's education and religious life seemed anything but progressive.

EARLY EDUCATION

Poteat was educated in the conventional mode for upper-class Southerners of his period. He had a privileged childhood and benefited from his wealthy family's resources. Randal Hall rightly indicated that by the time William Poteat was born in 1856 his family members had established themselves as part of the "southern aristocracy" of the Old South.[5]

The Poteats valued education. Formal education for the Poteat children began in the home with private teachers.[6] Their first teacher was an older cousin who taught them the basic rudiments of education. A subsequent teacher taught the children the core concepts of reading, writing, and arithmetic. William Poteat was precocious and claimed to have initially taught himself to read at a young age before his formal instruction began. He attended a school in the nearby town of Yanceyville for six months before being tutored in Latin by Lizzie Lowndes, who led a local academy for girls.[7] Suzanne Linder argued that the future contributions to education from the Poteat children suggested the quality of their early education. In addition to William Poteat's presidency of Wake Forest College, Edwin Poteat became president of Furman University in Greenville, South Carolina, and their sister Ida became chair of the Art Department at Meredith College in Raleigh, North Carolina.[8]

"THE COMING OF A COOL DEEP PEACE"

William Poteat first professed his faith in Jesus Christ in the midst of social turmoil. The late 1860s and early 1870s were difficult in the Piedmont region of North Carolina, and the wealth of the Poteat family could not completely shield it from the tumult of the Reconstruction period. Poteat was surprisingly reticent about the Civil War years and the hardest years of Reconstruction, both of which comprised the greater part of his childhood. He freely expressed nostalgia for the Old South of his early childhood. However, he seemed to prefer not to discuss the period's depressing aspects, including the loss of two brothers to the Confederate effort and the loss of the plantation lifestyle that he cherished when his family moved into town after the war. He portrayed his childhood as an idyllic one.[9] In reality local Democrats and Republicans fought for political control of the region to the point of assassinating rivals. White vigilantes terrorized Republicans, but African Americans suffered the brunt of the violence. In 1870 North Carolina's governor William W. Holden declared that Caswell and a neighboring county were in a state of insurrection. He sent militia under Colonel George W. Kirk to restore order, which was remembered as the Kirk-Holden War.[10] Despite the unrest, a religious revival arose in the region, particularly in the vicinity of the Yanceyville Baptist Church. William Poteat's mother Julia had been a compelling spiritual influence on him. He recalled his "mother's gentle, sometimes tearful, insistence reinforced by her life of sweetness and light." He said that she "awakened early in me the wish to be a Christian."[11] At the height of the local revival, twelve-year-old Poteat made a profession of faith in the conventional fashion of Baptist evangelicals.[12] He noted his absence of excitement, but he relished the calming peace that overcame him: "I recall no profound eruptive experience, only the passing of embarrassment and anxiety, the coming of a cool deep peace."[13] He "presented [himself] and was received into the membership of the village church" and was baptized along with sixteen others.[14] When Poteat left for college three years later he stood in the center of his family's traditional Baptist faith.

WAKE FOREST COLLEGE

Poteat entered Wake Forest College in 1872 when he was sixteen years old. Only recently reopened after the Civil War, the school had six professors and one hundred students.[15] He pursued the bachelor of arts degree, which focused on the classical studies of Latin and Greek, and secondarily on mathematics and science.[16] Students learned English composition and rhetoric by participating in one of two literary societies at the college. Poteat joined the Euzelian Society which, like the Philomathesians, had its own hall and library. The Euzelians debated political, social, and religious questions. Students learned parliamentary procedure, rules of debate, and the art of oratory. Poteat served as the society's librarian, recording secretary, and corresponding secretary, and eventually as the society's president.[17] He so excelled as a public speaker that the Euzelians chose him to be the senior orator. Poteat gave the salutatory address in Latin in 1877.[18]

Poteat experienced an impassioned reaffirmation of his faith in college. He strategically recounted the experience with great effect in a denominational address to North Carolina Baptists in 1922.[19] Although he made a profession of faith and was baptized at the age of twelve, he had a more intense spiritual experience during a college revival meeting. It was so memorable that he said, "I could point you out the pew on the back of which I wept my heart out."[20] He found himself lacking assurance in the conversion of his childhood, but "one thing was certain now, that He was mine and I was His forever." Although not at odds with his early evangelical faith, when Poteat recounted this testimony from his college years, he shared it with the subjective and experience-based emphasis that he later conceived to be the sufficient and only necessary grounding for the Christian faith. He articulated the mysterious nature of his encounter that defied theological explanation: "I do not know what occurred in the deeps of my nature then. I have no psychology of conversion. I do not have to understand it in order to be assured of its reality. . . . I only know that when I yielded my heart to Him my surrender was my victory."[21] But at the time Poteat seemed to remain firmly within traditional evangelicalism, which on its own had ample room for emphasis upon religious experience.

Poteat disclosed only one incident in college that shook his faith.[22] He recalled that a fellow student who was a "bright young chap" once whispered to Poteat in class and asked, "Why do so many brilliant men reject Christianity?" Poteat was stunned at the thought: "It struck me squarely between the eyes and I went down all in a heap." Poteat thought immediately of the chemistry professor who stood before him, whom he remembered as "Old Rab," and whom Poteat recognized as one of those brilliant men who had no use for religion. Poteat pondered the implications of his professor and others like him rejecting religion. He expressed however that "I suppose if nothing else had happened I should have carried all that I possessed in the way of religious inheritance to my mental garret and buried it alongside of the fairy tales of my childhood; but fortunately I soon came to myself."[23] Poteat remembered this experience, but he dismissed his doubts. A deeper crisis awaited him after graduation.

In college Poteat sharpened his mind and expanded his horizons in ways that prefigured his future leadership and influence, but he remained a traditional Southern Baptist. He encountered the progressive spirit that was arising in North Carolina, but only in nascent form. The New South was in its infancy in 1872, and progressive currents of thought were spreading slowly in 1877 when Poteat graduated.[24] The progressive spirit of the New South continued to develop into the 1890s, and it reached its height in the mid-1920s when North Carolina became a battleground for and against liberal ideology in society and religion.[25] The liberalizing college experience that Wilbur J. Cash described in *The Mind of the South* lay years in the future. Cash, a 1922 graduate of Wake Forest and admirer of Poteat, described the "phenomenon [that was] rising more and more clearly into view [that] inspired fear and hate" in the parents of southern college students. Perhaps with some overstatement he explained that students returned "home from school to say that they thought Mr. Darwin was right, echoing fearful ideas from that man Freud, who sounded as though [they] were in the pay for the Kremlin; quoting Henry Mencken and George Jean Nathan, and mocking the ministers."[26] Later as president of Wake Forest, Poteat referred to the crisis that many college students experienced when they encountered liberal ideas: "This sort of religious crisis is not peculiar to college students. It will be precipitated by preoccupation with intellectual or business pursuits and by any experience which gives one a new and startling view of things."[27] But Poteat argued that he had no such experience in college. He said for instance, "*The Origin of Species* had been out eighteen years when my Bachelor's diploma was handed me but I do not remember having heard of it. Certainly no reverberations of the fierce fight which evolution had fought and won disturbed our cloistral seclusion. . . . There was," he declared, "no intellectual crisis."[28]

However, in the values that were instilled at Wake Forest, we do see a touch of foreshadowing. In addition to an inquiring spirit Poteat's college education instilled in him a more cosmopolitan outlook and a concern for the public image that went with it. This occurred at a time when many Southerners were growing eager to overcome the public shame that hung over the region in the years after the Civil War and Reconstruction. As was mainstream in urban life in the North, Poteat embraced the Victorian ideals of refinement, polite society, and a spirit of progress as leading virtues. These seemed to be important factors in shaping the new direction that Poteat and others took in the late nineteenth century and afterward. But a more direct spiritual and intellectual crisis lay ahead when his career provoked a confrontation that shook his religious foundation and wrecked his faith as he had known it.[29]

A UNIVERSITY OF BERLIN EDUCATION

Poteat became a tutor at the college one year after his graduation. He provided remedial instruction in Latin and Greek for students who were not prepared for the standard college curriculum, which assumed a classical education as a foundation.[30] He excelled as a tutor and administrator and two years later, in June 1880, with the growth of the student body, Wake Forest added Poteat to the faculty as an assistant professor of science.[31] His appointment to teach in the field of science proved to be consequential for his career, but it also penetrated to the depths of his religious life.

The leadership of Wake Forest College endeavored to keep pace with the national trends in education, and its young professor became instrumental in this pursuit. Wake Forest began with the same disadvantages that most southern colleges faced in the postwar period: Its endowment was nearly gone, the student body was a fraction of its prewar size, the campus was in disarray, and most of the region was economically depressed.[32] But the administration and faculty were eager to make progress. They divided the college curriculum into seven schools, one of which was natural science.[33] Poteat and another professor shared the load of teaching chemistry, physics, astronomy, and natural history. In 1883 the faculty updated the curriculum to further emphasize the sciences. Poteat received a substantial raise in salary and was named professor of natural history. That summer Poteat toured the leading universities of the North: Harvard, Yale, and Brown. He returned with a microscope for his classroom, which proved to be innovative at a time when the classical method of recitation was still standard for scientific instruction in southern colleges. Poteat also attended lectures at Martha's Vineyard Summer Institute, where he studied botany.[34] Poteat pioneered the active learning model by bringing students into the laboratory and giving lectures rather than directing recitations. Students dissected specimens and viewed plant and animal tissue under a microscope. Courses like geology required fieldwork.[35] In 1892 Poteat became professor of biology and geology, and he updated the curriculum by combining zoology and botany into a single biology course. Randal Hall argued that "[both] the use of the term biology and the creation of a general biology class represented a cutting-edge understanding of his field."[36] Poteat proved to be a capable professor of science, but in addition to proving himself in the classroom he addressed the growing trends of higher education.

Poteat's early career paralleled the rise of professionalization and specialization in American higher education.[37] When Poteat joined the Wake Forest faculty in 1880, the expectation that professors have a graduate degree was still emerging. But Poteat compensated for his lack of specialized education with robust self-study, independent research, and interaction with other scientists. Poteat recounted his experience of independent research:

> I bought a microscope and began to penetrate. I verified what I had read in books—that the cell is the unit of structure and function throughout the living world and that every living thing is related to every other living thing in substance, action, and method of origin. And one happy day, poking about the world of the invisibles, I met my first ameba. I cannot forget the thrill of the apparition.[38]

It is most significant that in 1888 Poteat embarked upon research at the University of Berlin in Germany.[39] He, his brother Edwin McNeill Poteat, and Charlee Lee Smith, a recent Wake Forest graduate, studied at the university's Zoological Institute and focused primarily on methods of scientific instruction. In what was typical for that era Poteat earned no degree. Advanced studies at Berlin however qualified him as the pride of a small Baptist college in North Carolina.[40] To honor his achievements Wake Forest awarded Poteat an honorary master's degree.[41] By the end of his career Poteat had received five honorary doctorates.[42] Educated North Carolinians celebrated Poteat as a model for the New South. Southern Baptist leaders applauded the progress of one of their denominational colleges, but they could not have anticipated the series of controversies that eventually surrounded the young and promising professor.

CONCLUSION

Poteat's early familial and religious background hardly anticipated the path that he eventually took toward liberal Christianity. And his college education did not offer obvious signs of a progressive trajectory at the time. However, some of the values instilled at Wake Forest College, along with the emerging cultural and social currents of the day, offered a glimpse into the deeper impulses that later played a role when Poteat restructured his religious beliefs early in his career. But it was as a young professor that his studies provoked an inner crisis when the claims of modern science collided with his traditional Protestant faith. This crisis was shared by many of his generation in the North, but also in the South, which was not immune to the intellectual and social currents that were transforming American religious and cultural life.

Chapter Two

THE PATH TO LIBERALISM

Poteat's journey toward liberal religion began with his appointment as a professor of science, which precipitated an inner crisis when his study of modern science collided with his traditional Christian beliefs.[1] If this early crisis set Poteat on a path toward liberalism, the course of his journey was also clarified and reinforced by the rising currents of modern thought and a conviction to preserve a place for religion in modern society.[2] Poteat resolved this conflict by granting science sovereignty over explanations of the natural world, but the process of harmonizing the conclusions of science with his faith pressed him to reconceptualize Christianity. He reconceived of the Bible and its mode of revelation and developed an alternative religious epistemology. He identified experience as the source for religious knowledge and separated religious knowledge from scientific knowledge. He assigned religious knowledge to a subjective, spiritual realm and assigned science to an empirical realm, a realm based not on experience but on evidence and facts. Poteat envisioned an experiential Christianity without the doctrinal content of orthodox Christianity. Demonstrating striking similarity to modern thinkers like Friedrich Schleiermacher and taking his cues from the major intellectual currents of his day, Poteat aimed to save religion from the challenges of modern knowledge. He redefined his faith in an attempt to preserve the viability of Christianity for the modern world and for himself.

THE CONFLICT BETWEEN FAITH AND SCIENCE

Poteat provided an in-depth account of his early crisis in an article titled "An Intellectual Adventure: A Human Document."[3] He had no advanced training in science when he joined the Wake Forest faculty in 1880.[4] At the outset of his teaching career he knew little more than his students, but he was obligated to teach them nonetheless: "This anomalous obligation was hard for me; hard also for the victims of my inexperience." He promptly "set out to explore" his new field of study and found the experience to be both illuminating and troubling. With poetic flare he described the joy of scientific discovery: "Bird and beast and creeping thing came forward out of the dark to greet me, and alga and moss and fern and the radiant flowery host filled my days with delight and my nights with happy dreams. And above, the jewels flashing on the velvet breast of night kindled me to rapture at times, always melted me to reverence."[5] But Poteat simultaneously faced a growing crisis of faith: "For a period I was confounded & distressed."[6] He described the growing "cloud of doubt" that accompanied his explorations into modern science: "In the midst of these absorbing studies I cast a furtive glance at a cloud slowly spreading in one quarter of the horizon. It was small as a man's hand at first but big enough to suggest shadow and storm."[7] The further Poteat progressed in scientific study, the more paralyzed his faith became. Throughout the crisis he tried to continue exercising the outward forms of Christianity: "I was pretty faithful in religious duty personal and public, taught a Sunday-school class, participated in public worship, made religious addresses now and then." But his heart grew cold toward religion.[8]

Poteat's crisis centered on authority. Christians had held that the Bible delivered a truthful and authoritative account of the creation of the cosmos as part of God's revelatory message to humanity. Modern science claimed its own authority utterly independent of any form of religious authority or tradition. Poteat found it increasingly difficult to harmonize the Bible's account of creation with the Darwinian paradigm that came to dominate modern science.[9] Gradually Poteat accepted science's authority to explain the natural world, and he relinquished the veracity of the biblical account of creation as a matter of scientific or historic testimony. But Poteat remained desperate to find some means of retaining his Christian faith while embracing the authority of science. To do so he reconsidered the nature of the Bible by redefining the theology of revelation, and he devised a system that assigned scientific knowledge and religious knowledge to separate spheres.

Essential to his new vision of religion Poteat revised his conception of Christianity's holy book.[10] He described the gradual progress of losing confidence in the Bible's comprehensive truthfulness: "The absolute accuracy of the handling of scientific material in the Bible appeared exaggerated at first, then questionable, at last impossible."[11] Poteat spoke candidly of his revision: "Consequently, the opinions which I had inherited I was able to revise & that without discrediting the Bible quoted in support of them."[12] Poteat concluded that the Bible was a product of ancient culture, like other great works of literature. It "spoke the language of its time or it spoke not at all to its time."[13] The Bible contained the primitive understanding of science that characterized the ancient world, and this understanding implied that scientific and historical inaccuracies could only be expected. He denied that divine inspiration allowed the Bible's human authors to speak more than they could know within the confines of ancient knowledge. The Bible was a book about religion and spirituality, and all of its content beyond this realm was incidental.[14] Poteat was critical of some conservative Protestants' attempts to explain the Genesis account in scientific terms: "So far as such statements were concerned with natural objects and processes, which are open to investigation, they were inappropriate, ineffective, and injurious."[15] Perhaps in the early period unaware and in later years uninterested, Poteat did not engage with more nuanced and sophisticated approaches by evangelical scholars like those at Princeton Seminary. Benjamin B. Warfield and others took seriously the findings of science and remained open to the idea of an old earth and even to evolution itself while also insisting upon the infallibility of the Bible.[16] Poteat concluded that a reconceptualization of the Bible was necessary. He reasoned that the Bible had to be reimagined in light of modern science and research. He came to terms with a Bible that was exclusively relevant to inspire spirituality and morality. One could read it for spiritual guidance while recognizing its limitations in scientific and historical veracity.[17] Science spoke from evidence and facts, but the Bible and religion belonged to the spiritual realm of experience, and both held authority in their respective spheres. Poteat concluded that he had successfully preserved the Bible's authority by limiting it to the realm of religion. But his view of the Bible set him at a great distance from grassroots Southern Baptists and other southern evangelicals, which over time troubled many of his conservative brethren and led to a series of denominational controversies.

EXPERIENCE VERSUS DOCTRINE

Poteat determined that the Christian faith was rooted not in a body of doctrine, but in subjective religious experience. He argued that one's own encounter with God was the source of religious knowledge. Poteat survived his religious crisis by effectively divorcing religion from doctrine. He became convinced that the doctrinal content of Christianity was incidental and did not form its essence. Authentic religion, he argued, was not theoretical, but experiential: "I discovered the religious experience to be one thing and speculation about it quite another thing."[18] Poteat lamented

Christianity's history of elevating a standard of theological orthodoxy. Consequently he rejected a belief-based Christianity that charged anyone who dissented from theological norms with heresy.[19]

Poteat became concerned that modern people were rejecting Christianity because they did not believe in its doctrines. He considered this rejection to be disastrous since doctrine was not the "essential matter" of Christianity.[20] Poteat found peace in the idea that "religion is a way of life," rather than a set of beliefs. He described the enduring essence of Christianity: "Christ [in] religion is the way of life inspired by Christ. You take it [because] you are personally attached to him. You follow [because] you love . . . His way was the way of the Cross, i.e. the way of love & renunciation . . . Love & loyalty [are the] essence of [Christian] experience."[21] Poteat felt an apologetic burden and explained that modern people would embrace Jesus "but not the explanations which some of his friends have offered."[22]

Poteat argued that one's religious experience "and its testimony [were] valid and authoritative" for religious knowledge.[23] His former student, Gerald W. Johnson, explained that Poteat was unconcerned with how Wake Forest's young men might seek God or "with what ritual they worshiped" as long as they were sincere in their experience. Johnson admitted that conservative Christians were troubled by Poteat's convictions, but Johnson was confident that the sincerity of Poteat's religion vindicated him: "For this carelessness of rite and dogma he was blamed by sectarians; but I am sure that I speak for hundreds of his former students in declaring that 'Pure religion, and undefiled before God and the Father, is this.'"[24]

Theology offered indirect knowledge of God, but experience gave "immediate and untranslated" knowledge of the Divine.[25] Poteat rejoiced that thoughtful people were finding hope in "recognizing the legitimacy and the reliability of what the spiritual nature of man apprehends and delivers."[26] Poteat's new epistemology freed him from the "intellectual difficulties" that caused his crisis. He "postponed" all theological issues and would "solve them or not solve them at [his] leisure." Because religion inhabited a separate sphere from that of science, he resolved not to be troubled by its questions: "I will not permit them to shadow my personal relation to Christ." Also because of science's separate realm, it offered no answers to the deepest questions of life. Only religion through subjective encounter with the Divine offered answers.[27] Poteat preserved a form of religion, but it required a strict privatization of faith and an emptying of Christianity of much of its doctrinal content: "My religion was intact, tho' I was short on theology."[28] With his accommodation Poteat fit the characterization of liberal Protestants given by historian Christine Rosen: "These were preachers who embraced modern ideas first and adjusted their theologies later."[29] Poteat successfully reconceptualized Christianity to conform to modern thought, but this reconceptualization produced other challenges for his thought and life.

A few years after Poteat found peace from his crisis in the 1880s, he nevertheless felt a sense of alienation within the institutional, organized church. In 1896 he recognized that his heart had grown cold toward worship within the local church: "I go to church these days from a sense of duty. I expect neither to be refreshed nor to be informed. But for the obligation to lead the singing, it is likely the sense of duty would itself be insufficient to drag me out." He bemoaned the fact that his private spirituality offered more enrichment than worship within the church: "If the object of public worship is spiritual invigoration, I can secure that more certainly at home." Similarly he questioned the value of preaching. If church members gathered for the purpose of worshipping, then the sermon's "position and duration is a distraction & hindrance," rather than a benefit to religious experience. Poteat became uninterested in sustaining "the religious custom of the [ecclesial] community."[30] Personal religious experience would endure with or without the church just as essential Christianity would remain even if it were emptied of its doctrinal content and its outward forms of worship. Poteat wanted to preserve the viability of Christianity but found its forms of worship and instruction to be unnecessary and at times even unhelpful.

DOCTRINELESS RELIGION

Doctrinal Christianity troubled Poteat both intellectually and in his public life. But he argued that a religion without doctrine was safe from the challenges of the modern age. Modern Christianity would be free for individual interpretation without the hounds of orthodoxy charging after heretics.

Poteat remained a committed reader of the Bible and was aware of the biblical warnings about doctrinal error. In his personal Bible, he made a note by 2 Peter 2, which warned of false teachers, implicitly related to doctrine, and he noted the text's likeness to a similar warning in Jude.[31] But Poteat might have regarded these warnings as proof of the early corruption of the pure religion of Jesus. Having redefined biblical authority in a way that rejected the Bible's infallibility and with its usefulness redirected toward the subjective, he might have categorized such texts as unedifying for his own spiritual life.

Poteat imagined a Bible without doctrine. Although the New Testament Gospels were composed later, he argued that they reflected the earlier, purer spirit of Christianity when compared to the Epistles. The Gospels felt less dogmatic and less institutional. However Poteat denied the existence of any clear system of thought, even in Paul's writings. Contrary to the classical theologians Paul did not present a doctrinal system and only by imposition could one be formed. One could not even discern a coherent theology of salvation in Paul's writings.[32] Christians should not look to Paul's Epistles "for a consistent theory of the efficient cause in Jesus' work of reconciliation," because "it is, rather, the consequences of that work in and for the believer that occupies Paul's thought, and even here he has no consistent scheme of expression."[33] Paul was a spiritual guide who offered metaphors for Christ's work of redemption for encouraging men and women in their religious experience, not to teach doctrine or to communicate ontological realities. The metaphors that Paul used—expiation, reconciliation, redemption from slavery, and payment of debt—were not definite spiritual realities but rather reflections about God's work in the hearts of men and women.[34] A more doctrinally oriented religion, especially one that assumed the Bible's literal truthfulness, had little hope for survival in the modern age. Poteat said, "A more ignorant age might be dogmatic; not so this [one]."[35]

When Poteat spoke to seminarians at Southern Baptist Theological Seminary in Louisville, Kentucky, in 1900, he assured them that however much doctrine is revised or even abandoned in the future, "what is vital in the Christian experience will remain unaffected by it. For you will observe that theology is one thing and religion quite another."[36] One could have a vibrant religious life without knowledge of or concern for doctrine. Poteat declared that dogma was a dead end.[37] He distinguished doctrine from religion saying, "Religion is emotion; theology, reason. Religion is the response of the heart; theology, the logic of the head. Religion is the inward experience of God; theology, the intellectual account of it."[38] And Poteat stressed that whatever may change in modern religion, believers would always have Christ, the real Christ who was not dependent on theological formulations.[39]

By the turn of the century, Poteat had found peace in a Christianity without doctrine. He argued that it was a more dynamic religion with real potential to thrive in the modern age. And he believed that he was already witnessing the success of liberal Christianity, even in the Baptist South. In 1900 he declared that "hundreds of pulpits" were already representing the progressive view of religion, notably in the "liberally educated section of ministry," and with only "occasional exceptions."[40] Even if he overstated matters Poteat and others who shared his views found solutions to the intellectual challenges of the day with a new religious epistemology and through the inspiration of a movement that had influenced intellectuals, poets, and musicians in Germany and Great Britain before taking root in the United States, and even in the South.

ROMANTIC RELIGIOUSNESS

Poteat employed romantic ideas to ground his religious epistemology in experience. Romanticism was a broad movement. In addition to religion, it influenced music, art, and the broader ideas of love, work, and society.[41] Romantic thinkers balanced the Enlightenment's emphasis on reason by emphasizing "the affective, the intuitive, the mystical and the artistic."[42] They contended that knowledge, including religious knowledge, should not be limited to what one could prove by reason. Samuel T. Coleridge, a leading figure in English Romanticism, appealed to intuition as a way to discover religious knowledge.[43] Coleridge argued that religious knowledge proceeded not by rational proof, but by personal experience. Coleridge advanced the idea that Christianity was not a set of beliefs, but a life.[44] Poteat adopted these ideas and reframed Christianity into a subjective, experienced-based religion.

Romanticism offered Poteat a solution to the conflict that he experienced between religion and science. Poteat read Coleridge during a renaissance of Coleridge's ideas in the decades after his death.[45] Coleridge argued in his *Aids to Reflection* in 1825 that science and religion do not contradict one another because the two "do not move on the same line or plane" and "therefore cannot contradict."[46] Roger Olson expressed Coleridge's point well: "They cannot contradict each other because they are about entirely different matters" and they "cannot conflict any more than science and art can conflict."[47] Olson also explained how romanticism prepared the way for Protestant liberalism: "Partly because of [Coleridge] and Christian romantics like him, modernity had to make room for spiritual experience" and "romanticism forced the door of the Enlightenment open so that at least spiritual experience could not be ignored or brushed aside as sheer fanaticism."[48] Poteat found the approach compelling. He gave science the exclusive right to explain the natural world but allowed religion its own position to explain the spiritual realm of devotion, morality, and fellowship with God.[49]

The most influential Romantic thinker who developed the framework that Poteat employed was Friedrich Schleiermacher.[50] Robert Adams described Schleiermacher's approach as "romantic religiousness" in contrast to "rational religiousness."[51] Schleiermacher rejected the supernatural, propositional revelation of historic Christianity and argued that religious knowledge moved through the channel of feeling. One encountered God and learned about himself in relation to God through inward illumination via contact with the Divine. Poteat embraced Schleiermacher's idea that subjective illumination offered the authentic source of religious knowledge and forged a religion that was immune to the challenges of modernity.

THE FATHER OF LIBERAL CHRISTIANITY

Poteat agreed broadly with the father of liberal theology when he identified experience as the source for religious knowledge and the essence of Christianity.[52] Schleiermacher denied all forms of external revelation and rejected the adequacy of reason to answer the foundational questions of religion. He argued that religious knowledge moved through the channel of religious feeling. He made religious knowledge internal and personal. Schleiermacher argued that an inward illumination through encounter with the Divine was the foundation of all knowledge of God and religion and was the basis of spirituality.

Schleiermacher concluded that humanity's rational faculty was inadequate as a source of religious knowledge and presented feeling as an alternative. He criticized what he perceived to be rationalist forms of Christianity in the same manner that he criticized religion that was based on dogma.[53] Instead of reason Schleiermacher selected feeling as the faculty that provided direct access to religious knowledge. In his first edition of *On Religion: Speeches to Its Cultured Despisers,* Schleiermacher described the illumination of religious consciousness that consisted of feeling and intuition.[54] The philosopher Robert Adams explained Schleiermacher's idea of intuition as "a sort of mental seeing, distinct from any systematic theory."[55] In Schleiermacher's second edition and in his subsequent works, feeling displaced intuition as the dominant expression of religious experience.[56] Religious feeling was the channel for one's receptivity. It provided sufficient and authentic access to the questions of religion and participation in religious reality.

Schleiermacher conceived of something deeper than emotion or sensation when he referred to feeling—gefühl.[57] Gary Dorrien demonstrated that many of the continental Rationalists had recognized feeling as a form of knowledge, although they regarded it as a lower form of knowledge.[58] Schleiermacher elevated feeling as the most adequate means of apprehending religious reality and argued that it offered direct, unmediated apprehension of spiritual reality. Schleiermacher also argued that religion drew its life from feeling—not merely ideas but also energy.[59] According to Schleiermacher one's spirituality could be weighed according to his or her depth in this experience: "In whatever measure this actually takes place during the course of a personality through time, in just that measure do we ascribe piety to the individual."[60] Religious feeling was the source of religious knowledge and the measure of one's personal spirituality.

Schleiermacher preserved a place for theology in Christianity but considered it secondary to experience. In *The Christian Faith* Schleiermacher argued that the "Christian doctrines are accounts of the Christian religious affections set forth in speech."[61] Religious feeling offered direct access to God, but dogmatic assertions had value only to the extent that they corresponded to religious experience.[62] Schleiermacher argued that religious feeling was not conditioned on any prior knowledge of God: "[It was] independent of [any] original knowledge."[63] He proposed that feeling was preconceptual and as Dorrien explained, it made "possible all thought and experience."[64] Theology, as an articulation drawn from religious experience, was only indirectly related to God. To Schleiermacher doctrine was always secondary to and dependent upon experience. Experience was the authentic channel for religious knowledge.[65]

Schleiermacher grounded his system on the idea that religious experience involved an encounter with an objective Being. In *The Christian Faith* Schleiermacher called the essence of religion the "feeling of absolute dependence" or the "consciousness of being absolutely dependent."[66] In religious experience the subject became conscious of his dependence on God. This "God-consciousness" was relational and implied the objective existence of the Other. Schleiermacher stressed that "our spontaneous activity comes from a source outside of us."[67] Schleiermacher argued that the very content of the word "God" implied his existence and the authenticity of humanity's interaction with him: "This is for us the really original signification of that word."[68] The term "God," he said, "is nothing more than the expression of the feeling of absolute dependence."[69] Robert

Adams countered the charge that Schleiermacher's elevation of experience amounted to anthropocentric subjectivism: "We can hardly be absolutely dependent unless there is something, other than ourselves, on which we are absolutely dependent."[70] Schleiermacher stressed that experience was no more speculative than the grounding offered by the metaphysicians.[71] He defended the legitimacy of religious experience: "[It] springs necessarily and by itself from the interior of every better soul, it has its own province in the mind in which it reigns sovereign, and it is worthy of moving the noblest and the most excellent by means of its innermost power and by having its innermost essence known by them."[72] Schleiermacher's religious experience was subjective in the sense of being personal and inward, but through its referent was grounded in an objective Being, that is, in God.[73]

Poteat followed the general outline of Schleiermacher's theology of experience but without the depth of Schleiermacher's expression.[74] Poteat did not consciously operate at a deep philosophical level. He preferred to leave metaphysical questions to the metaphysicians.[75] However Schleiermacher's ideas entered the theological and broader intellectual atmosphere of modern discourse, and they made Poteat's new religious framework possible. Poteat's romantic piety came to hold a controlling influence on his thought and spirituality.

POTEAT'S PHILOSOPHY OF TWO SPHERES

Like Schleiermacher, Poteat provided a solution to the hostility between modern science and religion by framing religious authority and scientific authority as exclusive to their respective realms. He harmonized science and religion by classifying religious knowledge into the subjective, spiritual realm, separated from the realm of scientific knowledge. Poteat proposed that religious knowledge was personal and spiritual, and scientific knowledge was propositional and verifiable. He first articulated the basic contours of his two-realm philosophy in 1905. At that time he seemed to allow for minimal overlap between the two. Increasingly however he drew a sharper separation between the two realms and virtually removed any possibility of interaction between science and religion. Poteat made science sovereign over the natural world and made religion private and internal. Christianity could endure in the modern age but only by modifying its traditional framework of authority and by ceding truth claims to the realm of science.

The Path to Harmony

Poteat distinguished scientific knowledge from other forms of knowledge. He presented a nascent form of his philosophy of two spheres in *The New Peace: Lectures on Science and Religion,* which was based on a series of lectures that he gave at leading theological institutions in the North in 1905.[76] He argued that art contained a form of knowledge, but its aim was beauty rather than truth. Science exclusively had knowledge as its end and "was content with nothing short of the whole truth."[77] Edgar Y. Mullins, Poteat's counterpart at Southern Baptist Theological Seminary agreed and expressed Poteat's view well: "Art is the response of man's soul to beauty. Science is his response to truth."[78] Poteat located philosophy closer to science because it too had knowledge as a goal, but he limited the scope of philosophy and restricted it to metaphysical concerns, to that which transcended the physical world. He explained that science "discovers the orderly sequence of events in nature; philosophy asks why this sequence rather than another," and science "looks abroad and collates; philosophy looks within and thinks."[79] Poteat argued that theology was even further removed from science. He considered theology to be a "body of knowledge with which science is hardly to be identified."[80] One reason for the distance between the two was their separate emphases.[81] But their separation was primarily a result of the different "means of knowledge which they employ." Science was empirical, and theology was spiritual. But Poteat also distinguished theology from religion: "Theology is not religion, [just] as science is not nature."[82] Religious experience was authentic religion in itself, and theology was the commentary on the experience: "The religious experience is one thing; the explanation of it—theology in the restricted sense—is another." In this early period however Poteat argued that religion had an empirical quality: "Religious experience is a fact of nature, and as such it is clearly open to scientific investigation." Under this kind of investigation, science "coalesces with theology."[83] Poteat later relinquished this expression of an empirical quality and the legitimacy of science coalescing with religion and forced greater separation between the two, giving greater weight to the subjective nature of religious experience.[84] The benefits of removing Christianity from the challenges of science outweighed the benefits of proposing empirical legitimacy for religious experience. But even in this early period Poteat argued that science alone could explain the natural world.

Over time Poteat developed a starker division between scientific knowledge and religious knowledge. In a presentation before the Baptist Congress in 1910 he argued that religion and science functioned only within their respective spheres. In the realm of science scientists probed evidence to gain verifiable knowledge, but religion used a different means of knowing. Poteat echoed the Romantics and Schleiermacher: "The sphere of religion is not the sphere of knowledge, but of emotion; not of thought, but of will; not of truth, but of imagination and feeling."[85] He addressed the relevance of prayer in the age of science and argued that prayer continued to have value within its own sphere: "Whatever revolution may occur in the realm of science, strictly so-called, religion and its necessary support and expression, prayer, will retain their legitimate place in human experience."[86] The harmony of religion and science required that both functioned only within their respective spheres.

Achieving Harmony

Poteat achieved harmony for science and religion by isolating their authority. He was at the pinnacle of his influence in 1925 when he articulated the mature expression of his two-sphere philosophy at the John Calvin McNair Lectures at the University of North Carolina.[87] He argued that the Bible had once been "the compendium of all truth" in Western society.[88] As modern science arose it gradually ceded ground that religion previously claimed: "Religion, regarded as an explanation of nature, is displaced by science."[89] Poteat contended that science now held exclusive authority to explain the natural world. Only the "literalists" continued to regard the Bible as a source for understanding the natural world. Poteat lamented that the fundamentalists embarrassed educated Christians and limited the appeal of Christianity to thoughtful people. But Poteat judged that they acted out of ignorance. He distinguished their motives from their actions and advised his audience to "respect the one, [but] deplore the other." He sympathized "with their loyalty to the truth as they see it" but regreted "the havoc [that] they spread."[90]

Poteat warned that whoever attempted to force the Bible's "primitive creation pictures" to agree with science was committed to a fool's errand. He argued on scientific grounds that the biblical account of creation did not present scientific facts.[91] He contended that belief in the dictation theory of the Bible and its literal truthfulness previously led Christians to derive from Genesis a geological history of the earth. But in a more enlightened age anyone who questioned the unique role of modern science to explain the natural world could only expect ridicule from modern society. Poteat labeled those who did as obscurantists: "The attitude of resistance to the enlightenment of the world exposes itself to the ridicule of the world and can hardly hope to escape it."[92] Poteat's more conservative coreligionists might have responded that Jesus warned his followers to expect the world's ridicule.[93] But Poteat was committed to offering a religion that appealed to the cultured people of modern society. In the South these people were a new cultured middle class who were increasingly accepting the "assured results of science" and the unique authority of science to explain the natural world.[94]

Poteat accentuated the separation of the two realms to protect their respective interests. He declared that "religion is religion, and science remains science."[95] Because both science and religion were of supreme worth to humanity he declared that "we shall not be called on to surrender either." He differentiated them from one another as "two ways of relating oneself to reality, the intuitive, or religious way, and the rational, or scientific way" and added that in "the one case, you perceive without process; in the other, you understand by research." Science and religion used separate ways of knowing, as distinct as their separate subjects. Religion was based on private intuition and science on verifiable evidence.[96] Edgar Mullins expressed the same idea when he said that their "modes of knowing are not the same. In physical science sensation supplies the data; in religion, inward experiences of fellowship with God."[97] Poteat reasoned that science could not disprove religion any more than religion could inform science. He proposed that science "occupies itself only with second causes, and so is not an arbiter of religion."[98] For example science had no way to contradict the possibility of miracles because its authority did not extend beyond its own realm. Poteat's goal was "not proposing to accommodate religion to science, but that religious teachers recognize the authority of science in its proper sphere, just as scientific teachers ought to recognize the authority of religion in its proper sphere."[99] Poteat warned that Christian apologists who failed to respect the separation of the realms would only cheapen Christianity. They would "cheapen their object by the very means they take to render it credible." He warned that an attempt to bring "religious belief to the form in which science can smile upon it, [would] kill the nerve of religion itself." That is if conservative Christians tried to defend the Bible's ancient references to the natural world as scientifically true, they would discredit Christianity and demoralize its adherents. Scientists needed to recognize their limits as well. They held absolute authority in their realm, but as Poteat once wrote in a letter, scientists blundered when they failed to see that "there are spheres of reality to which their method and apparatus are inappropriate."[100] He was convinced that harmony would be maintained by separation.

Poteat contended however that science and religion were "not mutually exclusive."[101] Although he argued that the authority of science and religion rested only in their separate realms, he left the door open for their mutual appreciation. Poteat loved science and had dedicated his life to teaching it.[102] He called science God's poetry. He likened science to religion by calling science "a book of marvels," as was the Bible.[103] Even evolution, which caused so much social and religious controversy, was only a framework for understanding life. The theory of evolution could potentially help people better understand God by discerning his means of creation. "The modern idea of a God of evolution," he contended, "is bringing us back to the God of our fathers." The study of evolution would ultimately prove to be good for religious life.[104] Science and religion occupied separate realms, but that did not mean their interests were unrelated.

Poteat redefined faith by severing it from belief. He argued that belief was "assent to intellectual propositions supported by evidence."[105] When a person was "given a [sufficient] body of evidence" she or he "automatically [assented]."[106] But belief did not have the power to produce moral character. After all the Bible held that even the demons believed in God. Doctrine, particularly as it was preserved in creeds, was a human-made collection of religious beliefs that had accumulated over the centuries like "baggage." It could "neither save nor feed the soul."[107] As a young professor Poteat had argued that theology was "derived and partial, noble in its aim indeed, but limping with human infirmity and confused with human ignorance."[108] Edgar Mullins shared Poteat's unappreciative view of creeds although with less general pessimism toward theology. Mullins seemed to express Poteat's point when he said that creeds were merely secondhand expressions of "the doctrinal beliefs of the age or people who put them forth."[109] Poteat argued that faith was more powerful than belief and was tied to "the essence of the Christian experience."[110] Faith proceeded from feeling and not reason: "Faith sees what is not visible, makes real what is not yet a fact."[111] Like Schleiermacher, Poteat argued that the "apprehension of faith is immediate, intuitive, [and] non-rational." Poteat "ventured upon" a definition of faith as "the deep-lying capacity to apprehend the eternal world and respond to its appeal." He explained that reason "is convinced by evidence and argument," but faith "is evoked and won." Poteat likened faith to peoples' tastes and their "loves and hates," which are not decided by reason but inexplicably rise within them. Poteat distinguished reason from feeling when he said that people "admire with reasons" but "love without reasons."[112]

Poteat revealed his motivation for separating belief and faith: "The body of beliefs [that is, doctrine] is subject to the criticism of science. Faith is independent and is as reliable in its sphere as reason is in its sphere."[113] Poteat reframed faith to advance his mission of protecting religion from modern criticism by modifying the belief-based, doctrinal Christianity because of its vulnerability to modern criticism. Poteat signaled that this new form of religion was spiritually vibrant: "If you have faith in the Bible, you bathe in its spirit, [and] find its inward refreshment there. You confide with Abraham, you are loyal with Moses, you are responsive with David, weep with Jeremiah, aspire with Isaiah, flame with Paul, pray and love with Christ."[114] A religion of faith was deeper and richer than a religion of belief: belief was limited to reason, but faith was experienced and embraced.

Poteat discounted that the Bible seemed to link faith and belief. In the New Testament, Jesus's disciples believed in his bodily resurrection. They examined the evidence: They touched him, walked beside him, and shared a meal with him.[115] And they had faith. They entrusted themselves to the truthfulness of his words and the power of his sacrificial act. They were convinced that Jesus was Israel's long-awaited messiah, and they displayed faith in God by dedicating their lives to testify to what they had witnessed. Poteat however assigned belief to the realm of facts, and faith to an independent realm of religion so that neither could compromise the other. The challenges of the modern age supported such a move.

Poteat achieved immunity for religion from the challenges of the modern age. But to do so he surrendered religion's voice on matters of fact and its authority beyond personal morality and private spirituality.[116] Poteat had endeavored to preserve Christianity from what Roger Olson and others have called the "acids of modernity." The acids of rationalism, skepticism, scientific naturalism, and self-sufficient optimism threatened to dissolve traditional religion.[117] Poteat had removed the threat, and what remained was a religion of private spirituality. Olson explained that modern theologians were "intimidated by modern science" and "so intimidated that they redefined Christianity so that, in principle, it cannot conflict with science."[118] Olson argued that this "sounds good, but the cost is too high."[119] Poteat paid this price to maintain a place for religion in the public square and save himself and others from the ridicule of modern society. This pressure was felt by educated Southerners in the same manner as it was by intellectuals in the North.

At the end of *Can a Man Be a Christian To-day?* Poteat answered the title's question in the affirmative. A modern person could be a Christian by respecting the authority of religion and science within their respective realms and by pushing through the "darkness" toward "the light" of religious experience.[120] The modern Christian relinquished the baggage of traditional Christian doctrine and Christianity's claim to hold universal truth in its sacred text. Poteat made this exchange for a religion that was based on personal experience and private spirituality, and he left the facts to science and other forms of modern research.[121]

THEOLOGY OF RELIGIOUS EXPERIENCE

Poteat made religious experience the wellspring of religious life and thought. Personal encounters with God superseded the traditional authority of the Scriptures and attention to doctrine and theological orthodoxy. Similar to Friedrich Schleiermacher and the Romantics, Poteat characterized religious experience as an inward encounter with the Divine and the personal reception of illumination. This became the primary mode for religious knowledge and the source for and substance of religious life. Poteat reframed Christianity and made experience the enduring essence of Christianity.

Poteat formulated a mystical encounter of fellowship and illumination as the mode of religious knowledge and the source of religious life. He articulated it most clearly in his 1925 lectures at the University of North Carolina that became the book *Can a Man Be a Christian To-day?* He described the encounter as fellowship between God and humanity: "The spirit of man meets in harmony the spirit of God mediated and interpreted by Christ. God in Christ calls to the soul of man, the deep above us challenges the deep within us." When God and humans met together humans' hearts filled with "love and loyalty."[122] God confronted and beckoned: "Deep calls to deep, and if deep answers to deep, it is not because we are convinced, but because we are won."[123] Beyond anything that has been or that might be appended to religion in the future, this experience formed the substance of Christianity: "That fellowship of kindred spirits is religion, the Christian religion."[124] In the encounter God imparted illumination. In contradistinction to a verbally inspired Bible and an articulated doctrine, Poteat appealed "not to reason, but to faith." Poteat argued that faith did not emerge from the faculty of reason, but from feeling. It was not based in propositional truths like Jesus's resurrection or the sufficiency of his atonement, but in a mystical experience. The faith of religious experience was that "deep-lying central capacity to see the invisible, to apprehend the enveloping realm of spirit."[125] This encounter with the Divine revealed the foundational content of religion. It revealed that God existed and that he summoned humanity to fellowship. Poteat argued that religious experience provided all that was essential for Christianity. He drew a powerful illustration from botany to make his point: "If a . . . fire should worm its way through all the libraries of the world and destroy the last book of botany, if a malicious . . . infection should kill every botanist in the world, would the plants know about it or be seriously affected by it? Would they not still bloom in vigor and beauty . . .?"[126] The essence of Christianity would endure without the Bible, without its traditional doctrines, and without theologians or ecclesial institutions. The "life of the spirit in Christ" would endure through religious experience and so provide religious knowledge.[127]

Although it was short on theology, religious experience was rich in spirituality. Its illumination nourished and protected the soul. It was "the best medicine" and "the best policeman." The encounter also had the power to eliminate fear: "There is no fear in light, for all light is of God, and those who fear are in darkness." Poteat contended that illumination brought freedom: "There is no foulness and festering in the light, nor any tyranny. Light is emancipation." Poteat proposed that religious experience was sufficient to support the Christian life: "And never lose faith in light. It is the condition of life."[128]

Poteat invested the individual with the highest religious authority. He emphasized that because this was an "inward experience," only two parties were involved, and no outside authority could rightly evaluate another's experience.[129] On the surface this sounded similar to the theology of the new birth, that the Christian life began with personal conversion, which evangelical Protestants had emphasized since the eighteenth century.[130] And it might seem related to the Baptist theology of the priesthood of the believer.[131] But Poteat's theology of experience came without the institutional or doctrinal parameters of older forms of Christianity, in which the church facilitated discipleship, corporate worship, and theological orthodoxy.[132] Poteat warned about "the rabbis" who "confound you with their metaphysics."[133] He advised that "you will find peace if you discriminate between Christ and some of His interpreters." In religious experience, one learned from God in an unmediated fashion, which minimized the value of and eliminated the authority of theological tradition and institutional oversight. Even the Bible's authority became more personal than corporate. But religious experience offered "the immediate apprehension of moral and spiritual realities." This freed religious seekers to "discriminate between [their] personal attachment to Christ and men's explanations of it." The old orthodoxy unnecessarily burdened the modern Christian. Poteat advocated for a Christianity without doctrinal boundaries and with authority resting in the individual. Poteat's friend and colleague Richard T. Vann, a Baptist minister and president of Meredith College in Raleigh, North Carolina, expressed Poteat's view well when he described doctrine as a liability. Dogma might be necessary, but it was also an impediment: "It amounts to an effort to confine living and expanding truth in an iron mold."[134] Poteat encouraged those who were hesitant about the change: "Do not be afraid of the effect of enlarging knowledge upon acquisitions already made or upon long-cherished beliefs." And he called for boldness: "That sort of timidity is an impeachment of the majesty and harmony of the sum of things . . . Dare to look into the dark recess, to walk on any far-looking crest in God's universe, for you will find Him everywhere in proportion to the penetration and range of your vision."[135] Poteat's modernized religion empowered the individual to envision his or her own expression of Christianity.

Poteat used the theology of soul competency or "the competency of the individual" to support his subjective reframing of religious epistemology.[136] Edgar Mullins was a leading proponent of the modern theology of soul competency. Mullins argued that this doctrine was among the foremost contributions of the Baptists: "The sufficient statement of the historical significance of the Baptists is this: The competency of the soul in religion."[137] However Mullins cautioned against a form of individualism that overemphasized a "sense of human self-sufficiency."[138] Mullins conceived of soul competency as a product of the *imago Dei,* in which the individual was capable of knowing and being known by God without external mediation.[139] Poteat agreed but advanced soul competency beyond Mullins's more measured approach. Poteat offered textual support for Christian liberty and cited Luke 12:57, when Jesus asked, "Why do you not judge for yourselves what is right?," and 1 Cor. 10:29, "For why should my liberty be determined by someone else's conscience," as well as James 2:12.[140] Poteat argued that the individual should not turn to the "rabbis" for religious insight but should learn directly from Jesus: "Press through to Jesus . . . He has the words of eternal life, words possessing as well as imparting life."[141] There in the privacy of religious experience was the source of religious knowledge.

Poteat argued that religious experience had a universal quality. Although experienced by countless individuals in as many different places, religious experience was consistent: "The characteristic features of the Christian experience . . . have the universal quality of God and the human soul and are everywhere the same."[142] According to Poteat religious experience was more reliable than the traditional doctrinal form of Christianity, which was always under revision. Poteat displayed his general pessimism about theology when he argued that "the body of Christian doctrine and the organization of the Christian movement" had "suffered modifications and made acquisitions in the course of their passage through the centuries."[143] Experience was more stable than theology: "The Christianity of Athanasius is not the Christianity of Augustine, though they had the same Christian experience" because their theological "case needs to be revised with every important change of scene."[144] And "if it [theology] should be ignored, or discredited, or refuted in part or in whole, Christianity would not share its fate."[145] Poteat argued that the divine encounter as the unchanging essence of Christianity remained the same throughout the ages: "The experience is fundamental and universal. From that point springs the new life in Christ. I venture to think it the essence of Christianity."[146] William Poteat's youngest brother, Edwin McNeill Poteat Sr., president of Furman University in Greenville, South Carolina, explained the uniformity of religious experience by arguing that it was innate to all humans. Edwin Poteat agreed with his brother that this experience was the essence of Christianity.[147] Edgar Mullins also expressed William Poteat's sentiment about the universal character of experience by identifying it throughout the history of Christianity: "It is the source of power in the writings of an Augustine, a Clement, a Schleiermacher."[148]

Poteat asserted that religious experience though universal was distinctively Christian. In religious experience Christ mediated and defined the encounter: "The spirit of man meets in harmony the spirit of God mediated and interpreted by Christ. God in Christ calls to the soul of man."[149] Although mystical in its orientation, the encounter was grounded in the person of Christ. Jesus himself called to every religious seeker: "[Jesus] was King of all those who were open-minded to the truth. And this King of truth-seekers declared Himself to be the embodiment and illustration of the Truth."[150] Jesus as encountered in religious experience was the source of the religious life.[151]

Others in the Southern Baptist Convention agreed. Like Poteat, Alabama pastor Alfred J. Dickinson argued that the essence of Christianity was not a matter of historic facts—a miraculous birth or resurrection—but that one had experienced in his heart the redemptive message of Jesus.[152] Poteat argued that the fellowship and commitment one found in religious experience flowed from Jesus himself.[153] And experiential Christology had power. When Poteat preached a sermon in 1930 titled "The Radiant Christ" and proclaimed the Jesus of religious experience Archibald T. Robertson, professor of New Testament at Southern Seminary in Louisville, Kentucky, was deeply satisfied: "I have just read with great delight your fine sermon . . . on The Radiant Christ. Maybe you ought to have been a preacher instead of a scientist!"[154] And Jesus left a historical legacy too. Poteat argued that the New Testament Gospels revealed that Jesus exemplified the encounter between God and mankind, and it was this good news of religious experience that Jesus preached. However one was not dependent on a written record of Christ. Dickinson declared that one came to know Christ through experiencing the risen Christ directly. The theologian cast doubt on the importance and historicity of Jesus's bodily resurrection: "What became of the physical body of the risen Christ we may not know. It ceased to have any messianic significance or functioning after it had served to identify him to his own as the risen Jesus; and it is idle to speculate about it." Dickinson argued that what mattered was one's experience and the will to take up Christ's spiritual mantle. Instead of asking historical questions about the resurrection Christians should cultivate the experience of his presence now: "It is better to experience God than to know all the world's theologies." Alfred Dickinson echoed Poteat's view when he preached to Southern Baptists in 1907: "The value of religion is in empowering men to experience God; and this we do by our experiencing the risen Lord on his day." One came to know the risen Christ through experience.[155]

Poteat argued that an experience-based Christianity was vigorous. It was sufficient to support men and women through the challenges and questions of life: "It is a means of satisfaction in time of confusion and darkness, a means of hope when despair would otherwise possess us."[156] The faith that one received from his or her religious encounter "gives superiority [over] external circumstance." And this Christianity was active.

Although Poteat gushed with nostalgia for the simplicity of early Christianity he noted that the movement quickly and rightly became an active faith: "The inward experience required expression and imposed a task in the world outside."[157] Modern Christianity was equipped to fulfill the church's mission to bring the kingdom of God to this world. Especially after his retirement in 1927 from the presidency of Wake Forest, Poteat dedicated much of his life to the social concerns of the Progressive Era. He also endured seasons of intense controversy during his career. He might have argued that his life proved his faith was sturdy and active.[158]

Although Poteat's reconceptualized Christianity could appear similar to the Christianity of his childhood it was substantially different. William Poteat's younger brother, Edwin McNeill Poteat Sr., shared the same religious framework. Edwin Poteat confessed that the traditional, doctrinal religion seemed foreign to him. James M. Frost, the founder and first secretary of Southern Baptists' Sunday School Board wrote to offer Edwin Poteat a job and only asked if he could affirm the widely known New Hampshire Confession of Faith. Edwin admitted that he had never previously read it and after reading it found himself baffled by its contents. He told Frost, "As I read the articles today, I felt more and more that they were a harness that did not fit me. Not, I beg you to understand, that I differ on points of doctrine, but, rather that my whole method of approach is different." He politely turned down the job. The distance between Edwin Poteat and Frost was not a matter of one or two doctrines, but his entire framework was different and incompatible with the doctrinal confessionalism of historic Protestantism. Like his brother's, Edwin Poteat's faith was mystical and rooted in religious experience.[159]

Randal Hall recognized in some measure the extent to which William Poteat revised Christianity. Hall recognized for example that "Poteat had to dispense with the orthodox evangelical conception of God and the Bible." Hall, however, also argued that Poteat's liberalism was only a moderate form of liberalism. He considered it to be a "somewhat muddled half-acceptance of liberal theology."[160] Hall might have wrongly equated liberal theology with more aggressive examples of social Christianity, such as that of Walter Rauschenbusch and other social gospel figures. Or he might have misjudged the essential mediating nature of liberalism as a third way between traditional Protestantism on the one side and materialistic agnosticism on the other.[161] However regarding the new socially centered form of American Protestantism, Poteat's contribution was also quite substantial as Hall has demonstrated. In the end Hall followed the conventional picture of a South that was so resolutely conservative that even its most liberal leaders like William Poteat represented something closer to a mild form of theological modernism. But Poteat along with other Southern Baptist progressives was in the mainstream of a national movement of theological liberalism.[162]

CONCLUSION

Poteat's journey into theological liberalism began with a crisis of faith as a young professor, but ideas found in the currents of modern thought provided a satisfying solution for his dilemma. A combination of intellectual angst, fear of ridicule and ostracism, and a strong attachment to religion seemed to drive Poteat's quest to find a way to be a modern man of intellect and a Christian. His intellectual struggle was personal, but it proceeded in a professional context and an emerging social environment that made him reluctant to be left behind in age of progress. As he emerged confidently from his struggle, he felt a burden to help others and to defend Christianity in an age of skepticism. In an insightful study of Poteat's contemporary and counterpart in the North, Augustus H. Strong of Rochester Theological Seminary, historian Grant Wacker referred to a "complex blend of personal, social, and cultural factors" that led many thoughtful Christians to reconsider their religious beliefs and intellectual grounding in this period.[163] Although conflicted in the early years of his career, Poteat solidified his ideas by 1900, and he became an inspiration for others in the South who confronted the same challenges that he had.

Like Friedrich Schleiermacher, who addressed the cultured critics of his time and place when he wrote *On Religion: Speeches to Its Cultured Despisers,* Poteat embraced an apologetic mission to convince the cultured people of southern society that they could embrace the free spirit of the age and scientific knowledge without rejecting Christianity.[164] Poteat hoped to offer an alternative vision of an enlightened religion to a region that was urbanizing, advancing in education, and embracing modern ideas and sentiments. In the South, the cultured despisers were found almost exclusively among the educated. But much more numerous were Poteat's conservative Baptist brethren, most of whom could not have begun to make sense of Poteat's religious ideas. To them Poteat's views amounted to a rejection of the deeply held conviction that the Bible was a unique work of divine revelation, an authoritative source of religious knowledge, which also spoke truthfully of science and history, although care was necessary for interpretation. To Poteat this belief was as uncomfortable as it was necessary to overcome. To do so he appealed to a fluid, experience-based Christianity that focused on piety, morality, and energetic service for the kingdom of God on earth. This kind of religion offered less offense to the cultured people of modern society.

Poteat's acceptance of theological liberalism was a seminal part of the spread of modernism among Southern Baptists. He demonstrated how one could be a scientific and socially respectable person while also holding onto religion. Crucial to the social and cultural background of the period, Poteat embraced the rising New South spirit of progress and remade his faith in the modern image. He dedicated his career to persuading others to do the same. Modern progress did not have to come at the expense of religion. A modernized religion could make its own contribution in the greater drive for progress.

Chapter Three

A NEW RELIGION FOR THE NEW SOUTH

William L. Poteat joined a common cause with the New South visionaries to remake the South into a truly modern society. As the leading New South boosters focused upon economic, political, and social renewal, Poteat envisioned a new form of religion that would suit the modernized South emerging in the late nineteenth and early twentieth century. His adoption of liberal ideas in the 1880s roughly paralleled the rise of the New South movement. And the progressive ethos of the New South fueled and supported the growth of theological liberalism in the region. Liberal Protestantism did not originate within New South ideology. However the progressive vision of the New South reinforced the motivations behind Protestant liberalism and provided fertile soil for the movement to take root. New South ideals and southern liberalism emerged in the same places: the New South's rising towns and cities and the educational institutions that produced Southern society's new leaders. The impulse that drove the New South ambition for progress seemed to be related to the drive of the religious thinkers who reconceptualized Christianity for the modern age and this religious movement effectively became part of the New South drive for progress that transformed southern society in the late nineteenth and early twentieth century.

Poteat and other Southern liberals shared the ambition of the New South boosters who aimed to create a more progressive image for the South. Educated Southerners cringed at the stigmas that marked the South, and they became zealous to overcome them, whether the stigma related to a perception of economic provincialism or religious backwardness. A determination to overcome Southern marginalization animated the New South boosters and a fear of marginalization was at the heart of Protestant liberalism. Southern liberalism was a part of a broader movement in American religion that responded to the challenges posed by modern ideas. The regional transformation of the New South became the distinctive setting for the Southern wing of this American movement.

The New South produced a powerful new social class. This Southern bourgeoisie of professionals and businesspeople composed the new leadership of Southern society as the planter class, the old order, lost hegemony over political and social affairs after the Civil War and the abolition of slavery. Poteat and other Southern liberals exemplified the new professional class, although Poteat resisted the utilitarian impulse that became part of the New South creed. Among the new middle class, who embraced the cosmopolitan values of social respectability and modern modes of thought, Poteat encountered an ideal audience for his modernized form of Christianity. The growing towns and cities where his prospective audience lived were transforming the region, and they provided a suitable environment for the growth of Southern liberalism.

Similar to New South boosters like Henry Grady and Richard H. Edmonds who took their message for Southern progress to the cities of the North and key places in the South, Poteat spread his religious ideas widely. He delivered academic lectures at the leading theological institutions of the North, and he leveraged his extraordinary influence in the South by speaking at some of the region's key institutions of higher education, among many other venues. Several of his academic lectures were published as books. These books expanded the reach of his message and established him as a leading spokesperson for the liberal Christianity that he hoped would improve the image of the South on the national stage.

In perfect harmony with the New South spirit, Poteat's religious message had a robust social orientation. Although he eloquently advocated for the subjective, piety-based religion that had rescued him during his spiritual crisis, he also developed a distinct social vision for the Christian faith. He drew from the heart of the Christian mission when he envisioned the reconstruction of the world's entire social order to reflect the spirit of Christ. Armed with Jesus's principles of love, self-renunciation, and justice, human efforts for social progress would produce the gradual realization of the kingdom of God on earth and would produce a truly utopian society. An enlightened anthropology provided the necessary optimism that a dedicated people could indeed redeem society. Poteat's new theology of social salvation provided the vital religious motivation as people gradually produced the kingdom of heaven on earth. Because all of humanity shared an indivisible kinship as God's spiritual children, salvation in the traditional sense was unnecessary. But those equipped with the principles of Jesus could be the leaders of a movement toward an earthly utopia. This was a version of Christianity that Poteat hoped would appeal to the enlightened sensibilities of modern people. And among the New South boosters who proclaimed the transformation of their society Poteat did his part to establish a progressive faith that would suit the new age that was dawning.

THE RISE OF THE NEW SOUTH

The rise of the New South was the setting of Poteat's early career and his adoption of theological liberalism. He resonated with the New South vision that was transforming the South and revolutionizing North Carolina. When Poteat refashioned Christianity into a religion for the modern mind he contributed to a broader movement to remake the South into a more progressive society.

The South was in a depressed state at the end of Reconstruction in 1877.[1] Historian Paul Gaston described the postwar South as "desperately poor, alternatively despised, ridiculed or pitied and saddled with many unwelcome burdens."[2] But historian Edward Ayers rightly argued that although the Southern scene was bleak, signs of progress began emerging after Reconstruction that led Southern journalists to begin describing the emergence of a New South.[3]

The New South became a broad movement that embraced the energy, efficiency, and commitment to education that characterized Northern society, but with the values, morals, and faith of the South. New South boosters moved to compete with the Northern states to advance the South's standing in American life. If White Southerners could reconcile with the North and reenter national life they could create a new economic and social order that privileged industry and scientific advancement that, as Paul Gaston argued, "would enrich the region, restore prestige and power" and truly modernize the South.[4] The movement initially focused upon an economic vision. But the New South spirit inspired a broader movement for Southern progress that touched every area of life: politics, education, matters of race, and religion.

The Vision for a New South

Henry W. Grady, the editor of Atlanta's *Constitution,* cast the vision for the New South.[5] On December 22, 1886, Grady gave an address before the New England Society of New York that became renowned as an expression of the New South vision. Grady was thirty-six years old and he represented the rising generation of Southerners who had been too young to have participated in the Civil War and who also experienced the devastating effects of the war and Reconstruction.[6] He argued that the South, by which he meant White Southerners, had made peace with the outcome of the war and had resolved to move forward: "There was a South of slavery and secession—that South is dead. There is a South of union and freedom—that South, thank God, is living, breathing, growing every hour."[7] He stressed that Southerners had not been idle since the war. They "stepped from the trenches into the furrow; horses that had charged Federal guns marched before the plow, and fields that ran red with human blood in April were green with the harvest in June." Grady referenced Union General William T. Sherman, who was in attendance, and cited the rising city of Atlanta: "From the ashes he left us in 1864 we have raised a brave and beautiful city; that some how or other we have caught the sunshine in the bricks and mortar of our homes, and have builded therein not one ignoble prejudice or memory."[8] Grady insisted that Southerners had "fallen in love with work" and "have let economy take root and spread among us." The South was ready to "put business above politics." Grady contended that Southerners were also achieving racial harmony and equality and suggested that the Confederacy's defense of slavery had been the source of its inevitable failure. Grady assured his Northern audience that the sectionalism defining the previous generation of White Southerners was over. They had "smoothed the path to southward" and "wiped out the place where Mason and Dixon's line used to be."[9] The Northern press celebrated Grady's address and hailed him as the spokesperson of a New South. Grady did not stand alone as a leader of the New South movement, but Paul Gaston called Grady a "chief apostle of the New South movement."[10]

Although the New South movement was resolutely forward-looking it relied on Old South commitments more than it let on. The New South's promoters idealized and romanticized aspects of the Old South as they simultaneously promoted a fresh vision for the South's future. They portrayed the emerging South as a new civilization in place of the old, but it was not altogether removed from its antebellum roots, both historical and mythologized.[11]

Henry Grady and other New South boosters championed the economic model of the North and aimed to make the South into an industrial society. An industrial South would contain mills and factories but also required agricultural improvements.[12] Southerners' reliance on cotton had to give way to a more diversified agricultural economy, and farmers needed to incorporate the latest scientific advances to improve agricultural efficiency. Industrialization and increasing urbanization would give rise to a new market for a more diversified agriculture.[13] Another New South visionary, Richard H. Edmonds, argued that the South had unparalleled and untapped resources that were ready to be used: timber, iron ore, and coal, as well as the richest soil and most ideal climate in America.[14] But New South boosters knew that they could not accomplish their lofty goals without investment from the North and a greater supply of immigrant workers.[15] With optimism and some exaggeration Edmonds argued that Northern and European investors were pouring into the South. He suggested that Americans would soon exchange "Go West, young man" for "Go South."[16] The New South prophets promised prosperity for the South and collective triumph over what Paul Gaston called the "crushing poverty and heartbreaking disillusionment" of White Southerners.[17] Gaston argued that New South leaders fixed their eyes toward the future: "The New South prophets found their greatest pleasure in describing the nature of the future. They envisioned a balanced, diversified, dynamic economy that would produce incalculable riches."[18] William Poteat cherished the hope of progress, but he also became concerned about negative consequences from the New South vision for prosperity, namely in the form of materialism and a more utilitarian outlook on life.[19]

New South visionaries considered political reunification with the North to be essential to Southern progress. After the Civil War, White Southerners lacked significant political power in national affairs, and former Confederates lost local control in their own states. In the postbellum period White leaders experienced political and social isolation. Conservative Southern Democrats, called Redeemers, gradually seized control of Southern politics after Reconstruction and established a government for White persons only. This movement laid the political foundations of the modern South.[20] But the South remained politically weak on the national scene and this remained the case until the presidential campaign of Woodrow Wilson half a century after the Civil War.[21] For the South to achieve progress it had to overcome its isolation and find political allies beyond its borders.

New South boosters claimed that the impressive growth of towns and cities in the region was proof of the South's progress. Edward Ayers demonstrated that Southern towns and cities grew by five million people from 1880 to 1910, nearly doubling the national average for urban growth.[22]

Towns arose from the rural countryside, and older towns swelled into small cities, while several true urban centers like Atlanta, Birmingham, Nashville, and Memphis emerged.[23] Cities became regional commercial hubs in connection with the emerging towns. They were vitally dependent on the railroads, which were rapidly expanding in the South in the late nineteenth century.[24] In the New South's cities a rising middle class of professionals and businesspeople grew to possess great influence in society: economically, politically, and intellectually.[25] The new Southern bourgeoisie was largely young and educated, and it developed the sensibilities of urban life.[26] As a part of this new class Poteat and other liberal religionists used their social standing to promote religious enlightenment as part of cosmopolitan respectability. They became the hope of an improved image for Southern society.[27]

New South leaders seized upon education as a means for remaking the South. Paul Gaston argued that the New South visionaries believed "education is everyman's passport to success in a competitive, free enterprise society," and the business-centric and urbanized South of the future demanded exceptional improvement in education.[28] Historian Dan R. Frost examined the role of education in the New South and argued that Southern leaders, including former leaders of the Confederacy, "embraced innovative academic policies and developed forward-looking ideology for the South in the postbellum period."[29] Military defeat had impressed upon Southerners the superiority of Northern industry, material, and education. As a central feature of the New South vision, Southern educators produced a new generation of Southerners who could lead the South's economic and social advancement. The rising generation inspired hope that the South would soon share in the wealth and comfort of modern America and reassert itself as a powerful region in American life. Isaac T. Tichenor was a quintessential New South figure, an industrialist, a member of the new professional class, and also an educator. As president of Alabama's Auburn University he prioritized scientific instruction, agricultural innovation, and other skills that were important for business in modern America. Historian Michael Williams identified Tichenor as one of the leaders who "sought to blend the changes taking place in higher education with the adoption of New South ideals."[30] As an educator William Poteat stood in partial contrast to the New South trajectory. He insisted on the value of the sciences, but he also desired to maintain something closer to the classical model of education to form cultured individuals for a refined society. The purpose of education, he argued, was not to offer "knowledge of how to make a living." Instead education should produce "the man of liberal culture."[31] He thus resisted the more utilitarian approach of modern education in exchange for a classical and Victorian model, even as he celebrated the advancement of science and technology in modern education.[32]

A campaign for racial harmony also formed a part of the New South creed. But race relations grew steadily more tense during the New South era as Southern Whites sought social and political dominance while African Americans pushed for protection of Black persons' equal rights under the US Constitution.[33] Henry Grady recognized that racial harmony was necessary to meet the New South's broader goals. He expressed his relief that slavery was "gone forever from the American soil," but he indicated that the presence of two "dissimilar races on the same soil" was "a problem without precedent or parallel," particularly because the two were "terribly unequal in intelligence and responsibility."[34] Don Doyle argued that the New South leaders aimed to improve race relations and to better the economic and social conditions of African Americans. However, he also noted that they "accepted racist assumptions about the limited capacity of blacks and their inferior destiny in the South."[35] Racial segregation itself was a product of the New South. Its origins lay in assumptions of White superiority in the South's new environment: its rising cities, expanding railroads, and marketplaces.[36] In 1896 the United States Supreme Court case *Plessy v. Ferguson* gave national approval to local practices and legal arguments that were already at work in the South.[37] Doyle rightly concluded that "in the end, the New South's commitment to biracial social progress was compromised by the burden of racial prejudice."[38] Poteat was dedicated to the work of racial cooperation, but he also embraced a White supremacist worldview and acted from a paternalistic framework rather than acknowledging the equality of African Americans.[39]

The New South in North Carolina

Poteat's North Carolina became a leading state for the New South movement and likewise emerged as a leading state for liberal religious thought. Earlier in its history, North Carolina received the nickname of the "Rip Van Winkle State" for its underdeveloped landscape, slow economy, and lack of interest in national affairs. But it surged ahead in the final decades of the nineteenth century as a quintessentially New South state that was determined to achieve progress.[40] The progressive spirit of the New South revolutionized North Carolina and gave its leading citizens hope for overcoming its reputation of backwardness. Along with economics, urban growth, and education, a fresh consideration of religion would also have to be a part of establishing a progressive image for North Carolina.

North Carolina's transformation can be quantified in its growing towns and cities. Rural villages developed into bustling towns, and older towns grew into small cities. The town that became the city of Greensboro had a population of 497 in 1870 and grew to 10,035 by 1900. Salisbury similarly grew from 168 to 6,277, while Winston, near the old town of Salem, grew from 443 to 10,008. In 1870 Charlotte had a population of 4,473 but grew to 18,091 three decades later. Durham seemed to rise out the wilderness, having been too small even to appear in the 1870 census, but it grew to 6,679 in 1900.[41] North Carolina's urban growth was exceptional. But as C. Vann Woodward indicated, North Carolina remained a largely rural state: "North Carolina, one of the states most affected by the industrial movement, had 3.9 per cent of its population classified as urban in 1890. . . . By 1900 there was not a single city in North Carolina with a population of 25,000 and only six with more than 10,000."[42] But the transformation that occurred through the influence of the New South mentality was far more significant than the relative growth of urban space implied.

The rise of industry transformed North Carolina's economy and with it the lives of many of its people. It began with tobacco production, a crop that North Carolinians had grown for generations. But the invention of an automated cigarette machine in 1880 gave the industry fresh potential. Aggressive, New South-style businesspeople made North Carolina the leading state for tobacco production and gave rise to cities like Durham, Winston, and High Point.[43] As important as tobacco was in North Carolina, no form of industry better symbolized the New South than cotton mills. North Carolina's cotton textile production grew exponentially in the late nineteenth century, as the South outstripped New England, the historic leader of cotton textile production.[44] Leading North Carolinians surely felt they were on the verge of something great.

The New South vision inspired impressive advances in North Carolina education. As with industry North Carolina began at a substantial disadvantage in education and had the highest illiteracy rate in the South, with 19.5 percent illiteracy among White persons in 1900.[45] But North Carolina surged ahead in the twentieth century.[46] State leaders like Governor Charles B. Aycock, Charles D. McIver, and Walter H. Page led the state to remarkable growth in education, principally among White

North Carolinians. Historian James Leloudis argued that social reformers sought to create a New South through education: "Reformers viewed the classroom as the progenitor of a new culture and way of life."[47] The new approach to education aimed to create a new mind-set for the newly emerging society. Educators sought to instill ambition, industry, and individualism in their students.[48] Walter Hines Page, a significant force behind North Carolina's newfound progressive image, was one such voice for education. Paul Gaston argued that Page "provided a link between the [New South] ideology of the eighties and the public school campaign of the early twentieth century."[49] The rising tide of progress was exhilarating for educated White North Carolinians.

The admittedly limited nature of the New South movement's success was less important than the progressive spirit that it birthed. The South's progress was impressive in its own right. Edward Ayers noted that the South's industrial growth in the late nineteenth century consistently surpassed national averages.[50] Cities grew, schools proliferated, and industries created millions of jobs outside of agriculture, but the boosters' rhetoric exceeded reality. The South continued to be a largely rural region when compared to the more developed Northern states.[51] However Ayers explained that the cultural impact for Southerners was remarkable, and the "impact of industry in the New South needs to be measured in people's experience, not merely in numbers, not merely by debunking inflated rhetoric."[52] The South's backwardness showed some signs of diminishing, especially in regions like North Carolina. And educated North Carolinians celebrated as heroes those who elevated their state's reputation. They celebrated William Poteat for his refreshing and liberalizing influence in the state. Gerald Johnson, the esteemed journalist, praised Poteat for his contribution "to saving the intellectual honor of his state."[53]

AN APOSTLE FOR NEW SOUTH RELIGION

Poteat contributed to the New South movement by championing theological liberalism as a means to social and cultural progress for North Carolina and the South. He was one of the pioneers of Southern liberalism as recognized by both his admirers and opponents.[54] Religion held a prominent place in Southern culture and society. For many of the educated, professional class of Southerners who embraced the modern cosmopolitan values of social respectability and cultured refinement, the South's Protestant Christianity posed a problem in light of new science and historical research, as well as the changing sentiments of modern people. Poteat presented a liberalized form of Christianity that suited the modern mind, and he aimed to remove the obstacles that might jeopardize Christianity's social respectability. Like the New South boosters who labored to overcome the economic, social, and political marginalization of the South in American life, Poteat labored to protect religion's place in modern society and to avoid its marginalization in public life. Many educated Southerners prized his contribution to the movement for Southern progress in the form of his modernized religion.

Poteat fit the customary background for the leaders of the New South that significantly shaped their drive for progress. He was born in 1856 and was too young to have served in the Civil War, as had his older brothers. Instead of the glory claimed by veterans of the Confederate army, Poteat only experienced the devasting effects of war that lingered for years afterward as a reminder of the South's failure and the apparent inferiority of Southern civilization.[55] Poteat's family had belonged to the old planter aristocracy, but like many others, his family adapted to the changes brought on by the loss of the war. They abandoned their plantation and moved to the nearby town of Yanceyville, where they operated a small business.[56] And like most of the New South leaders, Poteat received a good education and graduated with a bachelor of arts degree from Wake Forest College in 1877.[57] Poteat cherished and idealized his Old South roots, but he was not occupied with the past.[58] His mind was fixed on the future and progress. He proposed that liberal Christianity provided a path to bring Southern religion into harmony with the best of modern society, and he believed that it could lead the South beyond the provincialism that had characterized its postbellum existence.

Poteat was an apostle for a New South form of Christianity. He presented a modernized form of Christianity and removed the obstacles that he believed traditional Christianity posed to modern progress. He began by reconceptualizing Christianity's traditional source of knowledge and its mode of revelation. He contended that God revealed himself through personal, spiritual encounter, not through an ancient text and theological declarations. With this subjective nature of the divine encounter, Poteat argued that the individual held a private accountability before God for all doctrinal and spiritual matters. Because the Bible was a human book of spirituality, it did not have to answer to science, nor was it problematic if it reflected a primitive understanding of science and history. Poteat separated religious knowledge from scientific knowledge to make religion immune from the intellectual challenges of the modern age. In addition to these intellectual challenges, Poteat was sensitive to modern people's changing sensibilities. He exchanged the traditional theology of human sinfulness for a more optimistic view of humanity and redefined Christian salvation by exchanging the otherworldly elements for a gospel of social redemption. Christianity's mission was to build a more just and peaceful world, which would transform society into the kingdom of God on earth. Poteat believed that this fluid and privatized religion of social transformation made Christianity immune from modern criticism and rendered Christians safe from the contempt of the more progressive society that was emerging.[59]

As the New South boosters imitated Northern industry, urban society, and education, Poteat provided a vision for religion that paralleled the liberalism that was transforming Protestant Christianity in the North. When William Newton Clarke declared that "Christianity is not a book-religion, but a life-religion," Poteat could not have agreed more.[60] Similarly Shailer Mathews argued that liberalism was not a new theology but represented "an attitude rather than a doctrine." Mathews declared that "the Modernist movement will never have a creed or authoritative confession," and he espoused the same subjective form of Christianity that Poteat advocated.[61] Theologian Gary Dorrien referred to Northern liberals when he concluded that liberalism was a movement to preserve social and cultural relevance for religion in the modern world. Shailer Mathews and other Northern liberals shared the same concerns as Poteat. They contended that Christians would have to "pass tests of moral and intellectual credibility" if they hoped to avoid marginalization in modern society.[62] In addition to supporting progressive Southerners, Poteat also hoped to enlighten some conservatives by convincing them to embrace liberalism, much like his counterparts did in the North. Thomas T. Martin, one of Poteat's most enduring critics, was not far off when he charged that Poteat was "but the Southern echoes from . . . Chicago University."[63] Poteat likely took this as a compliment and a sign of progress.

Progressive-minded Southerners praised Poteat for his contribution to the effort to overcome the South's intellectual backwardness.[64] In the late 1920s an unknown journalist praised Poteat as a liberalizing force in the South in "A Man Who Made It Easier to Think in the South."[65] He called Poteat "a symbol of the struggle for academic freedom and intellectual liberty." Poteat, he said, exemplified the great sacrifices that progressive

Southerners made in the effort to improve the Southern mind. And when Poteat prevailed against the conservative forces that sought to oust him from his position, "it meant that every honest teacher of truth in North Carolina would be free from badgering and from heresy-hunting."[66] When Virginius Dabney, a respected journalist from Richmond, Virginia, set out to write an account of liberal movements in the South, he wrote to Poteat, "As you are such a commanding figure among Southern liberals, I hope you will pardon me if I turn to you for help."[67] He asked for Poteat's input on religion and specified that he wanted "especially to have the names of those who were instrumental in freeing the churches from the tyranny of dogma."[68] In his book Dabney praised Poteat for his "magnificent fight . . . to save his state and his church from disgrace."[69] Gerald Johnson reflected on Poteat's willingness to spend his career at a small Baptist college in the South when he could have aspired to greater things. But he argued that Poteat's mission to enlighten Southerners' minds compelled him to stay: "Thus he threw his life away . . . [only] to lift somewhat the level of intelligence and to reduce somewhat the prevalence of bigotry in the most powerful sect in his commonwealth. Only to contribute to saving the intellectual honor of his State."[70] H. Shelton Smith, who was a professor of religion at Duke University's School of Religion, wrote to Poteat in 1937 and proclaimed Poteat's pioneering role as a force for modern religious thought: "You . . . represent a period of progressive thinking in the South that has not been set forth."[71]

Poteat's influence was significant, but the success of his program was limited to the new Southern bourgeoisie. Somewhat like the New South movement in general, his impact was substantial, even as the South remained a largely conservative society where many Southerners lived and worshipped as they had for generations with some actively resisting the changes proposed by the New South boosters.[72] Southern liberals like Poteat found a common bond with the New South spirit of progress, particularly in the regions of the South that saw the most economic and urban development. But to a great degree the South as a whole remained a traditional place, including religion. Southerners who did adopt the progressive spirit of the age and who embraced liberal Christianity, and there were many of them, stood far removed from the rank and file within the South's evangelical denominations, especially in Poteat's own Southern Baptist Convention. But the South's rising class of professionals provided a surprisingly receptive welcome to the modernized form of religion.

POTEAT'S ACADEMIC LECTURES

Poteat disseminated his religious ideas with New South ambition. He fascinated audiences in the leading theological institutions of the North, and his lectures at Southern institutions like Southern Baptist Theological Seminary, the University of North Carolina, and Wake Forest College offered a powerful regional influence. The most significant of these lectures were subsequently published as books. These expanded the reach of his message and established him as a leading spokesperson for the liberal Christianity that he hoped would improve the South's image. These books were widely read by educated Southern Baptists and by the cultural elites of the New South.

Laboratory and Pulpit. Poteat delivered the Julius Brown Gay Lectures at Southern Baptist Theological Seminary in Louisville, Kentucky, in March 1900. At the time Poteat was a professor of biology at Wake Forest College and was not well known beyond his native North Carolina. The lectures were published a year later in 1901 as *Laboratory and Pulpit: The Relation of Biology to the Preacher and His Message.*[73] In these lectures Poteat advanced quintessential theological liberalism to seminarians who would become the future leaders of the Southern Baptist Convention. However relatively little concern arose about the content of his lectures. Southern Baptist leaders and the seminarians in Louisville presumably sensed the novelty of Poteat's message, but they too felt the power of modern challenges, and Poteat was bold enough to offer creative if not also provocative answers.

In his lectures Poteat acknowledged that embracing the modern revisions of Christianity was difficult to bear, but it was also necessary and exciting: "The period of transition is, indeed painful and perilous, but that is how we grow from more to more. Let us rejoice in our growing apprehension of God, and when he pours us out the new wine of life, fetch us new bottles to receive it."[74] Poteat argued that if they embraced the new form of Christianity, it was not the essence of Christianity that was changing but only their apprehension of it: "Christianity is absolute, our apprehension of it is progressive."[75] Poteat struck a triumphant tone in these early lectures. He envisioned a future of enlightened and cultured society in which science was celebrated for its revelations, and religion was cherished for its cultivation of spirituality and moral virtue.

The New Peace. Poteat delivered a series of lectures in 1905 at several of the historic theological institutions in the North. In May he lectured at Hamilton Theological Seminary of Colgate University. The lectures were so well received that in October and November he delivered the same lectures at Crozer Theological Seminary, Newton Theological Institution, Rochester Theological Seminary, and the Divinity School of the University of Chicago. Poteat became president of Wake Forest in 1905. Due to his career advancement the publication of his lectures was delayed, even as William Newton Clarke encouraged their publication. In 1915 they were published as *The New Peace: Lectures on Science and Religion.*[76] This work presented a nascent form of Poteat's thought on the resolution of the conflict between science and religion. He argued this was an artificial conflict removed by recognizing the separate spheres of science and religion. These lectures were Poteat's first and only significant interaction with the major theological institutions of the North. But the eventual publication of the lectures gave his ideas a broader hearing.

Can a Man Be a Christian To-day? Poteat delivered the John Calvin McNair Lectures at the University of North Carolina in May 1925 at the height of his influence.[77] It was also the high point of the fundamentalist-modernist controversy in American Protestantism. Poteat himself had already endured two successive controversies related to his outspoken liberal views, and his McNair lectures provoked a third controversy.[78] Poteat spoke with bravado and delivered the mature expression of his religious thought about the liberal vision of Christianity.[79]

Gerald W. Johnson, by then a respected journalist and a professor of journalism at the University of North Carolina, covered Poteat's McNair Lectures.[80] Poteat delivered three evening lectures. Johnson accentuated "the quality of the lectures" and indicated that "the crowd was greater on each successive night, until Sunday night Memorial Hall was taxed to afford accommodations to the great throng that turned out."[81] Poteat estimated that fifteen hundred people attended on the third night.[82] Johnson noted that Poteat's third lecture progressed toward sermonic exhortation: "It moved the great congregation powerfully. Some were brought to tears, not students only, but faculty members and citizens from other towns, men who are not easily affected by emotion of that sort."[83]

Poteat perceived himself to be a guardian of religion and argued that his enlightened vision for Christianity offered a bright future for religion in the modern world. Johnson noted with personal satisfaction that the university's president, Harry W. Chase, introduced Poteat as a "Defender of the Faith."[84] Poteat stood against the true enemies of the faith: "Some men have been driven mad by a little learning, and have tried to use scientific truth to insult God and offend his people." Poteat lamented that one extreme tended to encourage extremism from the other side who "identify a divine religion with a man made theology, and brand every critic of their theology as an enemy of Christ." Poteat's call to safeguard Christianity meant opposition to fundamentalists: "It is time for educated Christians to oppose [the literalists], not harshly with bitter words, but firmly, without compromise."[85] Poteat went on the offensive against "extreme fundamentalists because, as he sees it, they are doing all they can to make it impossible for an intelligent, educated man to be a Christian today."[86]

To describe the current state of Christianity Poteat used the metaphor of a traveler who accumulated an increasingly cumbersome array of baggage. Johnson accurately summarized Poteat's central point: "The task now before the intelligent Christian is to disentangle the traveler from his baggage, because it is evident that much of that baggage cannot pass through the straight and narrow gateway of truth."[87] More than ever the modern age required the removal of the baggage: a supernaturally inspired Bible, doctrinal standards, and ecclesial authority. Poteat argued that modern knowledge demonstrated that much of the human baggage affixed to Christianity was faulty. The Bible was a human document, doctrine was open to revision, and religious authority was subjective and grounded in the individual and his or her experience with God. Modern Christians needed to disentangle essential Christianity from the nonessential baggage before modern people confused the two and discarded all forms of faith. Rather than hindering true religion, science was actually helping to free it so that educated people could remain Christians. To Poteat Christianity informed personal spirituality, morality, and civility, not the old questions of the dogmatists. Poteat stood in the middle between two extremes that threatened the future vitality of Christianity. One dismissed religion as backward and distasteful, and the other refused the revisions that were necessary for Christianity to thrive in the modern age.

The University of North Carolina quickly published the popular lectures, and the book sold relatively well. Within three months it sold more than one thousand copies and reached two thousand by the end of the year.[88] North Carolina Baptists' *Biblical Recorder* discussed *Can a Man Be a Christian To-day?* throughout the summer of 1925.[89] Poteat continued to receive praise for the book years after its publication. In 1935 one admirer wrote Poteat when he saw that the *New York Times* quoted the book.[90] Joseph Alling thanked Poteat for being a bright light for those who desired to hold onto faith while also accepting the claims of modern science. Poteat offered a powerful example for those who wanted to be modern and Christian: "For many people it should be a satisfaction to believe that they may 'retain your reverence before the Divine Authority of the Bible without embarrassment before the assured results of science.'"[91] Poteat's book helped thoughtful people adjust their religion to fit "the assured results of science" while also maintaining religious devotion.

The Way of Victory. Poteat delivered a series of lectures at the Chapel Hill School of Religion in October 1928. Although the school was independent from the University of North Carolina many of the university's students attended the lectures that were held at the Methodist Church of Chapel Hill. William Couch of the university's press published the lectures as *The Way of Victory* in 1929.[92]

In this book Poteat advanced a vision for social renewal based upon an appropriation of Jesus's teachings on the kingdom of God.[93] Poteat argued that the Christian mission for kingdom advancement was to redeem human society by infusing every area of life with the Christian principles of love and justice. Poteat advanced an imminent kingdom theology to energize a religious movement that would address the social challenges of modern society. He refocused Christian energy away from the heavenly minded blessed hope and the conservative fixation on eternity toward a mission for social redemption that focused on the imminent realization of the kingdom through the efforts of determined men and women.[94] He argued that the work of social salvation was progressively forming society into the kingdom of God on earth. This represented a recovery of the ancient message of Jesus.

Poteat's social vision harmonized with the emerging sentiments and values of modern society. He encouraged Christians to link arms with the reformers of America's Progressive Era to address the challenges of the age and ingratiate themselves to the cultured people of society who found traditional evangelical conversionism disconcerting. Poteat himself considered evangelicalism's theology of the new birth to be a disadvantageous appendage to authentic faith. Poteat, like other Southern liberals and their counterparts in the North, removed the stumbling blocks that traditional Christians had placed in the paths of modern people. Poteat's enlightened religion appealed to many of the cultured leaders of Southern society. But conservative Protestants eventually recognized the redefinition that was involved in liberalism. Poteat was hailed as a hero of the faith by many liberal Southern Baptists, but grassroots Baptists eventually determined that Poteat's Christianity was no Christianity at all. They saw him as a threat to the faith, not its savior.[95]

A NEW THEOLOGY OF THE KINGDOM

With a prominent interest in kingdom theology (transforming society into the kingdom of God on earth) Poteat and other Southern Baptist leaders bolstered a movement for social redemption.[96] Their vision to transform society into the kingdom of God on earth was religious. But it fit well with the New South impulse to remake Southern society, as well as with the more optimistic spirit of the age. A fresh optimism for human nature and humanity's relationship with God and a redefinition of salvation inspired renewed energy for expressions of kingdom theology. And the evolution of Southern society that occurred during the New South era offered tremendous hope for social progress. Poteat and others advanced an imminent kingdom theology and energized a religious movement to transform their society.

The theme of kingdom was familiar to Southern evangelicals, but Poteat suggested its reorientation. Southern evangelicals held that the church, whose mission was to evangelize and make disciples, was God's primary instrument for the advancement of the kingdom that Christ had inaugurated in this world. But they judged that the kingdom would only be consummated when the world to come arrived at the eschaton.[97] Poteat refocused what had been significantly an eternal hope into a temporal realization of the kingdom in this present world. Evangelicals embraced a stewardship for social transformation. However, they looked for divine consummation of the kingdom at the eschaton and the establishment of the new creation as the eternal home for the community of the redeemed. Poteat concentrated on the advancement of the kingdom in this world, which would be fulfilled by the efforts of men and women to redeem society. This fit well with the social activists of the American Progressive Era.[98] In Ritschlian fashion Poteat argued that Christianity's mission was the temporal redemption of society to be ordered by the principles of peace and love.[99] As with Southern progressivism, Poteat's optimistic activism harmonized well with the late Victorian spirit and its work for social progress, which were infusing the towns and cities of the New South.

Poteat addressed kingdom theology throughout his career. In 1913 he spoke to a group of Southern Baptist laypeople to inspire commitment to kingdom advancement. Anticipating a more individualistic mind-set,

Poteat urged that the kingdom started with the individual but did not end there: "[Jesus] saves the individual in order to make him a savior. He saves the man in order to save the world."[100] To critics who charged Christianity with insufficient concern beyond the individual, Poteat admitted "that Christianity as an experience is individual, but as a force it is social and organizes itself for social ends."[101] Jesus's mission had been a social mission. And his commandments for the kingdom were "principles which find their proper fulfillment only in the organized life of man." Poteat explained that the church was not synonymous with the kingdom and the kingdom was not dependent on the church. The church, in fact, had sometimes been an obstacle to kingdom advancement, for instance when it had been obsessed with doctrinal debates: "The battle of the sects has been the shame and often the defeat of Christianity."[102] He exhorted his audience members to surrender their comfortable lives for the cause of bettering society: "Off with your prim dignity. Wade in. No other cause is worthwhile. Nothing else is worthy of your intelligent, whole-hearted enthusiasm."[103] Poteat appropriated the charge of John the Baptist and Jesus to challenge his hearers' limited social action: "Repent for the Kingdom of Heaven is at hand."[104] Poteat exhorted, "This is enlistment day. Hand up to him now without delay your name on your heart."[105]

In 1930 Poteat made a compelling call for the immediate progress of the kingdom through social activism. He argued that Christians owed greater attention to the kingdom because it was "the central theme of our Lord's teaching."[106] Poteat defined the kingdom as "the reign of God in the life of man, or, the will of God realized in all human relations." Contrary to the otherworldly theology of evangelicalism, Poteat stressed a kingdom not for "the interstellar spaces" but for "this present world."[107] He argued that when Christians have been at their best, they were zealous to improve society. They worked for peace and justice. Poteat noted that some "Christian teachers, quite unaccountably, insist upon the other-worldliness of our religion." Such teachers should look to Jesus, who revealed the kingdom as a reality for this world. And the kingdom had no boundaries. It reached into business, politics, and social relations. Men and women who had embraced the spirit of Christ could gradually redeem every area of society. But much work remained: "A great part of it is yet to occupied. It is our task to establish His mastery over all, to infuse His spirit into all, to exact tribute from all for His purpose of universal redemption." Poteat's kingdom vision was a renewed version of the older postmillennialism of American Protestantism.[108]

Liberal Southern Baptist leaders redefined the kingdom of God the same way Poteat did. In 1931 Alabama pastor John W. Phillips preached a progressive message at the Southern Baptist Convention in Mobile, Alabama.[109] Like Poteat, Phillips stressed the greater importance of the kingdom over the church: "We find that Jesus mentioned the church on only two separate occasions but many times spoke of the kingdom. His sermons were about the kingdom. His parables were parables of the kingdom."[110] Joining the church was far easier than joining the kingdom. The rich young ruler and the Pharisees were in the church but not the kingdom.[111] The Old Testament priests too had missed the kingdom: "The priest confined God in a box, over which he presided, and from which he doled divine favors, for a consideration to Jews only. [But the] prophet took the wings of the morning and found God everywhere."[112] Baptist preachers, he declared, "are not the successors of the priests, but sons of the prophets."[113] Jesus shook the foundations of Jewish religion when he arrived with fresh articulation of the kingdom. In his Sermon on the Mount, Jesus perfected his kingdom ethic. The Jews opposed his message "because the principles of the kingdom jeopardized their special privileges, antagonized their prejudices, [and] opposed their orthodoxies."[114] Jesus's disciples temporarily embraced the kingdom, but "they seemed never to have seen it as [Jesus] saw it, and very soon it faded from their sky, until the word almost disappeared from their writings." The institutional church drove out the pure kingdom message from the beginning. But the modern age had brought a rediscovery of Jesus's original message: "More people are thinking, writing and talking about the kingdom than ever before. It is the biggest thing in the Christian thought of the world."[115] With the recovery of Jesus's message, Phillips suggested a fresh revision of Christianity: "We must restudy in light of the kingdom, some of our great words and favorite phrases. What do we mean by the atonement, by salvation and redemption? What do we mean by 'following Jesus' and 'accepting him as our Savior and Lord?'"[116] Phillips undergirded his kingdom message by redefining salvation just as Poteat did: "[It] is neither mystical nor magical, but the practical application of the principles of Christ and of Galilee and Calvary to the motives and methods of men."[117] Preaching to a room full of Southern Baptists, Phillips was not preaching to the choir, but neither was he ostracized for his message. He was elected vice president of the convention the next year.[118]

Like Phillips, Alfred J. Dickinson argued that he and others of his generation now understood the kingdom better than did the apostles.[119]

Previous generations had missed the pure kingdom message of Jesus, but Dickinson and other modern Christians had rediscovered it. Charles S. Gardner of Southern Baptist Theological Seminary seemed to agree. In 1911 Gardner preached the keynote message of the Southern Baptist Convention titled "Thy Kingdom Come." He said, "The Kingdom of God is a concept or ideal which no single age has adequately understood. But the enlarging experience of the human race reveals new depths of riches in it."[120] Dickinson defined the kingdom of God as "not merely an occasional evangelistic effort to enlist recruits for [one's] church, but the vital expression of Christian living in relation to morals, both public and private, in relation to crying human needs, and in relation to the administration of public offices."[121] The kingdom stood for the betterment of earthly society. It was primarily public and social, not to be confused with the church's exclusivism. Dickinson took his idea to heart, left pastoral ministry entirely, and dedicated his life to social work.[122] He shared Poteat's view: "[God] will therefore save each of us, even to the chief; but that he will through us save others and the whole world of men. Truly we have a task in the world as disciples of the risen Lord to bring in the reign of God and His righteousness to the world of men."[123] Like Phillips and Poteat, Dickinson deemphasized the role of the church and advocated a broader movement to reform society.

Poteat championed this mission that aimed to reconstruct the entire social order. By embracing Jesus's original kingdom message, human efforts for social progress could produce the gradual realization of the kingdom of God on earth and experience the emergence of a utopian society. Poteat never denied that there might be an eternal heavenly home, but that was beyond his reach. His mission was concerned with this world, and enlightened religion held the key to achieving heaven on earth.

THE CHRISTIAN MISSION OF SOCIAL SALVATION

Poteat and a cohort of liberal Southern Baptists attempted to reorient the center of the Christian mission. Rather than concentrating on the redemption of sinners through faith in Christ who was crucified to atone for sin, they centered on a more present mission for social salvation. Poteat argued that the Christian mission was to redeem human society by infusing every area of life with the Christian principles of love and justice. Instead of the conversionism that had been a prime occupation of American evangelicalism, Poteat reoriented Christian reconciliation to be primarily social in design and redefined salvation as natural and temporal rather than supernatural and eschatological. Men and women did not need saving in the traditional sense, since they already belonged to God's family. But the winning of individuals to Christ served to advance the kingdom of God in this world as Christians invaded every segment of society with the spirit of Jesus. Poteat's enlightened anthropology provided optimism that a dedicated people could indeed redeem society. The kingdom of heaven stood poised to advance on earth, and those equipped with the principles of Jesus could lead the movement toward an earthly utopia. This was a version of Christianity that Poteat hoped would appeal to the enlightened sensibilities of modern people. It was quintessential theological liberalism, and it was welcomed by many of the cultured people of the New South.

Poteat offered his most robust expression of social Christianity in *The Way of Victory,* in which he appealed to Christians to advance the kingdom of God with comprehensive social reform.[124] He reasoned that the hope for social progress rested in the changing of individuals: "Apart from this inward renewal of the units of society there can be no reconstruction of the social order after the mind of Christ."[125] He argued that individuals "must be won by Jesus and be infected with his ideal and committed to his purpose of redeeming the total life of man, before the group is transformed after the same pattern." Poteat declared, "A saved man means a saved society. Conversion socializes us."[126] Converted individuals received "a fresh consecration to [Jesus's] reign of righteousness and good will."[127] Poteat contradicted Christians whom he felt diminished the central social component of Christianity: "Pre-millennialists discredit or postpone the social program of Jesus to the catastrophic reconstruction at the imminent appearing of the Lord. And there is a large body of complacent Christians who demand what they call 'a pure Gospel,' which is probably a somnolent mixture of sentiment and theory appointing them no task, cracking the whip of conscience over their aimless lives."[128] Poteat criticized Christians who, he argued, aimed merely to be "ready for the next world and safely out of this [one]." Premillennialism was a rising movement in American Protestantism, but Poteat traced Christian negligence regarding the social mission of Jesus to the ancient church that "seems to have lost much of the rich and practical ideal embodied in Jesus' conception of the Kingdom of Heaven." Poteat argued that the social impulse of Christianity had never fully been lost and remained an impulse in Christianity throughout the ages. But Christians had often missed the centrality of the role that Jesus intended for social reformation as the advancement of the kingdom, and they gravitated instead toward an otherworldly faith.

In *Can a Man Be a Christian To-day?,* Poteat summarized the gospel mandate as "the redemption of all life in Him and to minister to all the forms of human need, forestalling them and correcting the conditions out of which they arise."[129] He urged renewed "consecration of the Christian movement . . . to the redemption of society according to the original ideal of Jesus."[130]

Poteat argued that the modern age presented the perfect "time for the recovery of Jesus' conception of the Kingdom."[131] Such a recovery required Christians to look to Jesus who was "setting up the universal reign of God in the earthly life of man."[132] Jesus's kingdom was not an institution or an organization or a state, but "a social spirit which will transfigure them all." Jesus announced "a perpetual period of the divine favor" while he gave the example of serving the needs of the "poor" and "degenerate types."[133] Poteat substantially explored how the principles of Jesus applied to the areas of business, government, and diplomacy.[134] He argued that the achievement of social righteousness was the central objective for social reform. He concluded that "the way of Christ is the way of victory for the individual and for society."[135] Randal Hall rightly concluded that Poteat's ambitious social goals "grew out of a social Christianity in which individual believers were to apply Christian precepts to social questions in the pursuit of an earthly kingdom of God."[136]

The social gospel movement was an American phenomenon with a significant Baptist contingent.[137] Usually associated with the Northern United States, the social gospel also took root in the South and influenced a generation of Southern Baptists.[138] Historians Thomas Kidd and Barry Hankins argued that social gospel theology penetrated the South, particularly in regions that were characterized by the spirit of the New South, where industrial growth created social conditions similar to that of Northern cities.[139] Kidd and Hankins rightly identified the growing industrial region of central Alabama and said, "There, preacher, professor, and editor L. L. Gwaltney appropriated the teachings of Rauschenbusch for his Southern Baptist context."[140] Gwaltney and Poteat were close friends and often discussed theological topics. Poteat considered himself to be more authentically liberal than Gwaltney, but in 1896 Poteat confided in his diary that he believed that Gwaltney was gravitating toward theological enlightenment if only he could more thoroughly surrender the old faith: "That led me to hope that [Gwaltney] was on the way to the light. He was not arrived at it, for he showed some confusion of thought, a mixture of his old view with the new."[141] A Baptist layperson in Atlanta, Georgia,

W. W. Gaines, advanced a vision for socially oriented Christianity in one of the leading cities of the New South.[142] Gaines served as chair of Georgia Baptists' Social Service Commission from 1911 to 1917. John Eighmy called him one of the era's "outstanding spokesmen for social Christianity."[143] Even more conservative Baptists like Edwin C. Dargan of Southern Baptist Theological Seminary were inspired by the rising social gospel theology.[144] His book *Society, Kingdom, and Church* offered a more conservative treatment of the subject.[145] Dargan's colleague Charles S. Gardner shared his interest in "Social Subjects."[146] Dargan requested that Gardner recommend a list of books on the subject, but asked that they not be "of radical tendency," although he hoped that Gardner would include works by Walter Rauschenbusch, whom he named favorably. Dargan, however, was not interested in reading a well-known liberal professor from the University of Chicago: "I could not commend Shailer Mathews."[147]

Poteat's North Carolina was a leading state for Southern Baptist social Christianity.[148] Eighmy observed that the "activities of the North Carolina liberals hold a unique place in Southern Baptist history. They represent the only group specifically organized to promote liberal social and theological ideas within the denomination."[149] William Poteat's nephew, Edwin M. Poteat Jr., was a leading theological liberal and social gospel proponent as pastor of Pullen Memorial Baptist Church in Raleigh.[150] Das Kelly Barnett, pastor in Chapel Hill and editor of the magazine *Christian Frontiers,* was a part of a younger and more aggressive generation that followed William Poteat's. According to Eighmy, Barnett became "the most outspoken critic of Southern Baptist social conservativism." Barnett eventually grew impatient with the largely conservative constituency of the Southern Baptist Convention and left it for the Protestant Episcopal Church.[151] There was room for liberalism in the Southern Baptist Convention, but progressive leaders had to be willing to tread carefully at times if they were going to stay within the broadly conservative convention of churches. Some of the most liberal chose instead to leave.[152]

Poteat lived what he preached and sought the renewal of the entire social order. He was involved in education, he addressed business and politics, and he worked to ameliorate immediate social needs in his region.[153] He served on the North Carolina Utility Commission.[154] He was a member of the National Economic League, based in Boston, Massachusetts.[155] He was an active member of Southern Baptists' Social Service Commission, led by Arthur J. Barton.[156] He worked with an orphanage in Thomasville, North Carolina.[157] He served with the YMCA.[158] Poteat was also an active member of the Commission on Interracial Cooperation.[159] And Poteat devoted substantial energy to the cause of temperance.[160] Randal Hall rightly concluded, "Perhaps more than any other person, William L. Poteat personified North Carolina Progressivism."[161]

CONCLUSION

By the time Poteat retired from the presidency of Wake Forest College in 1927, the New South movement had transformed Southern society. Central to its transformation was the growth of a broad progressive ethos that spread through much of the South. Poteat's modernized Christianity harmonized with the New South spirit of progress and contributed to the effort to remake the South into the modern image. Edwin Mims rightly characterized a part of Poteat's aspiration to update religion by "relating modern knowledge and progress to the faith of the fathers" so that the South had a chance "to make a real contribution to the nation and to the world."[162]

Poteat was also concerned about religion itself and aspired to preserve for religion a prominent role in American life against the forces of secularization. As Friedrich Schleiermacher had done a century before in Europe and as Poteat's liberal contemporaries were simultaneously doing in the North, Poteat addressed the cultured people of his society. In addition to his interest in improving the South's image beyond its borders, he aimed to persuade progressive Southerners that they could embrace scientific knowledge and the spirit of the age without rejecting Christianity. Poteat hoped that a progressive Christianity, with its enthusiastic social orientation and a new approach to sin and redemption, would appeal to the enlightened sensibilities of modern people in the New South. And to a notable extent, it did.

Chapter Four

THE MODERN CULTURE OF REFINEMENT AND PIOUS RESPECTABILITY

The New South's middle-class professionals adopted a culture of refinement and respectability that bolstered the growth of theological liberalism in the South. The South's emerging middle class aspired to cultivate a modern image of cultured sophistication, and this aspiration encouraged intellectual leaders like William L. Poteat to reshape Christianity to fit modern standards of respectability and modern notions of authority. Central to this mission was a reconceptualization of Christianity's holy book and a supremely subjective approach to religion and piety.

Poteat reconceptualized the Bible and its mode of revelation. He continued to affirm the inspiration of Scripture, but he redefined it and the nature of the Bible to harmonize the Bible with modern knowledge. Poteat rejected the traditional doctrine of inspiration, which held that the Holy Spirit supernaturally inspired the biblical authors to write a verbal message to humanity that was entirely true, invested with divine authority, and sufficiently clear for God's redemptive purposes. Poteat made revelation subjective. God revealed himself through personal, spiritual encounter, not through a supernatural revelation that included authoritative truth claims. Poteat believed modern readers would learn to overlook the Bible's culturally bound ideas and values that did not suit modern society. But the essence of the Bible would remain, unchanged and undisturbed, found in Jesus's teachings of love and self-renunciation. And Jesus himself would remain, waiting to be discovered through experience. Modern readers would come to terms with a Bible that was not a reliable source on science or history. The historical and scientific inaccuracies of the Bible, identified convincingly by scholars and scientists, were only an artifact of its ancient human authorship. They were to be expected. Such deficiencies however did not diminish the Bible's power as a religious book with real potential to sustain a vibrant Christian faith. But for Christianity to maintain a vital place in modern society, it required modernization.

Religious piety formed a distinctive part of the image of middle-class respectability in the South. Although modern in many respects, the South's new middle class was not secular. Religion continued to have a pivotal role in Southern society. The South's middle-class professionals prized religious devotion. Poteat's piety was highly regarded and served as a mark of his faith's authenticity and richness as well as proof of the enduring viability of liberal Christianity within a world that was undergoing transformation in the late nineteenth and early twentieth century. Absent from the new piety was the long-standing attention given to doctrinal fidelity and the essential role of the church in Christian spirituality. Modern piety was supremely personal, theologically fluid, and grounded in subjective experience.

Seeing education's formative powers Poteat devoted his life to it and envisioned the ideal of higher education as the formation of cultured individuals who would lead the movement for a more enlightened society. Education represented Poteat's greatest hope for a better South that would embrace the best of the modern world as he had. He wanted to prepare students for the challenges of the modern world, and he delighted in opening minds by introducing them to modern ideas, beginning with the authority of science. These ideas had shaped Poteat and compelled him to revise Christianity in a way that would suit the more cosmopolitan society to which cultured Southerners belonged.

Theologian Gary Dorrien insightfully noted the connection between liberal religion and social respectability: "The agenda of modern theology was to develop a credible form of Christianity before the 'cultured despisers of religion' routed Christian faith from intellectual and cultural respectability."[1] In the South, the new Southern bourgeoisie resembled the cultured class that Christian intellectuals encountered in the North, both of which seemed to echo the earlier experience of Friedrich Schleiermacher, the father of liberal theology, who made the original case to the cultured critics of Christianity.[2] Dorrien aptly explained that "the liberal tradition reconceptualizes the meaning of Christianity in the light of modern knowledge and values . . . and it is committed to making progressive religion credible and socially relevant."[3] Poteat determined to do just that and led generations of students toward the ideal of modern enlightenment.

THE SOUTHERN BOURGEOISIE

Middle-class Southerners, particularly professionals, cultivated an image of cosmopolitan culture marked by social refinement and respectability.[4] This Southern middle class was not defined primarily as an economic cross section of society but by a set of values, tastes, and habits of thought. Its members valued education, ambition, moral character, urbanity, and other symbols of refinement.[5] Related to the Victorian culture of nineteenth-century American life, the transformation of Southern society that the New South movement produced brought Southern towns and cities into closer alignment with the urban culture of the North.[6] Poteat exemplified the image of the Southern bourgeoisie, and its members cheered him for championing an enlightened form of religion to suit their modern tastes and ideas.[7]

The Cosmopolitan Image

Progressive Southerners were inspired to establish a more cosmopolitan South, and they celebrated the signs of cultural progress that they witnessed in the region's rising towns and cities. In *The Advancing South,* Edwin Mims, William Poteat's contemporary and a professor at Vanderbilt University in Nashville, Tennessee, characterized the motivation behind the "liberal movement in the South." He argued that it was a broad vision for a progressive society that would be marked by social refinement. The brave men who were "fighting for emancipation from outworn traditions" were "cheered by the vision of a new age and a finer civilization."[8] Mims argued that "open-mindedness and cosmopolitanism" were "the prime virtues of a progressive people."[9] Mims was confident that the South was achieving cultural progress: "The time is not far off when scholarship, literature, and art shall flourish, and when all things that make for the intellectual and spiritual emancipation of man shall find their home under Southern skies."[10] Historian Michael O'Brien rightly characterized Mims's *The Advancing South* as a celebration of "the arrival of the southern bourgeoise."[11]

Middle-class Southerners' cosmopolitan aspirations were based in the South's new urban spaces.[12] City centers rose as hubs of industry and transportation and suburbs extended outward from the business districts to make room for grander homes and country clubs. Historian Don Doyle demonstrated that the new class of Southerners promoted the arts and education in the pursuit of "high culture and its symbols."[13] Edwin Mims identified the new "cosmopolitan spirit" that was taking root in the growing cities of North Carolina.[14] He directed attention to Chapel Hill, the home of the University of North Carolina, and boasted that now the "currents of the life and thought of the world flow there."[15] Mims referenced a resident of Chapel Hill who reflected on the town's new atmosphere. He so relished its cosmopolitan spirit that a return to the old days was unimaginable: "I would not give twenty minutes of the Chapel Hill of 1925 for a hundred years of 'befo the war.' Great but narrow was 1875; 1925 is broad and universal . . . the spirit of the place is freer and finer and more democratic."[16] These cosmopolitan outposts of refinement and sophistication produced the South's liberal leaders, including religious leaders like Poteat who envisioned a new religion that suited their new environment.

Southerners found a more established cosmopolitan culture in Northern cities. Alfred J. Dickinson, pastor of Birmingham, Alabama's, First Baptist Church, traveled northward to Chicago for its cosmopolitan feel. In 1916 he spent a week at the University of Chicago where he savored the school's "cosmopolitan" character and its impressive "mental activity."[17] Dickinson's aspirations for urbanity and sophistication paralleled Poteat's, and they illustrated the longing within the new class of Southerners to achieve modern refinement and culture.

Poteat fully embraced the defining values and tastes of the professional class. Historian Randal Hall rightly argued that among Poteat's core beliefs was "respect for high culture and learning," as well as the South's need for "elite leadership."[18] Poteat envisioned a genteel community to be guided by Christian morality and led by cultured elites. But as Hall argued grassroots Southerners balked at Poteat's vision, and they resisted the leadership that he and other progressive Southerners assumed for themselves. The South's cultured citizens however were proud to call him one of their own, and they hailed him as a force for Southern progress. Journalist Wilbur J. Cash, although pessimistic regarding the extent of the progress yet made, applauded Poteat as a "civilizing influence" in the South.[19] And Virginius Dabney spoke for progressive Southerners when he praised Poteat for his "gallant" and "dauntless spirit" in the movement for a more enlightened South.[20]

A Southern Intellectual

Poteat exemplified the image of the new Southern professional. In addition to his status as a public religious figure, he was also an educator, a position that had come into its own in the early twentieth century. And he was a scientist, which was a profession that had newly risen to prominence in the late nineteenth and early twentieth century.[21] By the early twentieth century science held a place of authority in Southern society, and scientists had gained a position of legitimacy and respect.[22] Poteat's status as a scientist distinguished him as a symbol of intelligence and credibility.[23] He carried the cultural authority of religious leadership and the intellectual credibility of being a college educator and scientist. Poteat had the optimum professional credentials for social respectability in the early-twentieth-century South.

Poteat exemplified the bourgeois intellectual. He studied widely and became a respected authority on an impressive breadth of subjects: religion, science, race, education, politics, and social causes such as temperance. He wrote and spoke regularly on each of these.[24] Poteat was outspoken about his fondness for poetry and literature. And although he kept abreast of his specialized field of science, he reserved his evenings for broad reading and reflection rather than work in the laboratory.[25] Southern colleges and universities, as well as Providence, Rhode Island's, Brown University, awarded him a total of five honorary degrees to recognize his achievements as a public intellectual.[26] Few could rival the social gravitas that Poteat enjoyed among cultured Southerners.

A Victorian Middle Class

The transformation of Southern society that occurred in the New South era brought Southern towns and cities into greater comparison with the urban culture of the North and the Victorian culture that was rooted in the nineteenth century. Although associated with the reign of an English monarch and more rightly descriptive of British life from the late 1830s into the early twentieth century, the values, tastes, and sensibilities that defined Victorian culture became a part of American life in the late nineteenth century. The influence of Victorian culture reached the urban life of Southern towns and cities during the New South era.[27] The genteel and polite society that progressive Southerners envisioned for the South bore a strong resemblance to the Victorian image of modern respectability.[28] Poteat redefined Christianity in ways that suited the tastes and sensibilities of the polite society that characterized Victorian America.

Middle-class Americans of the Victorian era highly valued domesticity. The Victorian home was defined by familial nurture, the cultivation of moral character, polite manners, and religious piety. Randal Hall noted that Poteat was devoted to pursuing this "domestic ideal."[29] Poteat's dedication to his own intellectual pursuits was rivaled only by the attention he gave to his family. He read to his children, went on walks and bicycled with his wife, and the family played music together after dinner.[30] He emphasized the importance of learning and the value of character. Hall concluded that Poteat's family "epitomized in many ways the Victorian archetype of genteel domesticity."[31]

America's Victorian middle class also valued education. In the late nineteenth century, its members embraced college education as a middle-class foundational achievement. Poteat's career corresponded with American higher education's growth and standardization, and he recognized education's power to shape individuals and influence society.[32] Poteat seized upon higher education, especially Christian education, as the key to social transformation. In a 1922 address to North Carolina Baptists, Poteat defined Christian education as a form of enlightenment: "If I am asked for a definition of Christian education, I reply, Christian education is Christianity operating in the field of enlightenment." Educated and enlightened individuals would permeate society and lead its progress toward social redemption and the realization of the kingdom of God.[33] Poteat's vision of the new and better society that was appearing looked rather Victorian.

Poteat defined the Victorian era as a scientific age.[34] Science and technology had revolutionized American life in the nineteenth century, and science ascended to prominence as an authority in the modern mind.[35] Poteat strongly believed that religion must not conflict with the new authority of modern society. If Christians hoped to have intellectual credibility in modern America they needed to demonstrate that their religion did not conflict with the new authority. Christians had to learn to respect the special role of science to address all matters of the natural world, including the established fact of biological evolution from lower life-forms.[36] Poteat believed that those who resisted the authority of science in its realm necessarily surrendered the social respectability central to the culture of refinement of the Southern bourgeoisie.

Gary Dorrien has argued the liberal theology that took root in American religion in the late nineteenth century was Victorian. He contended that the Victorian values of refined society and social morality infused American liberalism:

> All of the major nineteenth-century liberal theologians conceived true religion in the way that came to be called Victorian. All of them were

> deeply concerned to provide an alternative to infidelism; all of them took very seriously the duty of good religion to cultivate civilizing moral virtues; all of them regarded religion as the cultivation of a spiritual self and a good society.[37]

The Victorian spirit left its mark on the religion of the professional class of Southerners who exercised substantial influence in the South's new urban life. Poteat championed the Victorian values of social progress, good morals, and a refined community, and they shone through in his religious thought. He became a model of Victorian respectability.

A SYMBOL OF RESPECTABILITY

Middle-class Southerners regarded religious piety as an important part of cultural refinement. Poteat became renowned for his piety. Admirers considered his external piety a mark of the authenticity and the richness of his faith as well as proof of the fresh viability of liberal Christianity. Progressive-minded Southerners praised Poteat for his intellectual power, his eloquence and gravitas as a public speaker, and his ability as an administrator. But many who knew Poteat admired him most for his piety. And his piety comprised a prominent part of his public image of refinement and respectability.

Historian Don H. Doyle described well the value that middle-class Southerners placed on religious piety. Doyle argued particularly about the businesspeople of the leading New South cities, that if they "were lionized for their worldly successes, they were no less praised for their character and religious piety."[38] These middle-class Southerners tended to assume that attaining material success and social standing depended upon their good character and religious devotion. Recognizing the social capital to be gained or lost very few of them overlooked religious affiliation and public expressions of religious devotion.[39] Southerners esteemed religion, and they admired models of faith. As progressive Southerners aspired to be modern, they were deeply grateful for men like Poteat who demonstrated that one could be both modern and pious.

Gerald W. Johnson, a prominent journalist and author, well defined the general nature of Poteat's liberal spirituality.[40] Poteat embraced a subjective spirituality in which individuals could discover their own sense of devotion and knowledge of God through their personal religious experience. Johnson explained that Poteat was unconcerned with people's methods for seeking God or "with what ritual they worshiped" as long as they were sincere in their pursuit. Johnson lamented, "For this carelessness of rite and dogma he was blamed by sectarians."[41] When Poteat claimed to have little interest in the outmoded theological questions that were traditionally thought to bear upon Christian spirituality, one critic, Thomas T. Martin of Blue Mountain, Mississippi, asked rhetorically, "Little interest in the question of whether Christ died for our sins or not? Little interest in the question of whether God is the father of sinners, or becomes our father by faith in the Savior?"[42] But to Johnson and other progressive Southerners, Poteat's religious sincerity rested not upon his theological beliefs but on the evidence of the outward piety that was a prominent part of his public image. And the subjectivity and fluidity of liberal spirituality provided a flexibility that seemed to suit the evolving society of the twentieth century as well as the individualism of the modern mind.

Those associated with Wake Forest College were Poteat's leading supporters, and their admiration centered on his piety. George W. Paschal, a professor at Wake Forest, believed he spoke for North Carolinians or at least for those with ties to Wake Forest when he defended Poteat during his first public controversy in 1922.[43] The controversy was based on a series of articles by Thomas T. Martin and called into question Poteat's theological orthodoxy and with it his fidelity to the Christian faith. When Paschal defended Poteat he said very little about his theology. Instead he offered proof of Poteat's "vitalizing Baptist faith" by pointing out Poteat's piety. When Wake Forest made Poteat president in 1907, Paschal argued, it was not concerned with a detailed examination of his theology. Instead its leaders "were much interested in being reassured that Dr. Poteat was a great spiritual force because of his daily walk and conversation with Jesus Christ." The leaders of Wake Forest had no question about the depth of Poteat's spirituality.[44] Even Poteat's adversaries acknowledged his piety. Martin said, "About President Poteat's noble pious life, no one has ever denied it." But Martin contrary to Paschal also argued that this was not proof of his faithfulness to the Christian faith. After all, Martin said, Crawford Toy and Horace Bushnell had also been pious men.[45] Poteat's supporters like Paschal rejected Martin's reasoning. They regarded piety as the all-important evidence of authentic religion and as a revered quality for a cosmopolitan Southern gentleman.

Wake Forest alumni praised Poteat for his spirituality. One 1928 alumnus who later became a professor at Wake Forest wrote a letter of admiration to Poteat: "You are the greatest Christian most of us have known, and the most spiritually influential man in North Carolina in the

Twentieth Century."[46] Another wrote Poteat to express his gratitude for Poteat's spiritual influence: "Your great life has always been an inspiration to me and I want you to know that I am greatly indebted to you for your fine influence while in Wake Forest College."[47] Some alumni nearly idolized Poteat, like one who said, "I always had such an extrordinary [*sic*] high regard for you all through college and since then. I was never able to let people know very well how much I thought of them as others doubtless are able to do, but my very near worship of you at college was a very real thing nevertheless."[48] Poteat held an honored position in the minds of many, and their esteem was generally linked to his piety.

Even more secular members of the Southern bourgeoisie admired Poteat's piety. Bruce Clayton, Wilbur J. Cash's biographer, noted that Cash's admiration of Poteat extended beyond his "shining example of intellectual integrity" to his spirituality. Cash did not attend church, and he deeply resented the conservative Protestants whom he considered backward and excessively concerned with doctrinal orthodoxy. But Poteat's liberal spirituality impressed Cash. To Cash, Poteat's piety only elevated his image of social respectability.[49] Similarly Gerald Johnson's biographer observed that "Johnson was never conventionally religious," and he felt antipathy toward the South's evangelical Christianity. But Johnson venerated Poteat for his piety.[50] In the towns and cities of the New South, many middle-class Southerners welcomed this new form of spirituality that suited their expectations of social refinement and respectability. But the new religious image was dependent upon a significant revision to the Protestant Christianity that had been rooted in American society for centuries.

LIBERALIZING THE BIBLE

William Poteat and the loose coalition of Southern Baptist liberals recognized that reconceptualizing the Bible was a foundational step to achieving the liberalized religion and enlightened society that they coveted.[51] Alfred J. Dickinson, a prominent pastor in Alabama and outspoken proponent of the new liberal theology, celebrated the new conception of the Bible and hoped to persuade others that his enlightened view of the Bible was beneficial for the church. He contended that a "modernized Baptist is a Christian with a larger, richer, more workable and efficient Bible than his fathers ever possessed." Dickinson believed the time was ripe for Baptists to embrace this more enlightened view of religion and its sacred text.[52]

Poteat wholeheartedly agreed with Dickinson and became the most public and outspoken advocate of liberal theology among Southern

Baptists. Letters came from across the South from men who agreed with Poteat's vision to reconceive of the Bible. Eugene Lankford, a judge in Cisco, Texas, wrote Poteat to express satisfaction with his critique of traditional Christianity. After reading Poteat's *Can a Man Be a Christian Today?* Lankford was delighted to correspond with someone who publicly challenged the outdated model of religion that both men rejected.[53] Lankford captured Poteat's apologetic motivation well when he said that the "age of 'supernatural religion' is passing," and this called for an updated form of religion. Since the traditional "church presents a supernatural gospel," Lankford argued, it "misses the mark."[54] Like Poteat, Lankford regretted that the "absurdities of 'supernaturalism' have driven [many] thinkers to Materialism."[55] Lankford worried that the simplistic, old-fashioned preaching of too many ministers was turning thoughtful people away from Christianity. When Poteat stated that the old religion did not suit modern society, the Bible stood at the center of the issue. He summarized his conception of the Bible in his reply to Lankford: "Intelligent people go to the Bible, I think, for inspiration and guidance, not because they think it scientifically accurate or final, but because it presents the record of gifted men's experience of God, and on the understanding that the same experience is open to them."[56] The Bible was not a supernatural book, but modern people should still look to it as a source of inspiration for their own spirituality.

David Morgan, a recent graduate of Wake Forest College, wrote to Poteat and revealed both the liberal views that emanated from Baptist colleges like Wake Forest and the distance of these views from that of rank-and-file Baptists. Morgan wrote to Poteat for a book recommendation that might prove the harmony of religion and evolution. Morgan asked for a book that advanced the argument that the Bible was "not a scientific textbook."[57] Morgan was dumbfounded when a conservative apologist, Harry Rimmer of Duluth, Minnesota, spoke at Ridgecrest Baptist Assembly in North Carolina where Morgan worked. Rimmer was a well-known fundamentalist preacher, and Morgan was alarmed, especially when students were receptive to Rimmer's conservative message.[58] Wake Forest had offered Morgan a more enlightened view of the Bible and religion: "I had forgotten that not all college students of the South have the opportunities that we do at Wake Forest."[59] Poteat responded to Morgan with his own frustration, saying that "some effort was made to get Mr. Leavel to cancel the engagement with Mr. Rimmer on the Ridgecrest program because it was known that he would raise and perpetuate a false issue and confuse and mislead by his distinct platform gifts. Your letter shows that he did do so. I fear the disaster was a serious one."[60] Poteat regarded men like Rimmer as out of step with the times and as obstacles to religious progress. Poteat recommended to Morgan his own solution to the problem: his published lectures, *Can a Man Be a Christian To-day?* Although he acknowledged the sincerity of many well-meaning conservatives, in the book he advocated passionate resistance to fundamentalists like Rimmer: "The issue is too grave, the perplexity of college and university men and women too deep, and the discredit of Christianity too shameful, for us to be mincing with our respectabilities." He urged that if "Christ is likely again to be betrayed in the house of His friends, however unwittingly, with however heroic a loyalty, the betrayal must be exposed at all risks."[61] Morgan ordered a copy of Poteat's book, but the rest of the Ridgecrest staff was not as open-minded on the subject. He told Poteat that "I have ordered your book and am looking forward to getting it about Tuesday. Poor, one-winged, Sunday-School-Board obsessed Ridgecrest did not boast a copy."[62] The network of progressives in the South was growing, but traditional Protestant faith continued to be the rule.

The movement to modernize the Bible raised important questions. Beyond the South Walter Lippmann, the acclaimed New York journalist, wrote to Poteat about the implications of the liberal conception of the Bible. Lippmann pondered whether the liberal view of the Bible still offered a foundation for morality. Poteat answered that "even if, as you say, Modernism does cast doubt upon the truth of the New Testament story, we still have [Jesus], for it is fair to distinguish between essentials and incidentals."[63] Poteat recognized various inaccuracies in the Bible, but he was confident that the Bible was correct about Jesus, and this was sufficient. Jesus represented "the standard of the good life and the efficient incentive of [moral] conformity."[64] Poteat believed that liberal Christianity still offered a basis for morality and meaning. His name was Jesus.

RECONCEPTUALIZING REVELATION

Poteat's view of the Bible was a modern phenomenon, perfectly primed for the cultural moment. For centuries Christians regarded the Scriptures as the written word of God. The biblical writings themselves made profound claims. In 2 Timothy 3:16–17 Paul claimed that all of Scripture is "God-breathed." Second Peter 1:21 suggested no limit to the scope of Scripture's inspiration: "For no prophecy was ever produced by the will of man, but men spoke from God as they were carried along by the Holy Spirit."[65]

This did not contradict the fact that the Bible was written and collected by humans, which itself posed no obstacle to God's superior and transcendent agency. Far from undermining inspiration the diversity behind the biblical writings only magnified God's wisdom and providence. Peter considered Paul's writings to have the same authority as the Old Testament (2 Pet. 3:16), and Paul claimed authority for his own writings (1 Cor. 14:37). Paul praised the Thessalonian Christians for receiving the apostolic message "not as the word of men, but as what it really is, the word of God."[66] Along with the Scriptures' own testimony, Christians had inherited from Judaism a belief in the authority of their sacred writings.[67] Early Christians assumed biblical inspiration and the corollaries of biblical authority and veracity. They regarded the Scriptures to be self-authenticating.[68] In the Middle Ages, Christians continued to revere the Scriptures in much the same way.[69] In the sixteenth century, Protestants proclaimed a divinely inspired and authoritative Bible with fresh vigor as they rejected church tradition, or anything else, as an authority equal with the Bible.[70]

William Poteat considered this a vexing problem. It was the source of conflict between science and religion and the reason that many educated people considered Christianity to be at variance with modern progress and enlightened sensibilities. A more advanced and skeptical age made revision necessary. But Poteat declared reassuringly that "at every stage in the intellcctual advance of the race requires the fresh authentication of fitting itself into the spirit and thought of the time."[71] Such change would require brave leadership. Poteat and other Southern progressives led the way by revising the doctrine of inspiration and with it biblical veracity and authority, in exchange for subjective illumination and privatized spirituality.

THE DOCTRINE OF INSPIRATION

Poteat came of age in the midst of a broad religious revolution and joined religious liberals who repudiated the traditional doctrine of inspiration.[72] Poteat's own denomination became the first in the United States to terminate a professor over the new theology when Southern Baptist Theological Seminary dismissed Crawford Toy over his revised theology of inspiration.[73] Following Toy's departure Southern Seminary's Basil Manly Jr. wrote *The Bible Doctrine of Inspiration Explained and Vindicated*.[74] Manly declared that "Christianity is a Religion of the Book."[75] Its book was divine, given by God, but it was also a product of human composition.[76] Manly argued that this double authorship made the Bible unique in all of world literature.[77] The Bible's inspiration was plenary—it applied to every part without qualification. Anything less would undermine the authority and truthfulness that the Bible claimed for itself. Jesus himself held a sacred reverence for the whole of Scripture, even down to the smallest jot and tittle of the text.[78] Manly pointed to the Bible's beauty when he asked how, except for Divine revelation, a people so obscure by the world's standards could deliver ethics so lofty and a story so sublime.[79] Manly said, "The student of the Bible feels himself lifted into a region higher than the boundaries of human exploration. It handles the loftiest themes with a quiet simplicity, a regal familiarity which betrays no consciousness of intruding into forbidden mysteries."[80] This was a point with which Poteat could agree.

At Princeton Theological Seminary, Benjamin B. Warfield undertook the same cause. He wrote voluminously in defense of the classical doctrine of inspiration. Warfield declared that "the religion of the Bible presents itself as distinctly a revealed religion."[81] For centuries Christians believed the Bible to be the oracles of God.[82] Warfield contended that "the Scriptures are throughout a Divine book, created by the Divine energy and speaking in their every part with Divine authority directly to the heart of the readers, [and this] is the fundamental fact concerning them which is witnessed by Christ and the sacred writers to whom we owe the New Testament."[83] But like Manly he argued that divine inspiration did not hinder human agency—the Bible itself affirmed both.[84] Warfield argued that just as in God's providence, God's unerring purpose and human agency were fully compatible.[85]

A generation before Manly and Warfield, John L. Dagg, Baptist minister, educator, and president of Mercer University in Georgia, gave a similar expression of biblical inspiration.[86] He asserted the compatibility of divine authorship with human agency: "The Bible, though a revelation from God, does not come immediately from him to us who read it, but is received through the medium of human agency."[87] Although given through humans, "what was spoken and written by inspiration, came with as high authority as if it had proceeded from God without the use of human instrumentality."[88] Dagg clarified that the "men who spoke and wrote as they were moved by the Holy Ghost, were the instruments that God used to speak and write his word. Their peculiarities of thought, feeling, and style, had no more effect to prevent what they spoke and wrote from being the word of God, than their peculiarities of voice or of chirography."[89] Dagg contended that inspiration was verbal—the very words of

Scripture were inspired, not merely ideas or impressions. He held that the "thoughts and reasonings in the minds of the inspired writers, were not a revelation to others until they were expressed in words; and if the Holy Spirit's influence ceased before expression was given to these thoughts and reasonings, he had not made a revelation to mankind."[90] Verbal inspiration however did not imply an ongoing miracle for preservation. Errors from copying and losses of manuscripts were "undeniable."[91] However the text that modern Christians held was sufficiently accurate and clear for "guidance in the study of divine truth."[92] Men like Manly, Warfield, and Dagg offered careful arguments for the traditional evangelical Protestant view of the Bible. But Poteat was unpersuaded by all such defenses of verbal inspiration.[93]

INSPIRATION REVISED

Poteat revised the doctrine of inspiration in substantive ways to harmonize the Bible with modern knowledge. He rejected any form of revelation that was, in the words of theologian Carl Henry, "objectively meaningful and true."[94] Poteat concluded that revealed religion in the traditional sense had become an impediment to religion. Modern Christians had no hope for religious and social progress if they insisted on conceiving of the Bible in the same way as its premodern readers had done. Equally problematic: When doctrines were regarded as sacred they too became entrenched and unyielding to improvement. Poteat had no use for a religion that looked backward rather than forward, as he was determined to do. Poteat warned that many ancient religions had become obsolete because of their failure to evolve: "Witness the obscuration and banishment of the Olympian hierarchy with the rise of Greek culture. Witness the successive decline of Zoroastrianism, Dualism, Magianism, in ancient Persia . . . The gods and goddesses to whom the Romans of an earlier day appealed in personal or national distress became for the poets of the Augustan age the mere toys of the imagination."[95] But he believed that modern Christians were learning to adapt.

Already in the 1880s Basil Manly Jr. noted the antisupernaturalist bias that had pressed against Christianity for at least a century. With insight into the approach of Poteat and others like him Manly referred to Christians who "would [seek to] gain the support of men of science for religion; and, without exactly denying miracles, have set themselves to pare down within credible limits the wonders recorded in the Bible."[96] Poteat rejected any form of biblical inspiration that entailed supernatural, propositional revelation. Like George B. Foster of the University of Chicago, who in his *The Finality of the Christian Religion* dismissed the doctrines of inspiration and atonement as hopelessly outdated, Poteat saw no place for the traditional view of inspiration in modern religion.[97] Nevertheless Poteat continued to identify with Southern Baptists despite their widespread commitment to the old theology. He would aim to convince others to abandon their outdated notions of supernatural revelation, and as he looked into the eyes of many eager students and mingled with the more cultured people in Southern Baptist life he was encouraged by the signs of progress.

Poteat envisioned a Bible that harmonized with the naturalistic presuppositions of modern science. In 1900 his Julius B. Gay Lectures at Southern Baptist Theological Seminary allowed Poteat to advance his views before persons who would lead churches across the South. In his lectures he blamed the Protestant Reformation for the "verbal theory of inspiration which in the next generation culminated in investing the Bible with the mechanical infallibility."[98] This theology became embedded in the Protestant tradition he complained, even down to the present when the Bible was widely used in its most rigid form to attack theological opponents. He referred to this as the "proof-text, utilitarian use of the Bible."[99] He called the "rigid theory of verbal inspiration" an embarrassment to the church and the source of its unnecessary conflict with modern knowledge.[100] The doctrine of verbal inspiration led Christians to embarrassing practices like deciphering the Bible for the details of the coming apocalypse.[101] Perhaps the greatest obstacle for Poteat, the theory of verbal inspiration, required a supernatural work of God, which "puts it outside of nature and violates the method of God's action so far as it has been discovered by us."[102] God worked in the world, but he did so only through natural methods—those discernible by modern science. Poteat was convinced that the old theology would soon die at the hands of a more enlightened society: "It is impossible for such a view of the Bible to survive."[103]

Poteat worked to free the Bible from superstition. Surrendering superstitious ideas like the existence of witches would only help the church's cause. Martin Luther might have thought that demons caused blindness and insanity, but modern people knew better. Retaining a view of the Bible that required belief in such outdated ideas would only drive thoughtful people away from religion. Poteat spoke of the Bible as a human document that offered men and women inspiration by more subjective means, without requiring belief in parts of the Bible that were out of step with modern thought, as well as removing any authoritative or orthodox interpretations. Poteat said that if "we refuse either to burn or to brand the man who dares avow religious opinion at variance with our own, it is not because we hold the truth of Scripture less passionately, but because we have absorbed the spirit of Scripture more deeply."[104] This "spirit" offered private, subjective religion, safe from criticism outside one's own experience with God. When people embraced the Bible as a human record of God's revelation "the more divine it grows, and the more universal and inviolable its authority."[105]

A series of articles in the *Baptist Argus* praised Poteat's Julius B. Gay Lectures, subsequently published as *Laboratory and Pulpit*.[106] W. R. L. Smith, pastor of Richmond, Virginia's, Second Baptist Church, who had himself previously delivered the Gay Lectures, offered resounding praise: "Professor Poteat has advanced the credit of Southern Baptists at the bar of the world's intelligence, and for one, I am profoundly grateful. His noble style is worthy of the great truths he brings. Scores of our pastors and hundreds of our educated laymen are smiling to-day over the strange music of his clarion peal."[107] Smith highlighted Poteat's effort to discredit the alleged antagonism between science and religion. Modern science did not overturn the Bible or undermine its usefulness even if it did invalidate some of the church's doctrines and the traditional conception of the Bible. Smith said that "the scientific method, which is triumphant everywhere, is invalidating systems of theology, and cherished traditions of men, but it does not harm the Bible, or the supreme dignity and glory of Jesus."[108] Poteat had argued that science dealt only with the natural world and the Bible only with the spiritual. He said that "science harbors no implicit denial of what is called the supernatural."[109] Even Thomas H. Huxley, Poteat insisted, acknowledged that the theory of evolution did not imply antitheism—scientists could not make such judgments.[110] The Bible held the utmost spiritual relevance, but it offered nothing related to science or other matters of fact.

Although Poteat could have counted many who praised these lectures, some conservative Baptists wondered how his lectures were instructive for students training for Christian ministry. In Missouri Baptists' *Word and Way* one critic questioned the priority that Poteat gave seminarians to become persons of science, more embracing of the spirit of the age, while he undermined the Bible's truthfulness and authority as traditionally conceived. Most of the students at Poteat's lecture were destined to be pastors. A pastor, the author said, is under a gospel obligation. He "is a preacher of the gospel. However much of the scientific spirit he may have, however open his mind and warm his welcome to the light of science, he belongs to another and distinct field. To this his thought and time must be mainly devoted. He is to deliver a message, and that message specifically, is in the Book."[111] A preacher was tasked with declaring the message of the book—an ancient book, but one still trustworthy. This conservative vision well represented the spirit of rank-and-file Baptists. But Poteat hoped to change that.

Throughout his career, Poteat remained steadfast in his mission to overturn the "man-made theory of inspiration."[112] Twenty-five years after the Julius B. Gay Lectures he offered the John Calvin McNair Lectures at the University of North Carolina, published as *Can a Man Be a Christian To-day?*.[113] He called the historic view "unfair to the precious documents of our faith."[114] In this later period, he showed less patience for those "committed to a bald literalism" who styled themselves as defenders of faith. Poteat deeply resented those who maintained a standard of theological orthodoxy as a test of Christian fidelity. Such was the way of medieval religion, and it had no place in the modern world.[115] Christians who tried to challenge science with the Bible were to be pitied. He said, "These earnest but misguided men are producing no effect whatsoever upon scientific opinion. Their solicitude comes in the wrong century. It might have been more effective in the nineteenth."[116] Fundamentalists were "compromising Christianity before the intelligence of the world."[117] Poteat was particularly concerned that so many young people were purportedly being repelled by an outdated form of Christianity. He argued that it put "in jeopardy the cause which it seeks to save."[118]

Poteat was primarily criticizing a caricature of the traditional doctrine of inspiration. Rather than engaging more sophisticated conservative arguments he reduced the conservative view to a dictation theory. He described it as "the very words of God dictated by Him to amanuenses whose responsibility ended with the prompt and accurate transcription of the transcendent Divine communication." The only thing required, he argued, "was careful penmen."[119] Protestant Christians, in theory, rejected such ideas. Basil Manly rejected the dictation theory since it ignored any meaningful human agency. He insisted on a double authorship for the Bible: the Bible is of God and of human composition—unlike any other book.[120] Poteat referred to dictation and the "embarrassments and grotesque absurdities" associated with it, claiming it made the Bible "reducible to a book of puzzles."[121] Theologian Daniel Treier clarified that this had not been the standard evangelical position: "At best (admittedly with popular aberrations), evangelicals reject a 'dictation' theory of inspiration, in which God directly communicates every word as if the writers were nothing more than impersonal divine pens."[122] Poteat claimed that the directness of his criticism resulted from a deep concern for young people who might be dissuaded from religion, perceiving it as obsolete. As a college president and public intellectual he offered an enlightened form of religion that harmonized with the progress of modern society. This kind of religion better fit the cosmopolitan image of respectability that Poteat and other middle-class Southerners so highly prized.[123]

Alfred J. Dickinson of Alabama held a view more acceptable to Poteat. In Dickinson's quasi-mystical view the word of God came to the believer when she or he was in fellowship with God. God's word was not written—it was not an objective message—but came as personal experience of and with God. Dickinson appealed to the experience of the prophet Jeremiah when he portrayed God as saying, "Behold I have put my words in thy mouth."[124] Dickinson declared that "it is a great thing for a preacher to have Jehovah's words in his mouth. They are his message and his gift, but can only be gather[ed] by contact with the divine."[125] Dickinson explained that God had not physically touched the prophet's mouth. It was a kind of "contact or fellowship when God endues one with the message of God."[126] God's true word was not verbal, but personal. It came directly from God to one in contact with the Divine.

Compared to Dickinson and Poteat, Edgar Y. Mullins, president of Southern Baptist Theological Seminary, expressed a more conservative view. Mullins's view of inspiration lay midway between Basil Manly's traditional view and Poteat's liberal view. In *Christian Religion in Its Doctrinal Expression,* Mullins argued that, in contrast to Poteat's view, the Scriptures offered propositional truth. Mullins said that the "Scriptures, with great uniformity, represent religion as a form of real knowledge."[127] And Christian theology, which drew from the Scriptures, was itself a science.[128] Mullins clarified: "Spiritual realities will not yield the same formulae for expressing their meaning as those found in the sphere of physics. But they are none the less real and may find interpretation in terms of truth."[129] The knowledge to be found in the Bible was religious knowledge but knowledge nonetheless. However, Mullins also clarified that the Bible was a record of God's revelation, not revelation itself. He said, "The Old Testament is the record of preliminary revelation. The New Testament is the completion of the record. Through these New

Testament Scriptures we maintain connection with the historical facts on which Christianity rests. These are the sufficient and authoritative source of knowledge for the great deed of the redeeming God who entered humanity to save through Jesus Christ our Lord."[130] Direct revelation existed but only through religious experience—the center of Mullins's spirituality. Like Poteat, Mullins rejected verbal plenary inspiration, but he believed that the Bible communicated objective truth nonetheless. He granted that verbal inspiration did "no doubt contain elements of truth, but [its adherents] attempt the impossible."[131] But Mullins's approach was too close to the traditional view for Poteat.

Regarding the distinction between general and special revelation Poteat accepted a form of general revelation as clearly as he rejected special revelation.[132] As a biologist Poteat treasured the study of the natural world as a way to know and experience God. Through the study of nature one could hear from God. Like special revelation general revelation did not reveal propositional truths about God, but it freely offered facts about the world that God had created.

Poteat and his fellow progressives revised the traditional doctrine of inspiration to offer a more enlightened religion that could be harmonized with modern knowledge. Liberal Christianity attempted to remove every stumbling block in the way of the cultured people of modern society, and the older view of inspiration was a sizable stumbling block indeed.

The Problem of Rationalism

Poteat repudiated what he considered to be rationalism within conservative Christianity. He was critical of metaphysics generally. He preferred to leave facts in the realm of science and to keep religion spiritual and personal. Tracing a historical trajectory Poteat argued that the rationalistic tendency of theologians began in the second century when Irenaeus began formulating a theory of "reconciliation," by which he meant a doctrine of the atonement. The church however did not develop a truly systematized theory of the atonement until Anselm in the eleventh century. Then in the sixteenth century an even greater rationalist impulse took hold during the Reformation and the era of Protestant Scholasticism as theologians systematized theology further and left the Protestant church captive to cold orthodoxy and dogma. Modern rationalists caused the same problems and were undermining genuine spirituality.[133]

Poteat stressed the limits of reason as well as the tendency of theologians to transgress those limits. He said that "if we must speculate, let it be with the clear recognition of the place and limitations of the rational process; for, as says [Samuel T.] Coleridge, 'Our faith ought to be larger than our speculative reason, and take something into her heart that reason can never take into her eye.'"[134] Poteat like most liberals of the era embraced Romanticism's conception of religion declaring that the poet "knows more of God than your theologian."[135] Poteat distrusted theologians: "To be quite frank, I will trust [Robert] Browning's instinct before Calvin's logic."[136] To Poteat religion was not about doctrine or truth, but about cultivating a spiritual life.

In *Can a Man Be a Christian To-day?*, Poteat declared experience to be the key to religion. Like Friedrich Schleiermacher, Poteat held that the "apprehension of faith is immediate, intuitive, non-rational."[137] To Poteat religious feeling, not reason, was the guide for faith and spirituality. An obsession with reason and dogma was the central problem with fundamentalism, he insisted. He accused fundamentalists of being "loyal to a closed logical system" and "repeating a blunder against which the past is full of warnings."[138]

John W. Phillips, a Baptist pastor in Mobile, Alabama, who had a PhD in Egyptology from the University of London, shared Poteat's outlook and was similarly outspoken.[139] Historian Wayne Flynt called Phillips "equally blunt" about his liberal views as his counterpart in Birmingham, Alfred J. Dickinson.[140] When challenged about the particulars of his theology, Phillips dismissed the entire framework of his critics. In a biographical sketch John H. Chapman of Howard College offered a summary of Phillips's religious thought: "The spirit of adventure is manifest in Phillips' theology. He does not spend much time constructing patterns of belief. He has the attitude of the biologist rather than that of the theologian. Enrichment of life for himself and for others is the consideration which gains his attention."[141] Like Poteat, Phillips believed that religion was not a matter of doctrine or logical precision but of life. Some Alabama Baptists raised questions concerning his doctrinal soundness, but Phillips nevertheless twice preached the annual sermon for the Baptist State Convention of Alabama and served as president of the convention. He also delivered the annual sermon for the national Southern Baptist Convention in 1931 and was elected its vice president.[142] Conservative theology was not always a prerequisite for service among Southern Baptists. Under the outspoken leadership of men like Phillips and Poteat liberalism was spreading.

Poteat defended himself from criticism of his views. In a letter to his former classmate at Wake Forest College, Amzi C. Dixon, Poteat responded to concerns raised about his doctrinal fidelity.[143] Dixon wrote to Poteat about his address before North Carolina Baptists in December 1922 called "Christianity and Enlightenment."[144] Poteat's response was revealing:

> I haven't time now nor do I feel disposed to write a theological essay in answer to your specific inquires. I am not a theologian and take little interest in the metaphysics of our theologians. I cannot avoid the impression that the invasion of an alien logic into the deeper things of the Christian experience, which do not yield themselves to logical treatment, is not justified by New Testament authority and has done a deal of mischief to the course of the Christian centuries.[145]

Poteat countered Dixon with his own question: "What do you think of the rationalism of [Christian] orthodoxy?"[146] The Bible and its message did not yield themselves to the rational deductions of the theologians. Poteat later said that the Bible "gives us, not metaphysics, but men; not logic, but life."[147] Poteat was convinced that the approach of conservatives like Dixon amounted to forcing an "alien logic" on the Bible and Christianity. Poteat aimed to avoid metaphysical questions and assumptions even if they seemed to be necessary preconditions for understanding.

Poteat dismissed the idea that logic had any relevance for religion. But he believed that this was not a loss for Christianity. It offered hope for religion in the age of science and skepticism.

Jesus Is Revelation

Poteat believed that Jesus revealed true religion. When he argued that Jesus himself was revelation he referred to Jesus the man but not an inspired text about Jesus.[148] Poteat said,

> According to Jesus, religion, *i.e.,* His religion, is love to God and man. According to His brother and apostolic interpreter, it is purity and kindness. According to the most gifted and influential of His successors, Christ Himself, in His own person, is all and in all. In other words, the essence of Christianity is an inward disposition, not an external connection. It is a personal attachment, not subscription to intellectual propositions. It is a close and easy correspondence with the Father through Christ.[149]

Poteat argued that the church gradually and increasingly moved further from the simple religion of Jesus, a religion of private fellowship with God, to a religion defined by institutional and doctrinal commitments.[150]

Conservative Protestants did not deny that Jesus himself was revelation—Jesus was God the Son revealed in flesh. Basil Manly Jr. explained that "in Christ the manifestation of the divine is personal, but in the Bible it is verbal."[151] But Jesus ascended to heaven, leaving the Scriptures as his testimony. Manly also explained the difference between revelation and inspiration: The first "imparts truth to the mind," but the second "secures the accurate transference of truth into human language by a speaker or writer, so as to be communicated to other men."[152] If revelation existed only in history, if it were only committed to individual proclamation or oral tradition, one could expect its corruption or even its disappearance in a matter of generations. And "if entrusted to unaided human record, it would have had neither unerring truth nor absolute divine authority at the very first."[153] And this was Poteat's position. Revelation was neither inerrant nor universal in authority. It was personal and provisional but no less authentic.

Poteat believed that the church had developed false views of Jesus. They had made him into a theologian, a teacher of dogma and metaphysics. The Christ constructed by the theologians was neither persuasive nor attractive in the cultured sphere of modern society. Misconceptions about Jesus discouraged modern people from embracing him. Poteat directed people to the Gospels for a fresh look for the authentic Jesus. He was there, waiting to be discovered. Poteat insisted that if they would read the gospels with an open mind, without the help of commentators or creeds, they could find the beautiful Jesus that was there. Poteat listed several things that might discourage someone from coming to Jesus: the need to surrender to him, hard sayings like cut off your hand or pluck out your eye, and to hate father and mother. Poteat apparently thought it unimportant whether Jesus actually said these things. Instead he said, "The open mind will find the dew of youth on all these pages [of the gospels] and the radiance of the morning investing the person of Jesus like a garment and glowing in all His teaching." Poteat pointed to a Jesus beyond the text of Scripture. The goal was not to answer the questions posed by reason but to encounter the person of Jesus.[154]

The Problem with the Literalists

Poteat found himself in a middle position between rank-and-file Baptists, who held no sympathy with his modernist approach on one side, and a rising agnostic materialism among cultural elites on the other.[155] He argued that a "man may be a Christian and accept the Divine authorship of the Bible for the religious life, and at the same time reject the worldview for which it is sometimes made responsible." This ancient worldview behind the Bible would never suit modern society. He declared that the "literalistic interpretation of the Bible" came into "vivid conflict with the assured results of modern science."[156] Embracing the theological revision that was liberalism he urged Christians to "revise [their] conception of the origin and purpose of the Bible and so retain [their] reverence before its Divine authority without embarrassment before the assured results of science."[157] All attempts to force the Bible to agree with modern science on an equal footing had failed. The expectation of ever making "primitive creation pictures" harmonize with science was hopeless.[158] Poteat stressed that the Bible's relevance was limited to religious considerations and to "interpret it outside the range of its religious purpose is as unfair as it is stupid."[159] Poteat charged conservatives with "causing the little ones to stumble—the little ones who have no defenses against official dogmatism."[160] This might have sounded ironic to conservatives, who themselves made similar charges against modernists for leading the vulnerable astray.

Poteat conceived of religion as a private matter. He advanced the modern notion that one's spirituality, including his interpretation of the Bible, was solely between him and his God, to be determined solely in subjective terms. Daniel Treier rightly identified the role that higher criticism played in religion's modern liberation. It freed men and women from any authority higher than themselves.[161] To be compatible with the conclusions of higher criticism revelation could not be objective. Therefore the interpretative authority of any particular person, group, or institution could be valid. Poteat shared the sentiment expressed by his counterpart at the University of North Carolina, president Harry W. Chase, who criticized "the religious bigot who insists upon his own interpretation of the Bible, his own conception of God and God's way with man, and who would damn to eternal torment anyone who disagrees with him."[162]

Poteat and his fellow liberals conceived of the Bible in vastly different terms than grassroots Baptists in the South. Fundamentalist church members eventually challenged the liberal reconceptualization of the Bible. But Poteat argued that the literalists actually limited the Bible's power by forcing it into a mold that choked it of its religious and spiritual purpose—one more profound than literalism offered. Many educated Baptist leaders adopted the liberal view but as they moved leftward their distance from the mainstream of Baptist life became increasingly apparent. But Poteat was convinced if Christians failed to modernize and to conceive of the Bible as a source for personal inspiration and private interpretation, contrary to the view of supernatural revelation and authoritative doctrinal standards, they would alienate modern, educated people and fade into irrelevance in the cosmopolitan world that was emerging.

CONCLUSION

Although intellectual questions played a central part in the rise of theological liberalism, social and cultural forces seemed to have a formative influence on the minds of middle-class Southerners in this new era. Though liberals in the South had their own Southern style they resembled the theological modernists of the North in a striking way that becomes less surprising when we consider that similar social forces were at work on both sides of the Mason-Dixon Line. Not limited by regional boundaries, the sensibilities of Victorian culture, a marked optimism and progressive spirit, the new authority of modern science and a scientific approach to academic research, and a culture of skepticism were reshaping the American mind. Most Southern evangelicals remained traditional in their religious beliefs as large numbers experienced a more marginal impact from the social evolution that was occurring in particular cities, institutions, and social circles. One's social class, level of education, and location seemed to reveal an observable correlation with the adoption of liberal ideas. The culture of refinement and respectability of the New South's middle-class professionals bolstered the growth of theological liberalism in the South. And Poteat perfectly embodied the image of cultured sophistication to which progressive Southerners were aspiring.

As conservative Christians encountered the ideas of liberal Christianity initial suspicion gradually turned into opposition. As they weighed the arguments made by liberal figures like Poteat, a growing number recognized that liberal religion represented a redefinition of Christianity. To rank-and-file Baptists the problem and the solution were simple. Someone mailed Poteat a clipping from a University of North Carolina Press flyer for his book, *Can a Man Be a Christian To-day?* The person scribbled an answer beneath the book's title: "Yes, if he believes God's truth, instead of the devil's lie."[163]

Chapter Five

THE RISE OF CONSERVATIVE OPPOSITION

In the 1920s William L. Poteat and other theological liberals faced a new level of opposition to their movement to liberalize Christianity.[1] Most Baptists in the South held to a traditional evangelical Protestantism. They were characterized by a tradition of biblicism and a simplified form of Protestant orthodoxy.[2] But a new spirit was rising within American evangelicalism. In the 1920s a movement of conservative leaders embraced a more militant spirit and actively opposed liberal theology and its advocates. Poteat and his fellow liberal elites were the natural targets for the new fundamentalists.[3]

In both the North and the South, a growing number of conservative Christians recognized that the liberal ideas of men like Shailer Matthews, William Newton Clarke, and Harry Emerson Fosdick in the North and William Poteat in the South represented a redefinition of Christianity. As more mindful conservatives turned attention to the theology of progressive leaders, they became alarmed at both the content and the greater implications of the new theology. Fundamentalists argued that the Christian faith and the hope of salvation were on the line, and they called for aggressive action against liberal theology.

In line with the mainstream of Protestant liberalism in America Poteat exchanged the traditional theology of human sinfulness for a more optimistic view of humanity, and he redefined Christian salvation by exchanging the supernatural and otherworldly elements for a temporal gospel of social redemption. Poteat argued that religious experience revealed one unequivocal truth: God is the father of all people, and all people are brothers and sisters. The only obstacle separating humans from God was their failure to recognize God's unreserved fatherly disposition toward all persons as his children. As brothers and sisters, humanity's mission was to build a more just and peaceful society. And this work of social salvation would progressively form society into the kingdom of God on earth.

Poteat carefully harmonized Christianity with the spirit of the modern age. Even in the South modern sentiment encouraged a revised outlook on human nature and humanity's relationship with God. Poteat obliged the cultured despisers of the New South when he offered a religion that did not offend their sensibilities and was devoted to the more agreeable aspiration of social reform. Just as Poteat harmonized revelation with modern modes of thought to make religion immune from the challenges of the modern age he formulated a revised theology of humanity and salvation with an apologetic mission to win educated people with a modernized version of Christianity.

A NEW ANTAGONISM

From 1890 to 1920 Southern liberalism took root and matured without any significant opposition, as historian Randal Hall observed. Beginning in 1920 however a forceful new movement of conservative Protestants challenged theological liberalism.[4] In the North, after World War I, factions of liberal and traditional Protestants began to fight for control of denominational institutions. These battles gradually gave way to the toleration of liberalism and ultimately toward liberal control.[5] In the South, North Carolina became one of the centers of the fundamentalist offensive against Baptist liberalism.[6] A conservative coalition of pastors, Baptist church associations, and itinerant evangelists challenged liberal leaders of whom Poteat was the most prominent. Popular evangelists like Thomas T. Martin and Mordecai Ham, North Carolina pastor J. J. Taylor, and Baptist layperson D. F. King wrote articles that charged Poteat with doctrinal heresy and especially expressed disapproval for his advocacy of evolution. They considered it scandalous that someone with such views could be the head of a Baptist institution.[7] But Poteat had a bulwark of support. Wake Forest College alumni, many of whom were theologically progressive and nearly all of whom sympathized with Poteat, came to dominate Baptist life in North Carolina. They triumphed over conservative efforts to challenge Poteat and the liberal Christianity that he represented.[8]

Poteat taught evolution openly for decades before he ever aroused significant criticism.[9] But the new fundamentalists lacked the polite restraint that had generally characterized Southern Baptist discourse in the preceding decades. North Carolina Baptist minister and educator Richard T. Vann argued that a "new species" of fundamentalists was causing trouble.[10] The student newspaper at the University of North Carolina proclaimed in 1925 that the "country is going fundamentalist" and noted the strangeness of the coalition that wanted to "make orthodoxy the test of good citizenship in this present world as well as the passport to the one to come."[11] Edwin Mims recognized the fervor of the new conservative movement in the South, which he called "the forces of reaction." He regretted that conservatives were "united and aggressive" while progressive Southerners seemed initially to lack the same level of cooperation.[12] Alarmed by the advance of liberalism, Southern fundamentalists became more determined to challenge liberal leaders like Poteat.[13] The fundamentalists aimed to awaken grassroots Southern Baptists by revealing how far leaders like Poteat had journeyed from traditional Protestant faith. They declared that liberal Christianity amounted to apostasy. A growing number of rank-and-file Baptists became determined not to stand by idly.

Baptists and the Bible

Because the Bible was central to evangelical and Baptist spirituality, views on the Bible became the first and one of most observable points of separation between conservatives and liberals. To traditional Baptists the Bible itself was divine revelation, supernaturally inspired by God. William Poteat rejected the view of a divinely revealed and authoritative Bible. In *The New Peace,* based on a series of lectures that he gave at several theological institutions in the North, Poteat criticized the traditional Protestant theology of Scripture: "The Reformers who scouted an infallible church set up an infallible book as the ultimate authority on all matters to which it referred. The Bible was assumed to speak the last word, not only on Hebrew history and religion, but also on the facts of physical nature."[14] Poteat criticized the "ultra-conservative theory" of "an original divine revelation transmitted" to humankind.[15] He recognized the long tradition represented by this view but deemed it to be out of step with modern knowledge. True to the essential spirit of modernism Poteat rejected all external forms of authority, most especially including divine revelation.[16] The traditional view represented a bygone form of religion. When fundamentalist preachers promoted the traditional view and declared the liberal view traitorous to the faith, conflict was certain to follow. And it did.

In an article in North Carolina's *Biblical Recorder,* Poteat uncharacteristically sneered at those who claimed to follow every letter of the Bible.[17] To show the inconsistency of such a claim he referenced the biblical command to tithe, the observance of the sacrificial system, and the Sabbath, among others things, which Christians had failed to follow consistently, while claiming to believe every word of the Bible.[18] Poteat's argument had rhetorical power but was disingenuous for he dismissed the carefully reasoned interpretative principles adopted throughout the history of Christian thought. Christians had long recognized the Bible to be a complex theological document revealed progressively over many centuries. Theologians reasoned that in the Bible's unfolding story line, Jesus fulfilled all the typological signs that preceded including the sacrificial system and the Sabbath. Christians had considered Jesus the ultimate sacrifice and source of eternal rest for God's people. The new covenant, fulfilled in the New Testament, did represent something new in the biblical story of redemption, but it came not in contradiction to earlier revelation but as its fulfillment. If pressed Poteat might have professed his ignorance on these theological points, since he was only a layperson. But in fact he had little interest in such matters.[19]

Many Christians in the South did conceive of the Bible in rather simplistic terms. Some were sensitive to any hint of innovation in religion however small. For instance William O. Carver of Southern Baptist Theological Seminary wrote to his colleague Edwin C. Dargan about a man who was deeply concerned about the new Revised Version of the Bible, believing the new translation's departures from the King James Version might destroy faith in the word of God. Carver considered this to be unfounded to the point of being humorous.[20] Virginius Dabney lamented the appearance of "rampant Fundamentalists, who suddenly became vocal over a wide area about 1920." He suggested that they believed "the Bible had been dictated by God in the English translation of the King James version."[21] This kind of traditionalism embarrassed Poteat and other progressive Southerners who cared deeply about their public image. It made their cause of liberalizing religion all the more urgent.[22]

Poteat was outspoken about his view and eventually provoked public controversy in the 1920s. An article in the *Charlotte Observer* alluded to Poteat's well-known evolutionism: His hermeneutic "reads into Genesis and other parts of the Bible a story of the creation of man that is not in accordance with the accepted and orthodox views of many of the Baptists of North Carolina."[23] The article addressed the upcoming Baptist Convention of North Carolina to take place November 17–19, 1925, during which two resolutions were expected, both of which potentially threatened Poteat's position as president of Wake Forest College. The Barrett Resolution would "lay the foundation for the ousting of Dr.

W. L. Poteat."[24] With the Barrett Resolution, the Bateman Resolution sought greater denominational control over its institutions, in this case over Wake Forest College, known for its liberal spirit. The article warned convention messengers to expect a stiff fight. But the controversy passed, and in the end Poteat emerged more secure than ever.[25] After this controversy ended fundamentalists admitted defeat against Poteat and the Wake Forest coalition and reluctantly turned their attention elsewhere.[26]

Denominational Education and the Seventy-Five Million Campaign

Grassroots Southern Baptists became aware of the distance between their traditional beliefs and those of leaders like Poteat in the same period that they embraced a greater sense of ownership over denominational institutions. In 1919 Southern Baptist leaders sought a heightened level of denominational cooperation with the goal of raising seventy-five million dollars over five years to be distributed for missionary work, education, and social ministries. The Seventy-Five Million Campaign failed to raise the proposed amount due to a depressed economy and an agricultural recession that occurred during the period. But the $58,591,713 that was raised inspired Southern Baptists to a greater sense of stewardship over the entities and institutions that received Southern Baptist money.[27] Historian Suzanne Linder rightly argued that "Baptists all over the South were becoming vividly conscious of their ownership and control of denominational colleges through publicity for the 'Seventy-Five Million Campaign.'"[28]

In 1925 Richard T. Vann, Poteat's friend and the associate secretary of the Education Board of North Carolina's Baptist State Convention, addressed the tension that had arisen as a result of conservative opposition toward progressive leaders at Southern Baptist colleges. He argued that conservatives and progressives needed to maintain harmony for the grand cause of Christian education.[29] Vann acknowledged that both parties had representation in the Southern Baptist Convention, and he demonstrated impressive insight into the differences between conservative and liberal Baptists. He recognized the fundamental differences to be rooted in distinct approaches to the Bible.[30] He also recognized that liberals tended to hold experience, rather than the Bible, as the epistemological foundation for religious knowledge.[31] Vann articulated the dilemma that Southern Baptists faced: "Now, with these two schools of thought before them, each clamoring for recognition and endorsement, what are the colleges to do? Both parties belong to our denomination, as do the college, and both, therefore, have somewhat to do with the colleges." In support of progressive leadership Vann argued that educators were called to lead as well as serve the denomination: "But in the nature of the case, a college must lead as well as serve. It sustains to its denomination somewhat the double relation of a pastor to his church. Servants though both are, they cannot serve their best without leading."[32] Institutional leaders needed to be brave enough to forge a fresh path into the future, which included the pursuit of truth wherever it might lead. He aimed to dispel fear by arguing it was only natural that a people's understanding of religion evolved over time, and he urged that scientists, as specialists in their fields, needed to be free to disseminate their conclusions. Vann reassured his audience that science could not ultimately undermine religion since the two operated in separate realms.[33] But Vann encouraged both groups to find common ground: "For it is well understood that each of the two holds some views that most of our people cherish, and all the truth held by either we are anxious to maintain." He acknowledged that it would be problematic if Baptist colleges lost touch with the denomination's people. But he contended that neither fundamentalists nor the most liberal leaders uniquely represented Southern Baptists: "And beyond question, so far, the mass of Southern Baptists are not lined up with either faction. Instead, they are generally indifferent to the whole discussion." Vann believed that most Southern Baptists would be satisfied to maintain harmony at their colleges and to allow latitude on the theological questions that separated traditional Baptists from liberals.[34] He argued that fundamentalists and modernists could join together to sing one of the great hymns of the faith, even if they did not believe the same theology: "Old truths have not changed any more than God has; but in accordance with all analogy and all experience, our conception of that truth must necessarily change. So when we sing about the 'Old Time Religion,' let us do it heartily; but remember that this does not necessarily mean old-time theology."[35] But the fundamentalists regarded the new theology as false theology. To make peace with it would mean disobedience to Christ. The divide had become deep, and both groups were determined to defend their opposing sides.

Poteat resented the fundamentalists who challenged his leadership, and he developed a reputation for boldness in the face of opposition. Poteat's contemporary Edwin Mims expressed his frustration with the many progressive Southerners who were unwilling to advocate publicly for their views: "And the most unfortunate fact of all is, that the enlightened man, be he a preacher or editor, or scholar or business man, either keeps quiet or is so interested in an institution or organization that he will not endanger his leadership by taking a positive stand for what he knows is right."[36] Mims used language from John Bunyan's classic *Pilgrim's Progress* to express his dissatisfaction with liberals who lacked the boldness to push for progress: "There are far too many men of the type which Bunyan had in mind when he drew Mr. Facing-both-Ways and Mr. Faintheart." But Mims called Poteat "Mr. Valiant-for-Truth" and "Mr. Greatheart" for his brave leadership. He admired Poteat for his skill at disarming his critics. Poteat could speak "to a Baptist State Convention assembled to condemn his views on evolution and leaving them so overwhelmed with his sincerity and his spiritual insight that no one dares to speak against him."[37] Poteat's supporters revered him for his steadfastness, but his opponents remained equally determined to push for his removal from a Baptist institution that Baptist dollars helped support.

AN APOLOGIST FOR MODERNISM

With the ambition of an apologist, Poteat used his leadership and influence as a public intellectual to advance liberal Christianity in the South. Although he was always considerate of his context when speaking Poteat's general forthrightness made him a target for the fundamentalists. His former student Gerald Johnson tried to capture Poteat's essence when he contended that Poteat was "fighting for the release of the human spirit from the thralldom of superstition and falsehood."[38] Poteat held that Christianity's relevance and respectability were dependent upon a more enlightened form of religion that was compatible with modern ideas and that suited the progressive spirit of the New South. He was determined to fight for it.

The apologetic bent of Poteat's progressive revision of Christianity was a fundamental characteristic of liberal Protestantism. Historian Gary Dorrien argued that "the agenda of modern theology was to develop a credible form of Christianity before the 'cultured despisers of religion' routed Christian faith from intellectual and cultural respectability"[39] Poteat defended his views by drawing on modern ideas with the hope of appealing to Southern society's educated leaders. Dorrien summarized the impulse well: "The liberal tradition reconceptualizes the meaning of Christianity in the light of modern knowledge and values. It is reformist in spirit and substance, not revolutionary. It is open to verdicts of modern intellectual inquiry, especially historical criticism and the natural sciences. It conceives Christianity as an ethical way of life . . . and it is committed to making progressive religion credible and socially relevant."[40] Historian Christopher Evans agreed and defined the movement as "advocating the need for a Christianity that could be reconciled to the modern forces of the natural sciences and post-Enlightenment reason."[41] Theologian Roger Olson observed that liberals reasoned the situation was urgent, believing that they faced "a permanent cultural revolution" that put Christianity at risk of "losing all credibility in the modern world."[42] Although historians have often overlooked the presence of liberalism in the South, Poteat advanced the same religious program in the South that men like William Newton Clarke, George B. Foster, and Walter Rauschenbusch did in the North.[43]

Poteat was not alone. Other Southern Baptists also advanced liberalism. Alfred J. Dickinson, as editor of the *Alabama Baptist* newspaper, attempted to enlighten his fellow Baptists. Dickinson's contemporary and fellow Alabama Baptist John Chapman recounted Dickinson's zeal "to open the eyes of his fellow-ministers to the treasures awaiting the diligent searcher for the truth of the Bible. . . . This consuming passion drove him to a life purpose of opening the eyes of 'blind leaders of the blind.'"[44] Dickinson was convinced that if traditional Christians devoted themselves to more serious thought they too would embrace liberalism. Dickinson judged that "God will forgive a preacher for ignorance . . . but will not forgivc him of laziness."[45] Dickinson aimed "to bring his brethren to a modernly sound view of religion and the Bible." However like Poteat's, Dickinson's "efforts brought him severe misjudgment from some quarters, and inspired in others an unrecognized suspicion born of a fear that he was leading them into positions that might trap their orthodoxy, and compromise their faith"[46] But also like Poteat, Dickinson was motivated by a sense of urgency to stave off disaster and save Christianity in the modern age.

Poteat felt a special responsibility to the students of Wake Forest College, and it was there that he had his greatest influence. Gerald Johnson recalled how Poteat helped students who struggled to make peace with modern ideas by introducing "a little gleam of light into some thousands of young minds that went darkling." And for students who were inclined to embrace a naturalist worldview, Poteat made "it forever impossible for them to reject utterly the things of the spirit."[47] Poteat's approach revealed how liberals saw themselves as a "third way" between atheistic materialism and religious fundamentalism.[48] The problem with materialism was that it ruled out the authenticity of religious experience and wrongly used science beyond its rightful sphere as a comprehensive vehicle for truth.[49] And the problem with fundamentalism was that it "makes no winning appeal to the young people of our day."[50] Poteat owed the coming generations an enlightened religion, and they represented his greatest hope for religious progress.[51]

Poteat's influence extended beyond his small denominational college and the Southern Baptist Convention. Progressive North Carolinians proudly remembered him as an advocate for social and religious enlightenment. A generation after his death in 1938 North Carolina's *News and Observer* published "Billy Poteat and the 'Watchmen on the Wall.'"[52] The article appeared as Hollywood released *Inherit the Wind,* which depicted the Scopes trial of Dayton, Tennessee.[53] The trial had humiliated progressive-minded Southerners who were working to overcome their region's backward stigma. The movie's release promised to reopen old wounds, but North Carolinians remembered Poteat as a powerful counterexample to the caricature of the South: "While the movie 'Inherit the Wind' is embarrassing Tennessee and ridiculing the Protestant religion in the South, it is good to remind ourselves that it was a vigorous Protestant layman who almost single-handedly kept North Carolina from this nonsense." The article noted that Poteat was giving the John Calvin McNair Lectures immediately before the Scopes trial, and they demonstrated the best of enlightened Christianity and cultured society.[54] The article praised Poteat for his dedication to enlighten Southerners when he could have left the South as many other progressive Southerners did. And Poteat endured considerable opposition for his advocacy of evolution and liberal theology. He was "on the hot seat for a period of ten years. He could easily have resigned—since his retirement age had come—or could have remained silent and safe. Instead, he chose the path of open commitment and defense of the truth."[55] The article noted Poteat's sense of determination and the level of influence that he had. It boasted that "Poteat and others kept North Carolina sane."[56] Poteat belonged to "a vanguard of religious thinkers, which in the case of North Carolina saved both the Baptists and the Legislature from making a monkey out of themselves over the 'monkey' business." *Inherit the Wind,* the article stressed, "does not represent the better side of the emerging Protestantism of the South." It declared that Poteat's *Can a Man Be a Christian To-day?* represented the very best of progressive society in the South.[57]

MODERNIZED THEOLOGY

Although Poteat embraced a form of Christianity that claimed to be a way a life rather than a series of doctrines, liberals revised Christian theology down to its foundational beliefs. The new ideas confounded many traditional evangelicals, and they provoked the fundamentalists to fight.

A New Redemption

Poteat revised Southern evangelicalism's soteriology and provided a theology that was more optimistic, self-sufficient, and suitable for modern society. He underscored the importance of an initial, personal experience with God, but he did so in strikingly different terms than those who held the traditional conception of conversion. Evangelicals conceived of conversion or "being born-again" as spiritual rebirth, most commonly conceived as a miraculous awakening from spiritual death to life. The idea of spiritual death assumed human inability and separation from God as a consequence of humanity's ancient fall from grace. Salvation was a work of God, but it also involved an active response from the converted in the form of repentance of sin and faithful devotion to the Lord Jesus Christ.[58] Poteat conceived of conversion without the prominent supernaturalism and the necessity of repentance and forgiveness. He defined salvation as a self-determined transformation of individuals for the cause of social redemption. Religious experience was private and internal, but salvation had a social orientation. Poteat viewed salvation as an eschatological hope for social renewal in this present world with the kingdom of God permeating society. In this way he provided a version of Christianity that appealed to the sensibilities of modern people.

Poteat redefined conversion. In a private journal entry from July 17, 1896, he defined conversion in simple terms as the "rising into activity & control of what was before present in the nature, but dormant."[59] At conversion a person embraced a heightened sense of personal responsibility and dedication for his or her spirituality. The awakening was not miraculous but was natural and self-determined and without fundamental alteration of one's nature. Many years later in his correspondence with Eugene Lankford, a judge from Cisco, Texas, Poteat seemed to make the same point when he defined what a Christian is without reference to grace, faith, forgiveness, or rebirth: "A Christian is one who loves God interpreted in Christ and walks in Christ's way."[60] On July 26, 1896, Poteat preached, as he had several times before, as a guest for Leslie L. Gwaltney, a prominent liberal Southern Baptist pastor and denominational leader in Alabama.[61] He preached on John 10:10 and proclaimed that the person and work of Christ were not principally for eternal benefit but for bringing abundant life to this present world.[62] Rank-and-file Baptists believed that conversion made Christians citizens of heaven as well as agents for Christ's kingdom in this world. But Poteat argued that at its heart salvation made one a better citizen of this present world in order to form a more just and peaceful society.

Poteat defined a new way of redemption in his book *The Way of Victory,* which was based on a series of lectures at the Chapel Hill School of Religion.[63] Christians had traditionally believed that people needed redemption because of the guilt of sin and God's righteous judgment against it. But Poteat argued that people needed redemption because society needed redemption, and society could only be redeemed by individuals' transformation. Men and women found the redemption that could transform society when they embraced the spirit of Jesus: "They must be won by Jesus and be infected with his ideal and committed to his purpose of redeeming the total life of man, before the group is transformed after the same pattern."[64] People received this renewal through religious persuasion and by the intentional alteration of their lives toward the Christian virtues of love and self-renunciation.[65] Poteat asserted that the Christian faith did not begin with a call to believe and repent: "[God] brings no moral code requiring obedience, [and] no doctrinal formulary demanding subscription." He argued that the idea that God expected obedience on warning of punishment "has no place in Christian morals."[66] Conservative Christians could have appealed to the New Testament's account of Peter's sermon at Pentecost. When the crowd asked how they might be saved Peter responded, "Repent and be baptized every one of you in the name of Jesus Christ for the forgiveness of your sins."[67] They might have recalled the prophetic forerunner to Jesus, John the Baptist, who declared, "The time is fulfilled, and the kingdom of God is at hand; repent and believe in the gospel."[68] But Poteat advanced a private spirituality and subjective morality and appealed to love as God's only requirement: "And all He requires of this 'new creature' is the happy slavery of love: 'Son, give me thy heart.' Love me, and do as you please. Love me, and think what you must. Love me, and choose your own task, set up your own standard of the good life, and look within you for the effective incentive to be good."[69] Rather than Jesus achieving salvation for his people Poteat proposed that Jesus saved by inspiring a new way of life: "It appears therefore, that personal attachment to Jesus is the essence of our religion and the secret of the new way of living which he came to inspire."[70] To the redeemed God gave "the opportunity of ennobling service" and "fresh consecration to his reign of righteousness and good will."[71] In Poteat's formulation, the themes of salvation and the outward practice of one's faith appeared similar to that of traditional Christianity. But the theological content of Poteat's way of redemption was different from orthodox Christianity.

Poteat rejected the theology of original sin and guilt. He argued that men and women did not need the Holy Spirit's miraculous rebirth or repentance because no breach existed between God and humanity.[72] Protestant Christians had generally taken the Pauline language of being "dead in your trespasses" as a spiritual reality that was true of everyone who had not been spiritually reborn by the Holy Spirit. Salvation was necessary because humans carried the guilt of sin, and all people eventually became personal transgressors, which separated humanity from God. But doctrines like the fall of humanity, imputation, and propitiation did not fit into Poteat's framework. He denied that people were born with a sinful nature. In a private diary from the mid-1920s, he implied that deficiencies in human conduct were not the result of a sinful nature but rather came from bad examples: "Children are naughty [because] adults are stupid."[73] In an earlier journal entry from 1896 Poteat explicitly rejected the doctrine of the imputation of Christ's righteousness. He appealed to Romans 4 and argued that Abraham was independently righteous. Abraham had no need for Christ's vicarious righteousness. God considered Abraham righteous because he was in himself actually righteous, although Poteat allowed that Abraham's external conduct might have sometimes fallen short.[74] Righteousness was well within the possibility of people's own efforts.

Poteat therefore disapproved of the gospel invitation that was a common practice in conservative Baptist circles. In a diary entry from December 17, 1896, Poteat privately objected to a preacher who gave "the plan of salvation."[75] Poteat criticized it as reminiscent of a "legal proceeding." The preacher had declared "justification on account of the vicarious death of Christ made available by faith, which was defined as 'simply believing what God says.'" But Poteat argued that the traditional doctrinal content of the gospel was an unnecessary obstacle to prospective disciples: "I said in my heart, 'Thank God! The saved state does not depend upon having a correct theory of how it is brought about.'"[76] In his reshaped soteriology,

Poteat presented a mystical mode of redemption, which was designed for humanity's self-improvement. He prioritized a social version of Christianity over the more otherworldly theology of evangelical Protestantism.[77]

Alfred J. Dickinson of Alabama similarly discounted the evangelical theology of conversion. Historian Wayne Flynt noted that Dickinson was "[not] much interested in evangelism." Perhaps unsurprisingly Dickinson's congregation gradually declined in membership during his time as pastor of the First Baptist Church of Birmingham.[78] Dickinson increasingly focused his thought and energy on social ministry and grew to lament the years he spent in pastoral ministry. Dickinson resigned his prominent pastorate in 1918 to run for a state congressional seat to advocate for economic and labor reform. He lost the election but dedicated the remainder of his life to social causes.[79] In 1923 he explained that social work liberated him from his "high pulpit where preachers talk of narrow doctrines and faith and vague traditions." Suggesting a single-minded passion for social outreach he illuminated the distance between his convictions and those of most Southern Baptists when he confessed his regrets: "I have spent a number of years in the so-called pastoral work and from a standpoint of good done, my time was worse than wasted."[80] Poteat also dedicated substantial energy to social ministry. But he was resolutely committed to his ministry as an educator and the work of bringing religious enlightenment to Southerners.[81]

Poteat's liberal piety seemed to lack the kind of assurance that evangelicals expected from the Christian faith. After a moment of anxiety from an episode of an irregular heartbeat Poteat reflected on what awaited him after death.[82] He did not appeal to the Christian hope of eternal life, and he expressed uncertainty about what awaited those who died. Instead he spoke with theoretical and conditional language: "If there is a good God, & if he has the power to order things after his mind, I know that I am in harmony with him & that there can be no risk in 'meeting him.' If there is no good God, if it should turn out that my preference for goodness actually brings me into conflict with the powers that be, I accept that issue & whatever fate may wait upon it."[83] Poteat's public persona exuded confidence about his religion. But in his private thoughts some uncertainty seemed to remain about fundamental religious questions: Who is God, and what is God like?[84] At a brief moment of crisis Poteat comforted himself with his religious experience—he knew God by personal encounter. However Poteat's religious epistemology of experience offered only limited knowledge and apparently also limited assurance of God or salvation.

The Universal Fatherhood of God and the Brotherhood of Humanity

Throughout his career Poteat contended that Jesus revealed God's universal fatherhood. Exemplified in the theological motif of "Jesus' revelation of the fatherhood of God," Poteat appreciated that enlightened Christianity was leading away from the undesirable modes of Latin and Greek thought, which he argued had supplanted the original modes of Christian thought.[85] Two decades later in *Can a Man Be a Christian To-day?* Poteat summarized the pure message of Jesus to humanity: "God is our Father with a genuine solicitude for His wayward children."[86] Poteat argued that no breach in relationship separated humanity from God for any reason except a failure to recognize God's unbroken fatherly disposition toward his children. Jesus revealed that "commerce" with God was "open and easy."[87] Poteat's brother, Edwin M. Poteat, agreed: "We must sweep our minds clean of all such ideas as that God needed to be changed in his disposition toward sinners."[88] When God looked at humanity he only saw his precious children without any defilement by guilt or sin. They only needed to know of his fatherly love. The biblical picture of God as holy judge and righteous king whose heavenly family was composed of those who had placed their faith in Christ, belonged to a bygone era that must now give way to a higher understanding of humanity and its relationship with God.

Poteat's theological motif originated with the nineteenth-century German theologian Albrecht Ritschl, who employed familial language to define comprehensively God's relationship with humanity.[89] As Roger Olson has said of another theologian, "Similarity is not always evidence of influence," but Ritschl's ideas took root among theological liberals in America. Poteat appropriated Ritschl's motif to define his more optimistic view of humanity and relationship with God.[90] Theologian John Frame explained that "Ritschl promotes a concept of the kingdom of God based on the fatherhood of God and all mankind as God's family. *Redemption, justification, regeneration, adoption, forgiveness,* and *reconciliation* are all essentially synonyms, referring to God's action in restoring the broken family relationship."[91] Ritschl argued that Christians had a mission to extend their family influence for the transformation of society.[92] Ritschl's theme of social activism appealed to American liberals, and Poteat adopted this framework for his vision of social redemption. A Ritschlian theological framework and its connected activism supplanted the older theology Poteat considered to be unnecessary baggage that had accumulated around true Christianity.[93]

Poteat seemed to reject orthodox conceptions of God. He never used language that suggested that he embraced the classical doctrine of the Trinity.[94] Such a formulation was too metaphysical for Poteat. Instead he used expressions that verged on pantheism. He emphasized God's immanence and implied divine interdependence with creation.[95] These ideas became influential among some thinkers within Poteat's circle. At the Baptist Congress Meeting in 1910, one of Poteat's colleagues advocated pantheism as a decidedly modern option: "There is another school of modern thought, however, which refuses to depersonalize nature. The God who sits on the far-off circle of the heavens is giving place to the immanent God. . . . He does not need to project himself into his world at times of special crisis—he is already there. The natural order is the expression of his immediate will."[96] Poteat argued that modern science ushered in a new worldview that suggested the unity of all things: "There is no chasm between them; the supernatural is natural, and the natural is supernatural. Even the inveterate antithesis of matter and spirit shows signs of dissolving."[97] And he stressed the unity of God and humanity: "Moreover, the divine and the human nature draw into a close fellowship, the human nature being divine in its origin and aspiration, and the Divine nature expressing itself in the human."[98] Poteat favored Georg W. F. Hegel and expressed satisfaction after reading Hegel's *Philosophy of History*.[99] Poteat also favored other Hegelian authors, especially the American philosopher Josiah Royce.[100] A pantheistic framework proved helpful to Poteat for framing his evolutionary worldview: Creation and all history slowly but progressively advanced toward God's designs. This framework could alleviate the burden of explaining miracles if Poteat exchanged the categories of natural and supernatural for God's immanent work in history.[101] If orthodox theism proved to be an obstacle for Poteat then a Hegelian framework complemented his thought.

With these views Poteat stood at a distance from the evangelical Protestantism that was deeply rooted in the American South. Protestant Christians, including Southern evangelicals, in theory maintained that they had responsibility to love their neighbor, which Jesus clarified to refer to all people without distinction. But they treasured the ideas that they were uniquely bound together as spiritual brothers and sisters in Christ and that God was father to a particular people whom Christ purchased with his blood.[102] Baptists had long called one another "brother" and "sister" as an expression of this familial affection within the "household of faith."[103] But Poteat rejected such exclusivity and the insufficient social vision he believed it fostered. He affirmed God's familial embrace for all humanity. Since God was father to all without distinction, all men and women belonged to an indivisible kinship as God's children. The modern acceptance of this theology fueled the optimism of Poteat's mission for social redemption. Roger Olson's summary of Ritschl's theology was also true for Poteat's: "Christianity is not an otherworldly religion but a religion of world transformation through ethical action inspired by love."[104]

Theology of the Atonement

Poteat's first public controversy arose in 1920 when the popular preacher Thomas T. Martin challenged Poteat's orthodoxy on the doctrine of the atonement. As part of Poteat's larger reconceptualization of doctrine and the Christian life he dismissed the standard objective theology of the atonement as too theoretical and ultimately unnecessary for fellowship with God. He considered the doctrine of penal substitution to be distasteful and representative of an outdated mode of Christianity out of step with modern society. Any theory of the atonement that advanced an objective work for the forgiveness of sins missed the mark. Poteat proposed Christ's subjective work to win humanity to fellowship with God by a grand display of his love.[105] Martin captured the nature of Poteat's views. However he failed to dislodge Poteat from his position in North Carolina Baptist life.

Poteat's views placed him at great distance from rank-and-file Southern Baptists who generally held to the penal substitutionary view of the atonement.[106] Gary Dorrien accurately defined the content and relative importance of the doctrine of the atonement to evangelical Protestants: "Traditional Protestant orthodoxies placed the substitutionary atonement of Christ at the center of Christianity, conceiving Christ's death as a propitiatory sacrifice that vicariously satisfied the retributive demands of divine justice."[107] Randal Hall noted the disparity between progressive leaders and those in the pews: "The gap between leaders and membership continued to plague southern churches throughout the overwhelmingly conservative South."[108] Poteat and other liberal Baptists like Alfred J. Dickinson, John W. Phillips, and Edwin M. Poteat Sr. had discarded the traditional view, but their conservative brethren eventually noticed and raised concerns. Those who challenged leaders publicly were labeled fundamentalists.[109]

Evangelist Thomas T. Martin of Blue Mountain, Mississippi, ignited a public controversy when he published a series of articles in Kentucky Baptists' *Western Recorder* that challenged Poteat's theological fidelity on the atonement.[110] The controversy stemmed from Poteat's 1900 Baptist Congress address titled "Wherein Lies the Efficacy of Jesus' Work in the Reconciliation?" Poteat advocated for a subjective view of the atonement against the consensus among grassroots Baptists.[111] In the years following the address some Baptists in North Carolina expressed misgivings but usually with a spirit of restraint.[112] However in 1907 D. F. King of North Carolina charged Poteat as being a higher critic and thus unfit for leadership at a Baptist institution. But King failed to generate substantial pressure against Poteat. In 1919 he wrote an article to declare Poteat's heterodoxy. But the editor of North Carolina's *Biblical Recorder,* Livingston Johnson, a friend of Poteat and trustee at Wake Forest College, refused to publish it. Instead King printed and circulated copies of Poteat's address. Martin's reception of the address put the evangelist on the offensive.[113]

Thomas T. Martin argued that the theology represented in Poteat's address was beyond the pale of Baptist orthodoxy and that Poteat's views were not a private concern. Martin argued that "his teachings can contaminate the young men of Wake Forest and especially the young Baptist preachers who are educated there."[114] Martin recognized that Poteat's atonement theology derived from the affirmation of the universal fatherhood of God and the denial of any need for atonement in the objective sense: "The breach [between God and humanity] is healed when the cause of it ceases to exist. The essential and sufficient condition of reconciliation is the change of man's attitude to God—that is, repentance—God's attitude being already favorable . . . The work of Jesus in reconciliation, therefore, must be concerned with the change of man's attitude only."[115] Martin recognized also that Poteat redefined repentance, denied original sin, and conceived of Christ's atoning work principally as a display of love with the goal of disarming humanity's disaffection toward its adoring father who waited with open arms. When Poteat's defenders offered his undeniable piety as proof of the sincerity of his faith Martin argued that piety could be misleading: "[Livingston] Johnson says that President Poteat is devout; no one denies it; so was Professor Toy of the Southern Baptist Theological Seminary, who held similar views to some of the views of President Poteat's published address, and yet he was compelled to leave the Seminary. So was Horace Bushnell devout . . . [Johnson] says President Poteat is faithful as a church member; no one denies it; so was Horace Bushnell."[116] Martin also connected Poteat to the University of Chicago's infamous liberalism: "The reader will have perceived that these expressions are but the Southern echoes from Dean Shailer Matthews and Prof. Ernest Burton and other and weaker voices from the Chicago University."[117] The question was fundamentally "whether God is the father of sinners, or becomes father by faith in the Savior [alone]."[118] Martin argued that the idea that "God is the Father of sinners, of all men, [stood] squarely in the face of the Savior's teaching, 'If God were your Father,' and of God's word, 'as many as received him to them he gave [the] power to become the children of God.'"[119] Poteat had offered a view of God and the Christian gospel that bewildered Southern evangelicals. But Poteat argued that none of the ideas explored in his address were "against essential Christianity, but [only] against an outworn mode of conceiving it."[120] But to Martin and most Southern Baptists, Poteat's views struck at the heart of Christianity. Willard Gatewood accurately reflected Martin's concern: "His main quarrel with Poteat, therefore was that the latter's theology blinded sinners to the need for redemption by holding that God was already their father without it."[121]

Poteat and his supporters successfully defended him. Livingston Johnson of the *Biblical Recorder* published a letter in which Poteat expressed that he was faithful to "the fundamentals of our Christian faith." Poteat carefully crafted his language to ease fears and disarm his opponents while not conceding any ground.[122] Poteat leveraged his redefinitions of traditional theological ideas.[123] He could claim fidelity to the fundamentals of the faith, but he meant something strikingly different than what conservative Christians understood the fundamentals to mean.[124] When he said that he accepted the "New Testament as the law of [his] life and the standard of [his] thinking" he sounded like his conservative brethren, but he had redefined revelation to be subjective rather than objectively authoritative. When Poteat's defenders claimed that the old address no longer represented his beliefs Martin claimed to take them at their word, although he continued to challenge the views themselves as originally expressed in the address.[125] But Poteat had never repudiated his earlier views. And later he reasserted a subjective, moral view of the atonement and again challenged the view of penal substitution.

Poteat rejected objective atonement theology as distasteful. Five years after the initial controversy with Martin, Poteat publicly declared his rejection of penal substitution in the University of North Carolina's John Calvin McNair Lectures. He argued that an objective view of the atonement was profane and stemmed from vain theological deductions instead of the embracing of the simple beauty of Calvary:

> The tragedy of Calvary, where our Lord laid down his life to win ours,—the wonder of infinite love and the mystery of Divine suffering do not protect that most sacred spot in history against vulgar invasion, and one hears even there the clatter of logical apparatus seeking to determine how the Cross becomes efficacious, a clatter only a little less profane and alien than the gambling of the soldiers for the seamless robe.[126]

Poteat followed the liberal pattern that exchanged substitutionary atonement for the moral influence theory.[127] In 1928 he argued that the suffering and death of Christ were intended to inspire moral and social transformation. The cross did not objectively change one's status before God nor alter his or her nature, but "personal attachment to Jesus is the essence of our religion and the secret of the new way of living which he came to inspire."[128] Poteat said, "[The cross] was the symbol of a love which went beyond the gates of death to succor and redeem."[129] Poteat believed in the redemptive power of Christ and the cross, but his redefined soteriology sharply separated him from rank-and-file Southern Baptists who continued to preach the older way of redemption.

Poteat's objectors failed to understand that he had not merely rejected any number of doctrines but had reconceived the very nature of doctrine. Thomas T. Martin rightly sensed the distance between traditional Protestant theology and that expressed by Poteat, but he failed to recognize that Poteat had redefined the role and meaning of doctrine in the Christian life. Historian Tom Nettles explained that with "all these doctrinal changes and rejections, the central contention for the modernists was not just a change in doctrine. Their worldview demanded a complete change in attitude toward doctrine."[130] And Nettles rightly applied this to Poteat: "The basic liberal contention that 'Christian faith is not a doctrine or system of doctrines, but a personal attachment' permeates all that Poteat writes."[131] Poteat opposed the idea of doctrinal norms or expectations of theological orthodoxy and he instead emphasized religious experience, morality, and the mission of social redemption.

Poteat was a kindred spirit with Albrecht Ritschl.[132] About Ritschl, Roger Olson concluded, "Although he explicitly rejected any doctrine of the atonement that would make Christ the bearer of divine punishment for the sins of the world, Ritschl did not deny the special significance of Christ's death. Kevin Vanhoozer rightly explained, "With Albrecht Ritschl . . . we might speak of a corporate variation on an 'Abelardian' theme, moving from individual to social morality—a turn to the *intersubjective,* as it were."[133] Poteat agreed and emphasized the social nature of salvation and God's work of establishing his kingdom in this world.

By the 1920s a growing number of educated Southern Baptists had little regard for the old theology of the atonement. The bloody cross did not fit well with the polite society that was emerging in the New South era. Gary Dorrien's argument for earlier liberals was also true of Poteat: "The nineteenth-century liberals refused to accept religious teachings that offended their moral, intellectual, and spiritual sensibilities."[134] Poteat's soteriology better harmonized with the rapidly urbanizing and progressive-minded New South, but it remained at odds with the majority of Southern Baptists.

CONCLUSION

In the 1920s the liberal ideas that Poteat and others advanced provoked a new breed of fundamentalists in Baptist life who rose in protest against the new theology. The heart of their opposition centered on key leaders at denominational institutions, and no one faced greater scrutiny than William Poteat as the president of a prominent Baptist university. As the sheer distance between progressive leaders and the rank-and-file majority came into focus, further and heightened conflict seemed inevitable. Alternative conceptions of the doctrines of salvation and atonement, sin and religious exclusivity, and the essence of the Christian mission revealed a remarkable divergence in Baptist life between a number of educated leaders and the grassroots majority. What the outcome of the coming conflicts might be, however, was anything but clear.

Chapter Six

AN IMPREGNABLE LEADERSHIP

William L. Poteat prevailed against two movements that sought to remove him from leadership over a Baptist institution because of his outspoken advocacy of evolution. In doing so he helped secure space for theological liberals in the Southern Baptist Convention. Poteat stood firmly against his opposition, and he was determined to avoid even a suggestion of capitulation to his conservative critics. He triumphed over his opponents with the wide support of Wake Forest alumni, his esteemed reputation for piety, and by carefully misleading rank-and-file Baptists. Poteat's position grew stronger with each controversy to the point that it became impregnable. He overcame his opponents in part by successfully convincing the majority of North Carolina Baptists that his religion was ultimately in harmony with theirs. Weary of conflict they were content to put an end to controversies and focus on denominational cooperation.

Poteat recognized the peril of being a progressive voice in a broadly conservative denomination. He was unsurpassed as a public intellectual in North Carolina and his prominence and influence in North Carolina Baptist life only increased through the 1920s and 1930s. But Poteat, like most theological liberals, was not a radical in a way that led him to establish rival institutions. He recognized that the loose coalition of liberal Southern Baptists, although influential and growing, constituted only a small minority of Baptists in the South. He was content to work within the denomination of his upbringing. The decentralized nature of Baptist life and Baptist principles like local church autonomy and a fresh emphasis on private spirituality allowed substantial freedom for people like Poteat to maintain liberal theology in relative peace. To Poteat what mattered most was not one's denominational affiliation or membership at a local church but rather one's private spirituality. Poteat's theology of religious experience made formal affiliations relatively insignificant and more a matter of convenience.

But Poteat's theological path was not always peaceful. During the first half of the 1920s Poteat endured the antipathy of militant conservatives. These conservatives came to be called fundamentalists. Poteat weathered these controversies by regarding them as a necessary burden on the path toward progress. Poteat's contemporary Edwin Mims expressed the idea well when he said that "the liberal leaders of whom I have written are bearing the burden that forward-looking men have always borne."[1] Wake Forest College alumnus Gerald W. Johnson expressed the same sentiment when he commended Poteat for his sacrifice for the cause of progress: "Poteat was an intellectual, but he was more than that—he was an educator who staked his career, not once, but daily for forty years on the proposition that, in a collision between truth and dogma, truth must prevail."[2] Both parties considered themselves to be fighting for truth, which inspired a form of sacred devotion to their causes. Driven by a sense of duty Poteat resolved to endure the fundamentalists' scorn. At the same time, he made the case to educated Southerners that Christianity should be and rightly could be modernized.

THE FIRST MOVEMENT FOR POTEAT'S REMOVAL

In 1922 Poteat overcame the first of two challenges to his position as president of Wake Forest College. Two years earlier North Carolina Baptist layperson D. F. King had raised concerns about Poteat's theology. Evangelist Thomas T. Martin publicly challenged Poteat's theology of the atonement as well as his advocacy of evolution in a series of articles in Kentucky Baptists' *Western Recorder.* But Martin eventually relinquished his attack, and the movement lost momentum.[3] In subsequent controversies evolution shifted from a secondary issue to the main concern among Poteat's critics. He had been an outspoken advocate of evolution since the 1890s, but in early 1922 Poteat published an article titled "Was Paul an Evolutionist?" that reignited the fires of controversy.[4]

In a provocative article first printed in the New York–based *Watchman-Examiner,* Poteat made the case that the apostle Paul gave signs of being an evolutionist.[5] He focused on the account of Paul before the Athenians. In Acts 17:26 Paul said, "All nations he has created from a common origin, to dwell all over the earth, fixing their allotted periods and the boundaries of their abode." Poteat interpreted this description of humanity's "common origin" as meaning that Paul referenced both the great length of time needed for evolution, when God fixed the "allotted periods," as well as the "boundaries," which implied the isolation of species essential for evolution, as Charles Darwin argued based on his research on the species in the Galapagos Islands. Poteat argued that Paul's language might lead to the conclusion that he was an evolutionist: "I am quite unable to frame a neater statement of the doctrine of the descent of existing organisms from earlier organisms under the divine impulsion and guidance."[6] Grassroots Baptists considered Poteat's interpretation outrageous. It was deeply troubling that these statements could come from the president of a Baptist college.

Responses to Poteat filled the pages of North Carolina's *Biblical Recorder* for weeks. Pastor J. J. Taylor of Leaksville, North Carolina, argued that teaching evolution was not a question of "liberty in teaching" but in this case one of accountability to a Baptist denomination. If professors wanted to teach evolution they had the same right as anyone to articulate their positions, but they should do so at institutions that were not founded and supported by Baptist resources: "Evolutionists and their supporters also have their rights, and they are at liberty to establish and maintain schools that promulgate their views."[7] Randal Hall well expressed Taylor's and of many North Carolina Baptists' sentiments: "No one denied Poteat's right to believe as he wished and be damned; however, his opponents disavowed his right to do so as an employee of the Baptist denomination."[8] Taylor argued that North Carolina Baptists had a stewardship over the teaching at Wake Forest.[9] Historian Willard Gatewood seemed to be correct when he linked Baptists' heightened concern for stewardship to the Southern Baptist Convention's Seventy-Five Million Campaign.[10]

Taylor argued that from its inception evolutionary theory was based on philosophical materialism and the motivation of envisioning a world without God. Thinkers like Hume, Voltaire, Schelling, and Darwin led the way. The term "evolution" really belonged to them: "These agnostic gentlemen have a right to their term." Taylor had no room for Poteat's theistic evolution and believed the idea to be oxymoronic: "The fact is, evolution and unbelief are inevitably linked together both logically and historically." Robert H. Spiro of West Asheville, North Carolina, concluded that either evolution is true or the Bible is true, but both cannot be. Evolution, he argued, was the product of humanity's fallen mind.[11] Historian James Thompson explained that fundamentalists were convinced that evolution would corrupt the minds of young people. Even so-called theistic evolution necessarily perverted the creative work of God as revealed in the Bible and removed the foundation for morality.[12] Another North Carolina Baptist offered a clear answer to Poteat's question of whether Paul was an evolutionist: "Did Paul believe that he came all the way up from a clod by means of spontaneous generation? He did not."[13]

Poteat responded with two articles that defended the veracity of evolution as well as its compatibility with the Christian faith. He seemed astonished that his article provoked such a "remarkable revival of controversy."[14] His critics, he contended, were resisting an idea that had been settled in professional circles for at least thirty years. With a hint of ridicule Poteat asked rhetorically, "One wonders where these excited gentlemen have been? Were they asleep when the procession passed?" Poteat rejected the idea that modern science was clashing with faith. Those who pressed an either-or alternative were hurting rather than helping the cause of religion. In its simplest form evolution claimed that all plants and animals were the offspring of earlier plants and animals, and this in no way undermined essential Christian theology. Poteat discredited those who offered lists of supposedly reputable scientists who rejected evolution. He contended that the scientific community had an overwhelming consensus on evolution and showed no signs of faltering.[15]

In a subsequent article Poteat made the case that evolution in no way threatened Christianity. One could be a Christian and an evolutionist without any compromise of faith. Those who argued otherwise were motivated by fear and ignorance.[16] Poteat made his case by providing examples of reputable evolutionists who were also people of faith. He cited several scientists including Charles Darwin himself but his argument proved weak on this point. Instead of demonstrating that these scientists were Christians he only provided statements that implied that they remained open to theism. However Poteat cited the renowned Princeton Seminary theologian Charles Hodge who had argued that evolution did not necessarily imply naturalism.[17] He also cited the Baptist theologian Augustus H. Strong who argued that Genesis did not disclose the precise details of how God created the world, which left open the possibility of evolution.[18] Above all Poteat pointed to Wake Forest and claimed many such persons who maintained a warm Christian faith while also accepting scientific facts. Poteat challenged his critics' character and argued that those who held to this controversy were guilty of unchristian behavior: "It is not right. It is not fair. It is not Christian. It ought to stop."[19] But Poteat's opponents were not swayed.[20]

After weeks of debate D. F. King argued that the stakes were clear. North Carolina Baptists would either tolerate evolution at Wake Forest or they should demand Poteat's resignation.[21] King considered Poteat dishonest when he claimed that evolution and Christianity were compatible and that evolution represented no threat to faith. He implied that the state of Northern Protestantism was proof enough: "I am surprised at any brother's taking the stand that the teaching of evolution is not fraught with danger when almost half of the students who have been taught this pernicious doctrine in the Northern schools have become infidels." King called North Carolina Baptists to take official action at the next state convention.[22] A sizable contingency of grassroots Baptists prepared to do so.[23]

But Poteat held an impressive level of support from Wake Forest alumni. One alumnus, Bernard W. Spilman, wrote a very personal defense based on intimate knowledge from when he was a student at Wake Forest thirty-five years earlier. He had known Poteat as a Sunday school teacher, worship leader, preacher, as well as his biology professor. He argued that Poteat's piety was unquestionable: "If there is a devout, humble servant of Jesus Christ who believes his Bible from lid to lid; if there is a man who holds to the deity of Jesus in its fullness; if there is a man on the earth who is trying to lead men to Jesus for salvation, if there is a man who lives the religion of Jesus day by day, that man is W. L. Poteat." If anyone doubted Spilman's testimony, "there are easily a thousand men in this State who can be brought forward as witnesses to testify the same thing." The army of devoted alumni were their own source of proof and they occupied prominent posts throughout North Carolina and the South.[24] Wake Forest's student newspaper *Old Gold and Black* defended Poteat largely by pouring scorn on his opponents. The paper likened the fundamentalist coalition to the historic forces of persecution: "The forces of intolerance are never asleep. The spirit that brought forth a Spanish Inquisition and the persecution of John Wyclif—the very spirit that nailed the Son of God himself to a cross of pain—still lives and stalks among us." Modern methods of persecution were more humane, they acknowledged, but the same spirit of suppression was behind the current controversy.[25] The *Raleigh Times* defended Poteat as a hero for the freedom of thought. The article recognized the volatility of the controversy but expressed confidence in the security of Poteat's position. Poteat could take care of himself. But if Poteat chose to leave Wake Forest he would have no trouble finding a promising position in the North. And the people of North Carolina would pay the price in the loss of their leading voice for enlightenment.[26]

In May, Wake Forest trustees appointed a committee to evaluate Poteat in light of the controversy. After questioning him on the fundamental doctrines of the faith and after hearing testimonies from alumni about Poteat's character and devotion to Christianity the trustees fully exonerated him and reaffirmed his leadership of the institution. When asked doctrinal questions Poteat leveraged the liberal redefinitions of theological terms. When he affirmed doctrines like "Redemption from sin through [Jesus's] atoning death" and the "divine inspiration and final authority of the Bible," he meant something different from the traditional beliefs of the vast majority of Southern Baptists.[27] Whether the trustees recognized this and overlooked it or whether they lacked theological comprehension to recognize it is unclear. But in this stream of Baptist life what mattered was not the specifics of one's theology but his or her own religious experience and piety. By the 1920s, this framework had become deeply rooted among educated Southern Baptists.

The evolution controversy dominated the 1922 Baptist State Convention of North Carolina. An impressive 498 messengers gathered, which was nearly double the number of the previous year.[28] The first day of the convention passed routinely, but on the second day Poteat was slated to give an address on education. Richard T. Vann, a Wake Forest trustee and close friend of Poteat, introduced Poteat, and every eye in the convention hall fixed upon him. Everyone who had ever heard Poteat give an address knew that he was a masterful speaker. In his address Poteat made brilliant use of rhetoric, personal charm, and intellectual gravitas without ever mentioning the topic on everyone's mind. Poteat instead tried to demonstrate his sincerity as a Christian and his commitment to the sacred cause of Christian education. He attempted to persuade his hearers that he was one of them. As he did before the Wake Forest trustees months earlier he affirmed his belief in the Bible, and he did so with gripping language: "I love this little book and accept all it says. It has been the light and joy of my life. I commend it to you. It is our final authority for faith and practice." Poteat stressed his loyalty to the Bible: "If you hear of anybody who flouts its authority and threatens to destroy it and to dislodge it from the minds and hearts of men, blow your trumpet, turn the bell of it Wake Forest way, and our little company, little but loyal will be at your side on the dot."[29] Poteat also shared his testimony when as a young college student he encountered God in a fresh way, which was sure to resonate with evangelicals' conception of the new birth.[30] Poteat emphasized the weightiness of Christian education especially at a time when so much seemed to be at stake in American society. He declared that Christianity was the great hope for society, which he meant as a mission for enlightenment and social morality, but even the most conservative Baptists could appreciate the point that the Christian message offered hope to the world. Poteat urged his audience to be newly consecrated to the sacred cause of Christian education. He communicated that he had the resolve and the intellect necessary to lead an institution in this sacred task. Questions about theological particularities and the nature of scientific theories seemed small before so momentous a calling. He convinced his hearers that he was still the man for the job.

In this speech Poteat turned the tide against his opponents, but it was a temporary victory. Instead of censuring him North Carolina Baptists adopted a resolution to publish his address.[31] In his address Poteat uncharacteristically masked his liberal views. In an attempt to endear himself to his audience Poteat carefully misled his hearers when he articulated his belief in the Bible. What he said was not untrue from his perspective, but he exploited the surface-level similarities of the liberal view of the Bible to convince his hearers that he shared their convictions. Poteat leveraged the redefinitions that constituted liberal theology and successfully disarmed his conservative opponents. Randal Hall was correct that Poteat "overwhelmed the convention" and that his "persuasiveness left his conservative opponents no opening for combat that did not look petty."[32] But Poteat had not addressed the most pressing issue that precipitated the controversy in the first place. Hall rightly concluded that because Poteat's victory was more rhetorical than substantive the victory was sure to be short lived.[33] Poteat's brother Edwin warned him: "When they have forgotten your superb eloquence, they will come home to their own house of life and see again Evolution mocking their faith in the uniqueness of their Lord. And President Poteat will be more a puzzle to them than ever."[34] Edwin Poteat's words seemed prophetic. In a few years Poteat faced essentially the same conflict for a second time.

THE SECOND MOVEMENT FOR POTEAT'S REMOVAL

Poteat reignited denominational controversy when he delivered a lecture series at the University of North Carolina that underscored his liberal vision of Christianity along with a fresh apologetic for evolution. In response conservative Baptists organized again to push for Poteat's removal at the 1925 Baptist State Convention of North Carolina. Poteat had kept a lower profile for two years but grassroots Southern Baptists were no more contented with evolution and liberal theology than they were two years earlier, and Poteat and his supporters were no more willing to compromise their convictions than were conservatives. Conflict was inevitable. But at the conclusion of the conflict Poteat suffered no loss of influence, and his position remained as secure as ever.

Progressive Southerners praised Poteat's lectures with the same level of intensity as the conservatives who denounced them. The John Calvin McNair Lectures focused on the relationship between science and religion, which made Poteat a natural choice. He delivered the lectures in June 1925, and the university press quickly published them as *Can a Man Be a Christian To-day?* Randal Hall observed that Poteat "presented his ideas with unusual aggressiveness." Poteat felt secure in his position at Wake Forest, and he was likely also energized by recent political victories in North Carolina against anti-evolutionary forces.[35] Fundamentalists seized upon *Can a Man Be a Christian To-day?* as their best source of proof for the illegitimacy of Poteat's leadership over a Baptist institution. A conservative coalition aimed at the upcoming Baptist convention as a second attempt to censure the evolutionists in their midst and if possible remove Poteat from leadership. One conservative from Asheville was so incensed by Poteat's defense of evolution that he challenged Poteat to a fight. He told Poteat to "get three other Scientists and yourself, and put gloves on, and have a few rounds just for 'fun,' and, if I fail to knock the four of you out in two minutes I will give to you each $25.00 in gold, proving to the public that Scientists are weak in mind and body." Poteat had thirty days to respond or else be exposed as "a coward."[36] But Gerald W. Johnson, a 1910 graduate of Wake Forest College, praised Poteat's McNair Lectures.[37] He gave eager approval to Poteat's challenge to "fundamentalists because, as he sees it, they are doing all they can to make it impossible for an intelligent, educated man to be a Christian today."[38] Johnson agreed with Poteat's call to resist the fundamentalists: "It is time for educated Christians to oppose [the literalists], not harshly with bitter words, but firmly, without compromise."[39]

During the summer, rumors spread that Poteat might resign. Perhaps Poteat's forthrightness in the McNair Lectures represented one last declaration before imminent retirement. Poteat's opponents waited eagerly for news of what they would count as surrender. But Poteat had no intention of resigning lest it suggest defeat. As opposition grew he showed full determination to remain.[40] But Poteat had been mistaken if he thought that conservative members of his denomination had lost the will to fight.

Roused to indignation conservative Baptists decided that if Wake Forest trustees refused to remove an avowed evolutionist from leadership, North Carolina Baptists should aim to institute a new form of denominational accountability for their schools. W. C. Barrett, pastor of the First Baptist Church of Gastonia, North Carolina, proposed that trustees be elected directly by the convention. Up to this point the board of trustees was essentially self-perpetuating. Barrett argued that the state convention supporting colleges like Wake Forest deserved greater accountability in keeping Wake Forest in Baptist hands and maintaining doctrinal fidelity in Baptist schools. Barrett argued that this accountability would spare Baptists from losing their schools the way that Methodists had lost Vanderbilt University.[41] Barrett said, "These institutions, we call Baptist Institutions in North Carolina, either belong to the Baptists, or they belong to somebody else." He pressed, "The name Trustee certainly indicates that the Institutions do not belong to the Trustees . . . If they owned the Institutions they would not be Trustees, but owners."[42] The denomination had a right and duty to hold its institutions accountable. Some observers expected that Barrett might call directly for Poteat's removal.[43] Others apparently hoped that if the Barrett resolution passed "Dr. Poteat will then accept this as a verdict of North Carolina Baptists and immediately present his resignation as president of Wake Forest."[44] Through the summer and fall the situation simmered, and both sides braced for a showdown in Charlotte. An article in the *Charlotte Observer* reported that an unprecedented number of messengers were expected to gather in November and warned readers to "Expect [a] Stiff Fight."[45]

More than a thousand messengers converged in Charlotte for the 1925 convention.[46] The first day was quiet. On day two, R. J. Bateman of Asheville introduced a resolution or rather a series of five joint resolutions that challenged liberal theology and evolution. Bateman affirmed the literal truthfulness of the book of Genesis and insisted upon its literal interpretation: "That we interpret the record of Genesis not as myth but as God's inspired revelation. We believe that it is literal and unassailable as to the fact of creation by God." Bateman emphasized the special creation of humanity as distinct from that of animals and lower life-forms. And this was essential to uphold humanity's creation in the divine image: "God by special act, created man in His own image apart from the rest of the animal creation." Bateman argued that God's special creation of humanity was "fundamental as a background for the superstructure of Scriptural revelation; that it holds the underlying conception of the redemptive program." The denial of a historical Adam compromised the New Testament motif that pictured Jesus as the second and final Adam.[47] Bateman expressed conservatives' argument that evolutionary thought was not an isolated concern but was related to other points of Christian theology.[48] Bateman addressed theological liberalism directly, calling it "Modernism," and he responded with a confessional declaration of traditional Protestant theology. Bateman called Baptist colleges to pledge themselves to this faith. They should agree to teach only "the attested facts of Science," by which Bateman meant to exclude evolution, which he regarded as "insufficiently substantiated to be taught as [fact]." The convention adopted Bateman's resolutions without discussion.[49] Conservatives could claim that they had made their voice heard, but in fact Bateman's resolutions enacted no meaningful change.

Both sides recognized that the Barrett resolution threatened to effect substantial changes if adopted by the convention. Before W. C. Barrett introduced his resolution on Wednesday evening Wake Forest alumni gathered to hear an address from their beloved president. Poteat demonstrated a calm steadiness against his opponents. Failure was not an option: "I decline to be whipped out on a false issue which involves the respectability of my Alma Mater." Poteat declared unequivocally that he would stand for "Truth." A deep sense of conviction and affection for Wake Forest College compelled Poteat and his supporters to resist the conservatives' agenda, which amounted to the suppression of intellectual progress.[50] Messengers at the convention seemed to take careful notice of the fierce determination of the Wake Forest coalition.

The convention passed the highly anticipated Barrett resolution Wednesday evening, but the resolution's lasting significance seemed uncertain. The motion required the convention to appoint a committee to amend the charters of the colleges that were "owned and supported by the Convention." The new process for electing trustees read: "The trustees shall be elected by the Baptist State Convention of North Carolina, and hold office at the will of the convention."[51] The convention passed the resolution without conflict. But a subsequent motion was immediately voiced by Bernard W. Spilman, a Wake Forest alumnus and supporter of Poteat. Interestingly however Barrett himself seconded Spilman's motion, and Spilman seconded Barrett's motion.[52] Spilman created a resolution that qualified Barrett's directives by clarifying that the current members of the board of trustees would themselves make the initial nominations to the convention to fill any vacancies on the board. Only then would the convention retain "the right to elect or reject anyone thus nominated" as well as exercise the power to substitute nominations.[53] The convention passed Spilman's resolution as it had Barrett's without discussion. Together the adoption of these resolutions brought a puzzling and anticlimactic conclusion to months of controversy.

After the convention both sides claimed victory, but the situation was essentially unchanged. Illustrating the confusion that initially set in, an editorial in the *Charlotte Observer* asked, "Did the Anti-Evolution Forces Win or Lose in the Action of the Baptist Convention?"[54] Bateman's resolution was a clear declaration of the conservatives' traditional Protestantism, but it made no functional changes or challenged any person or institution by name. Conservatives were proud to point out that the convention passed the Barrett resolution, but Spilman's resolution removed the bite from Barrett's. In practice Wake Forest's board of trustees would continue to fill its own vacancies along with the formality of the convention's approval.

When conservatives recognized the strength of Poteat and his supporters they softened their demands. Randal Hall seemed to be correct when he concluded that when the time came denominational leaders "wanted to avoid the divisions and bitterness of an open battle."[55] The *Raleigh Times* seemed to regret that the convention turned out to be less exciting than many had predicted.[56] The article argued that the convention skirted the real issues at hand: "The Barrett resolution was a complete camouflage and fought shy of evolution entirely. Neither did the Bateman resolution mention evolution directly; and after slightly hinting at it, went out of its way to so sugar-coat its reference to it that even Dr. Poteat himself would gladly have endorsed it."[57] One conservative indicated defensively that the convention passed no positive statement in support of Poteat or his view either.[58] But it was clear that Poteat was secure in his position, and his influence was unshaken. North Carolina Baptists moved forward with the unchanged predicament of a progressive denominational leadership and a conservative rank-and-file majority. Hall agreed when he described the outcome of the 1925 convention: "The gap between leaders and membership continued to plague southern churches throughout the overwhelmingly conservative South."[59]

SAFE AND SECURE

The 1925 convention marked the final organized attack against Poteat and his leadership. Edwin Mims reflected on Poteat's tenacious leadership as a liberal intellectual in the South. Mims knew well the fierce opposition that Poteat faced in the first half of the 1920s. But Mims expressed his confidence that Poteat had become absolutely secure in his position, holding such commanding support from Wake Forest's trustees and an army of alumni. In 1926 he wrote with satisfaction that Poteat was "too firmly intrenched to be dislodged."[60]

Already during the months leading up to the 1925 convention there were signs that Poteat was becoming unassailable. In June 1925 an editorial in the *Winston-Salem Journal* indicated Wake Forest alumni's wide support of Poteat: It "undoubtedly accounts for the ease with which he triumphs over his foes every time there is anything even remotely resembling a showdown." The article argued that Poteat's opponents should recognize the strength of his position. Conservative efforts against him were doomed to failure:

> The opponents of Dr. Poteat, it seems to us, have reached the point where they are forced to recognize that the fight on him is largely futile and will degenerate, if, in fact, it has not already degenerated, into a nagging campaign, unless they can cause something to happen that will change the attitude of nine-tenths of the Wake Forest alumni and a majority of the Baptist men and women who have made modern Wake Forest possible.[61]

Gerald Johnson also credited Wake Forest alumni with Poteat's strength. Although conservatives were energized and organized in 1925 hundreds of Wake Forest alumni came in force to the convention hall in Charlotte. Johnson characterized them in surprisingly stark and admittedly overstated terms, but his point regarding their aggressive devotion was clear: "[Poteat] merely stood his ground and whistled, and instantly around him sprang up a thousand alumni, grim alumni, with red eyes and no scruples about flying at a Fundamentalist throat."[62] A theological liberal could survive and even thrive in Southern Baptist leadership. Randal Hall was correct when he concluded that Poteat prevailed because of his personal charm and his irrefutable piety, but the most significant factor for his triumph was the robust support of the people of Wake Forest College.[63]

The final organized attempt to hold denominational leadership accountable to doctrinal standards proved ineffective. Liberals had established themselves among Southern Baptists, and they held prominent positions within denominational life throughout most of the rest of the twentieth century.

CONCLUSION

Poteat retired from the presidency of Wake Forest College in relative peace in 1927 at the height of his influence. Far from being pressured to retire Poteat went out while he was on top. When he announced his retirement to the trustees they tried to persuade him to defer it until a successor could found, but he declined.[64] As president emeritus he continued for a decade to be active as a professor of biology. He also devoted an impressive amount of energy to social activism, working to address the social challenges of modern society: poverty, education, sanitation, and alcoholism.[65] Two weeks after his retirement Poteat received an honorary LLD. from Brown University, having already received honorary degrees from the University of North Carolina and Baylor University. Educated North Carolinians brimmed with pride.

Poteat obtained a symbolic vindication in the twilight his career. North Carolina Baptists elected Poteat to serve as president of the North Carolina Baptist State Convention in 1936 to recognize his faithful career of Christian service including throughout the years of bitter conflict.[66] After the 1925 convention fundamentalists essentially conceded higher education in North Carolina to progressive leadership. At the national level Southern Baptists formulated their first convention-wide confession of faith, the Baptist Faith and Message, which gave the impression of doctrinal accountability. But in the coming years Southern Baptists fostered denominational unity by emphasizing cooperative mission over theological clarity and doctrinal accountability. This unity and an emphasis on private spirituality provided space for liberal Southern Baptists to shape an alternative theological tradition that accommodated modern streams of thought and was inspired by modern sensibilities. At the same time, it maintained shared forms of worship and ministry with the conservative majority, which became sufficient for Southern Baptist consensus for decades to come.

Chapter Seven

A SOUTHERN PROPHET OF EVOLUTION

William L. Poteat championed Darwinian evolution as a part of the bedrock of modern thought and one of the established tenets for the intellectual elites of the New South. Poteat's advocacy of evolution and the social ideas that seemed to extend from Darwinism significantly defined his public image among both progressive Southerners and his conservative opposition. As a member of the New South elite Poteat aimed to enlighten Southern society. He argued that society should defer and give leadership to those who possessed a higher intellectual and cultural sophistication rather than trusting the common people of society to lead simply by virtue of their majority. Progressive Southerners praised him as a prophet of intellectual and social progress and as a symbol of enlightenment. Many Southerners, however, resisted his self-appointed leadership and viewed him as a threat to their civilization.

In the 1920s conflict erupted among Southern Protestants in North Carolina over teaching evolution in public schools. Progressive leaders clashed with the more conservative rank-and-file majorities, just as they did in larger denominational matters. David Scott Poole, a devout Presbyterian, introduced a bill in the North Carolina legislature that challenged the teaching of evolution in tax-supported schools. Issues of local democracy and popular rule versus academic freedom and the priority of experts to guide American society arose. In his religious conflicts Poteat led the progressive wing within the Baptist State Convention of North Carolina, and he secured space for liberal ideas in a broadly conservative denomination. But in the political conflict Poteat avoided a direct role and essentially became a spectator during the Poole bill debates. However because progressive Southerners so associated Poteat with the fight against religious fundamentalism and anti-evolutionism many credited Poteat with being among those who defeated the Poole bill.

Although he was a public religious figure Poteat's evolutionary thought and his advocacy of Darwinism shaped his public image more than any specific theology. Poteat was in the mainstream of American theological liberalism, and his views were comparable to those of his contemporaries in northern Baptist life. But most of the criticism he faced during his career was less explicitly theological. Poteat tended to be more careful not to speak too freely about his liberal views on the Bible, the atonement, or sin. But as a biologist he was outspoken about his support of evolution, which he regarded to be essential to modern education and social progress. This made evolution the most obvious target for those who were troubled by Poteat's liberal views, and they recognized that Poteat's affirmation of evolution had significant theological implications. Both sides agreed that truth itself was at stake, which conferred a kind of sacred relevance to the conflict.

As a witness to the formative power of education Poteat devoted his life to education and envisioned the ideal of higher education as the formation of cultured individuals who would lead the movement toward a more enlightened society. Education represented Poteat's greatest hope for a better South that would embrace the best of the modern world as he had. He carried a burden to prepare students for the challenges of the modern world, and he delighted in opening minds by introducing students to modern ideas beginning with the authority of science. A more enlightened society would be a flourishing society, and he hoped that this could be achieved by a devoted group of cultural elites. And Poteat's victories over conservative opposition suggested that enlightenment was advancing.

POTEAT'S VISION OF ELITE LEADERSHIP

Poteat held a view of the social order that placed educated elites over the common people.[1] He argued that society should grant leadership to those who possessed a higher intellectual and cultural sophistication. This order would benefit the whole of society. The wise leadership of the elites was needed especially in light of the tumultuous changes of the modern era, as American civilization endured the growing pains of progress. In the early twentieth century the common people of North Carolina lived in a dramatically different milieu than did people like Poteat. The refined tastes, cosmopolitan outlook, and progressive thought life of the New South elites set them apart from common Southerners. But many Southerners resented the suggestion that they should defer to the leadership of a class of educated elites. Poteat's paternalism was met with resistance by many of the rank-and-file members of his own denomination. But he skillfully maintained his influence, through which he shaped generations of leaders who adopted his convictions regarding elite leadership.

Historian Randal Hall argued that Poteat embraced a set of core values that reflected an elitist view of society: "Poteat maintained throughout his life . . . respect for high culture and learning, the need for elite leadership, and a love of order and hierarchy."[2] Hall also recognized the tension that this created, particularly over the issue of Darwinism. As one of the elites and as a scientific expert Poteat contended that evolution was settled science and therefore warranted universal incorporation into the modern scientific curriculum. But this led to conflict in both church and state when many North Carolinians dismissed Poteat's expertise and resisted the leadership of evolutionists in their state.[3]

Poteat possessed a low estimation of the intellect of average Americans. In a commencement address for United States military cadets in 1932 Poteat bewailed the state of American education.[4] A reporter summarized Poteat's disparaging assessment of the common American mind: "He deplored the fact that, despite rapid advance in the mechanics of education, this country is still 'a stronghold of illiteracy, a nation of eighth graders,' a fertile field for demagoguery." Poteat blamed teachers as part of the problem for playing it "safe" and "taking orders" from administrators, rather than bravely teaching children to think for themselves. Poteat argued that the "purpose of education . . . was not to teach the student to conform, but to enable him to adjust himself to new conditions."[5] Because of ill-equipped intellect, most Americans lacked the ability to make the best decisions for themselves and society. Poteat outlined this concern in an address at Vassar College in Poughkeepsie, New York, in 1927: "The untrained masses have had no defenses against misinformed enthusiasm, and their response to the appeal of the Christian faith harried by science has demonstrated at once their docility and devotion."[6] Driven by their passions and commitment to outworn traditions the unlettered masses of society needed to be led by a class of people that possessed intellect and modern sophistication.

In the modern world science especially was too lofty to be entrusted to anyone but the experts. Poteat was among the evolutionists in North Carolina whom historian Willard Gatewood argued refused to surrender science to a "mass gathering," whether it be religious or legislative.[7] Those who dismissed evolution because it contradicted their religious beliefs only embarrassed themselves and impeded social progress. Gerald W. Johnson, an alumnus of Wake Forest College, remembered fondly that Poteat was known to say, "No man has any right to an opinion until he has first made himself acquainted with the facts."[8] And once a person acquainted himself with the facts, he was sure to acknowledge the veracity of the experts. But many North Carolinians judged otherwise. Randal Hall observed that Poteat "chafed at the lack of respect given expert knowledge."[9] When concern arose about the possibility of grassroots Baptists protesting Poteat's public involvement at an upcoming Southern Baptist convention because of his outspoken advocacy of evolution, Poteat complained to his brother Edwin that "I have a deep seated resentment against Paul's weaker brother determining policy for the whole bunch."[10] Poteat had to acknowledge the joint power of his many weaker brothers, but he refused to compromise his fundamental principles, especially regarding the authority of science.

Journalist, author, and Wake Forest alumnus Wilbur J. Cash shared Poteat's frustration with the lowly state of the Southern mind and the need for enlightened leadership in society. Cash concluded that the condition of the South's common people resulted from a long history of unengaged minds. He lamented that in general Southerners were unreflective and uninterested in cultivating higher forms of thought. Cash seemed to share Poteat's conviction that those who had transcended the backward patterns of Southern society represented an elite class who could lead the South into a more progressive future.[11]

Poteat's elitism applied to the church as well as broader society. And to Poteat elite leadership meant liberal leadership. Those enlightened persons who had learned to appropriate the best of modern thought were alone suited to lead Christianity into the future. Liberals represented a small minority of Southern Baptists, but they grew to hold great influence within the denomination, particularly in its educational institutions. These elite leaders deserved deference and authority, and it was a present lack of appreciation for this ideal order that was impeding religious progress. Poteat and other liberals regarded themselves as bold defenders of the faith at time when Christianity was vulnerable to losing its relevance in the modern world.[12] Gerald Johnson grumbled about the democratization of American religion that persisted in many quarters. He deplored that eminent leaders of the faith were given no greater weight than an unlettered preacher with his English Bible: "A Cornelius Woelfkin, a William Herbert Perry Faunce has no more authority in matters of faith and doctrine than is possessed by the semi-literate pastor of some Little Bethel in the remote backwoods."[13]

Poteat's Wake Forest College supported the elitist ideal despite great pressure from rank-and-file Baptists. Walter Lippmann, the acclaimed New York journalist, visited Wake Forest in the 1920s when Poteat was under pressure for his progressive views. Lippmann praised Wake Forest as a "place where the long, laborious unrewarded and often dangerous search for truth is still honored."[14] Wake Forest was unimpressive "in material things, yet none richer in the spirit which makes men seek higher things in life." Lippmann expressed alarm at the popular contingent in North Carolina that challenged the school's tradition of "seeking the truth." He asked rhetorically, "Shall Wake Forest succumb to the siren song of the populace or shall it continue to make America for itself by reaching out for the truth," and would truth be "denied and cast down and trampled under the foot of the horde"? Lippmann exhorted Wake Forest against surrendering its heritage to retain the support of the denominational mob. The school's mission was more important than "the golden calf" of financial support.[15] There was never any question about Poteat's priorities. He would hold the line for a more modern and more progressive South. Such was the burden of the elite.

POTEAT'S PHILOSOPHY OF EDUCATION

Poteat envisioned the ideal of higher education as the formation of cultured individuals who would contribute to the formation of a more enlightened and genteel society. Education represented Poteat's greatest tool to form a better South—a society that embraced the best of the modern world. But Poteat also demonstrated genuine concern for the students themselves. He aimed to prepare them to be leaders in the modern South, and this goal required that students find intellectual enlightenment for the sake of overcoming tradition. It necessitated that leaders provide students with a modernized religion that met the standards of modern respectability. Poteat was genuinely concerned to convince young people that they could be both modern and religious. If educators and other intellectual leaders failed to shape students into the modern image, graduates could expect to face the contempt of modern society. Poteat and other liberals were convinced that those who failed to conform to the modern world would surrender any hope of maintaining social respectability. This surrender would be too heavy a burden to bear.

Poteat argued that educators needed to prepare students for the unique challenges of modern society. Virginius Dabney described the disruption that had occurred in the nineteenth century: "Fatal in its implications for scriptural orthodoxy, Darwin's evolutionary hypothesis burst upon a mid-Victorian world with shattering effect . . . and relegated Adam and Noah to a place beside Thor, Vulcan and other mythical personages of antiquity."[16] Modern thought had shaken the foundations of religious authority and the traditional worldview of most Americans. Christians needed to respond to the challenges modernity posed, and progressive educators could light the way for students. Thoughtlessly dismissing modern ideas would only be counterproductive. Poteat argued that modern education should provide students with a solution that harmonized an updated form of Christianity with modern ideas. Edwin Mims well defined this effort as the "adjustment of religion to modern scholarship and thought."[17]

Poteat was deeply concerned about providing students with a form of religion that would be credible according to the standards of a modern thought. Poteat believed that his position as the head of a Baptist institution entailed a stewardship to do just that. Students needed answers to "the questions that are sure to arise in the minds of young men who are here thrown into the current of the world's thought."[18] Institutions and educators that failed to provide a respectable solution for students roused his indignation. Poteat said bluntly, "I am indignant only when I saw misinformed men erecting a false issue and making it hard for intelligent young people to be Christians."[19] He resolved to counter the conservative influences that placed unnecessary obstacles in the way of young people, like those who implied that students should question the conclusions of modern science or those who claimed that Christianity was dependent upon a set of doctrines. Poteat focused his energy on presenting an enlightened form of Christianity to reassure young people of religion's viability in the modern world. He advocated for religion, and he argued that students might be able to achieve some level of culture without religion. But such culture would be deficient without the enlightened religion of Jesus: "It is He who enlarges the volume and enhances the quality of life. He is the secret of the harmonious expansion of our powers which we have called culture. You will not find the highest culture apart from Him . . . without Christ your culture will want consistency and elevation; it will be empty and aimless and cold."[20]

Edwin Mims recognized Poteat's apologetic concern with and burden for young people as well as the hope that he placed in them. Mims called

Poteat's *Can a Man Be a Christian To-day?* a "vision of the light shining in the minds and hearts of the young."[21] Like Poteat's optimism, Mims's optimism for a more progressive South rested in the younger generation: "Best of all, the younger generation in the best colleges and universities is freer of traditions and prejudices and feels the stirring of the impulses that are surging in the minds of all other young people of the world."[22] Poteat expressed his satisfaction that the young tended to "substitute vigor for decline, teachableness for unteachableness, the spirit of adventure for conformity, initiative for the love of comfort, which prefers that things remain as they are."[23] Randal Hall similarly noted the hope that Poteat placed in young people to create a more progressive society: "Poteat labored diligently to educate the Baptist youth of North Carolina. The only hope he always sustained was that a cultured and religious leadership could bring into being the new community to replace the lost island worlds of the nineteenth century."[24] Poteat hoped to harness students' enthusiasm and convince them that religion could be progressive and enlightening. Poteat's arguments and his grand vision won the hearts of many students at Wake Forest and beyond.

Poteat regarded character formation as an essential part of education. In this way he followed an older model of education that viewed learning not merely in intellectual terms but also as spiritual and moral.[25] Historian Joseph Stetar well summarized this philosophy: "Concerned with educating the whole man, advocates of mental discipline also necessarily addressed themselves to the development of character and the inculcation of Christian values, often fearing a student's mental development might outpace his moral growth." Traditional educators argued that the mind might be a loss "if moral and religious stamina were lacking."[26] Poteat told students that their "primary need is to be good; after that to be intelligent."[27] Randal Hall rightly argued that Poteat considered the cultivation of morality to be essential for the achievement of social progress. True progress necessitated an "environment conducive to Christian middle-class morality."[28]

Poteat aimed to produce modern people who were marked by intellect and culture. He demonstrated his standard for evaluating a person's quality in a diary entry from 1896. He reflected on the caliber of Franklin H. Kerfoot, a professor of theology at Southern Baptist Theological Seminary in Louisville, Kentucky.[29] Poteat reasoned that Kerfoot seemed to be a "sensible man." But he was also "a conservative." If Kerfoot was sensible but still conservative he must therefore have been unacquainted with the best of modern thought and literature. Poteat judged that Kerfoot was insufficiently modern and lacking in culture: "I feel that he is chiefly lacking in the feeling for literature & in acquaintance with the thought of the modern world."[30] Poteat concluded that Kerfoot's shortcomings made it unlikely that he would accomplish anything of great worth. The modern world needed leaders who embraced modern thought. Conservative persons did not fit Poteat's vision for a genteel and enlightened society. Randal Hall noted a similar example when Poteat opposed the election of a president to Raleigh, North Carolina's, Meredith College, at which Poteat served as a trustee. He disapproved of the candidate because he lacked culture and intellectual gravitas.[31] Poteat resolved as an educator to produce enlightened people of modern intellect who fit his standard of social respectability. He seemed to expect that cultured people would eventually come to the same liberal conclusions that he had.

Poteat presented the pursuit of culture as a religious cause. In addresses to his students at Wake Forest he argued that a life rich in culture was the abundant life that Jesus proclaimed.[32] Poteat and the faculty at Wake Forest sought to maintain an atmosphere that inspired students to aspire to higher culture: "Someone has defined culture as the harmonious expansion of all the powers which make the beauty and worth of human nature. It is a sort of beneficent infection which you catch out of the atmosphere of the Best, the best things, the best men. Here for four years you have been in such an atmosphere."[33] Poteat encouraged students to develop the "habits of the mind" that led to a cultured life characterized by beauty and refinement.[34] But Poteat contended that the highest achievement of culture depended upon religion, even as religion was aided by culture: "For religion without culture is partial, austere, inefficient, superstitious. Culture without religion is partial, unsatisfying, aimless, anarchic. But when they are combined, each in its highest development, they guarantee the happy and the victorious life."[35]

Christianity was in need of some soul-searching in light of the changes modern thought had wrought. In an address to seminary students in 1905 Poteat had argued that because Christianity's doctrines were formed "before the rise of modern science," it was not surprising that it "contained implications and sometimes explicit statements sharply opposed to assured scientific results"[36] Traditional Christianity's theology needed to be revised and in some cases outright rejected to recondition Christianity for the modern world. The South's Protestant Christianity in the form of what Poteat called "the ultra-conservative theory of an original divine revelation" was not an option for modern people.[37] Poteat advocated liberal Christianity as a form of intellectual enlightenment to help students embrace the life of culture that Poteat cherished as the good life.

A SAGE OF MODERN ENLIGHTENMENT

Poteat took pleasure in his strategic position as a professor and president of Wake Forest College to introduce students to modern ideas and thereby enlighten their minds. In the early decades of his career, Poteat instructed the first generation of Southerners who had significant exposure to modern ideas. Throughout his career he oversaw a steady stream of students who first encountered modern ideas as students at Wake Forest. Poteat revealed to students what Edwin Mims called "the enlarged freedom of the modern world."[38] He introduced the ideas that defined the modern mind: individualism, suspicion of tradition, the subjectivity of religious knowledge, and the authority of modern science. The critical spirit that characterized modernity became a mark that one had been awakened to modern ideas and that he or she had joined the enlightened class of Southerners who were leading the South into the future.[39]

Edwin Mims described Poteat's method for opening the minds of students. Poteat affirmed the enduring importance of religion but aimed to persuade students that Christianity could reasonably be accommodated to modern thought. Poteat spoke "with the evident desire to help them adjust their inherited faith to the best of thought of to-day."[40] This adjustment involved the reorientation of religious authority, a deemphasis on doctrine, and the exaltation of private spirituality. But Poteat reassured students that these modifications did not alter the essence of Christianity, which was rooted in religious experience. However Mims seemed to recognize that Poteat's methodology placed Christianity in a subservient position to modern thought, but he approved.[41] He referenced Gerald Johnson as a prominent example of the power of Poteat's enlightening influence: "[Johnson] attributes his emancipation from traditionalism and conformity to President Poteat of Wake Forest College, whom he regarded from his student days as an 'amazingly lucid and convincing teacher and a personality still more amazing—a veritable high priest of truth.'"[42] Poteat was a sage for enlightened Christianity.

Poteat appealed to his Baptist roots to justify his progressive views. He argued that Baptists were formed from a plea for religious freedom. Baptists proclaimed "their release from the coercion from belief, from the coercion of ritual, and from the coercion of ecclesiastical authority."

Poteat contended that the Baptist spirit of freedom was permeating all of modern Christianity, and Baptists were poised to be leaders in the modernization of the Christian faith.[43] Poteat was correct that Baptists, especially in the North, were leading figures in the emerging movement of theological modernism.

Gerald Johnson argued that Poteat's work of unsettling minds was the pinnacle of his legacy. Johnson highlighted the extent of Poteat's influence:

> Such was the man with whom some thousands of men of North Carolina were in intimate daily contact for years. These men have since become leaders in their communities, in their churches, in the State's political affairs, in its educational affairs, in its commerce, in its professions, in all its intellectual, and social, and material activities.[44]

Johnson described Poteat's power to open young minds and the irreversible nature of his influence: "A critic complained, 'He unsettles the boys' minds.' It is true—splendidly, gloriously true. He did unsettle boys' minds and men's and women's minds, too. He unsettled them so thoroughly that never will they settle back into the old complacencies, the old prejudices, the old ruts and ignorance and partisanry from which he lifted them."[45] Poteat agreed with Edwin Mims, who said that colleges like Wake Forest were "the hope of the South." Mims said, "They kept the light of the altar of truth burning through many a dark night, and now eager-hearted young men and women are bearing this light to the dark corners."[46] The truth referenced by Mims and Johnson represented a modern and enlightened spirit more than any explicit idea or proposition. Poteat inspired many Southerners to embrace this progressive spirit as a foundation for the modern image of cultured respectability.

With the pursuit of social respectability forming a personal ambition for Poteat, he remade Christianity into a religion that appealed to the cultured people of Southern society. The more objectionable elements of Protestant Christianity had to be modified in the face of a culture that considered traditional concepts like original sin and hell to be distasteful and that regarded standards for theological orthodoxy to be too constrictive. Educated Southerners could not ignore that many respected institutions of learning had challenged the historical veracity and scientific relevance of the Bible and that many of the brightest minds of American society regarded Darwinian evolution as a settled fact. It would be increasingly difficult to maintain the image of social respectability without accepting the unique authority of science and modern research over the realm of facts.

Those who were most insistent and outspoken in holding to traditional Christianity and its outdated modes of thought were labeled fundamentalists, and the contempt that the fundamentalists faced and the prospect of their social marginalization were precisely what Poteat was determined to avoid. Poteat exemplified the image of cultured refinement and sought to harmonize Christianity with modern thought. And the Southern bourgeoisie cheered him for his commitment to elevating the South toward greater respectability.

POTEAT'S THEISTIC EVOLUTION

Poteat enthusiastically advocated Darwinian evolution. He recognized it as a part of the bedrock of modern thought and one of the established tenets for the intellectual elites of the New South. Because evolution had become foundational for modern science Poteat argued that spreading the knowledge of evolutionary biology was essential to social progress. And the elites of society were positioned to lead the drive for progress. Poteat felt a special sense of duty to disseminate the knowledge of evolutionary science in his state, but he would do so in a way that preserved a vital role for faith and spirituality. Poteat made a way to harmonize Christianity with Darwinism; this harmonization arose from his early crisis of faith. In this way he presented himself as proof that a person could be a man or woman of science and also of faith.

Poteat had been outspoken about his advocacy of evolution since the 1890s, making him an early exponent of evolution in the South.[47] In *The Mind of the South,* Wilbur J. Cash praised Poteat for his early stand for science: "In the early 1900's William Louis Poteat . . . had begun to teach biology without equivocation, to set forth the theory of evolution frankly and fully, as having, as he said, more evidence behind it than Copernican theory." Cash argued that Poteat had provided the South with "the first wholly honest and competent instruction of [evolution] in a Southern evangelical school, and the first in Southern schools of any sort save such exceptional ones as I have before noted."[48] When Poteat faced criticism from fellow Baptists in the early 1920s, he explained with a sense of disbelief that he had been teaching evolution for years: "The doctrine of evolution as the divine method of creation has been taught here frankly for many years."[49] Cash recognized the risk that Poteat had taken and this increased his reverence for him: "What is more wonderful, he survived, though a storm swirled about his head all the years of his life, and though he needed all his quite unusual gifts as a diplomat and orator to accomplish it—and not only survived but in a few years was made president of his college."[50] Because Poteat prevailed against his opposition he took on a legendary status among progressive Southerners.

Poteat considered evolutionary biology the backbone of modern science and a modulating force for the whole of modern education. In an early article for the prestigious magazine *Science,* Poteat dated the beginning of scientific education in America to 1859 when Charles Darwin published *Origin of Species.*[51] The temporary "ferment" that arose in education after Darwin's theory eventually compelled a "spontaneous adjustment to [the new] external conditions." And the new biology breathed fresh life into the other academic disciplines, even including theology which was "the most rigid and unprogressive of all the systems of human thought."[52] But Poteat stressed that evolution was not merely an invention of Darwin or any modern thinker. Balanced with the cultural authority of modernity Poteat also attempted to strengthen evolution's footing by establishing for it a distinguished history. In an article for *Popular Science Monthly,* Poteat argued that although Darwin introduced momentous advances in biology, he did not discover the process of natural selection. Evolution was known by the ancients, he argued.[53] Poteat cited Lucretius from the first century BCE as a "pre-Darwinian writer" who "sets forth the ideas of the struggle for existence and natural selection in terms of remarkable clearness."[54] Aristotle too recognized that "nature proceeds by gradual transitions from the most imperfect to the most perfect, that the higher species are descended from the lower, that man is the highest point of a long and continuous ascent." He argued although without substantiation that theologians throughout the Middle Ages had perceived an evolutionary process in nature. This process extended to the time of Jean-Baptiste Lamarck, who in the early nineteenth century introduced "the first elaborate exposition of the means or factors of evolution as applied to the origin of living forms." Then Charles Darwin finally "closed the question and won at once the almost unanimous assent of the naturalists of the world."[55] Poteat contended that a modern curriculum needed to feature this centerpiece of biology as a central part of human knowledge.

North Carolina Baptist educator Richard T. Vann shared Poteat's view of Darwinism and argued that the best of modern science should drive Christian higher education. More than anyone else Christians had discovered that they could learn about God both from his word and from his world.[56] Scientific instruction needed to be in the hands of the experts, scientists themselves, and not theologians: "Neither priest nor prophet, nor apostle, nor even our Lord Himself ever made the slightest contribution to our knowledge of natural science. For enlightenment on this subject, then, we must go, not to the cathedral, nor the Theological Seminary, but to the laboratory." Vann followed the same two-sphere philosophy as Poteat and other Baptists like Edgar Y. Mullins. The Bible essentially made no contribution to topics other than religion and morality. Scientists needed to have absolute freedom for research without hindrance or even input from theology.[57] Vann warned that science always prevailed over faith: "We must concede, and we shall do well to remember, that in every conflict between scientists and religionists, the latter have been defeated." And he argued that "Christianity has probably suffered more from its ill-informed defenders than from unfriendly scientists." The "Book of Nature is only another volume in the Book of God, and consciously or unconsciously, every real teacher of science is a professor of theology."[58] Poteat agreed and defined science in poetic fashion: "I think of Science as passing to and fro in God's garden, busy with its forms of beauty, its fruits and flowers, its creeping thing, its beast and bird, the crystal shut in its stones, the gold grains of its sands, and coming now at length in the cool of the long day upon God Himself walking in His garden."[59]

Poteat esteemed Thomas H. Huxley, the famous English evolutionist as a source for evolutionary thought and as a prototypical modern intellectual. Instead of the more utilitarian image of the isolated laboratory scientist, Huxley represented the kind of broad-minded intellectual that Poteat himself typified.[60] Huxley had pursued specialized studies in marine zoology, paleontology, primate anatomy, and physical anthropology but also became a respected voice in religion, politics, culture, and social issues.[61] And Huxley was among those who reoriented science as a discipline. Huxley popularized science for broader application in educational curricula as a boon to social progress, just as Poteat advocated.[62] Poteat cited Huxley as an authority when he insisted that evolutionary science did not threaten Christianity: "Prof. Huxley himself has admitted that evolution is neither antitheistic nor theistic, declaring that it has no more to do with theism than the first book of Euclid has."[63] In these ways Huxley inspired Poteat as a modern man of science.

In the most famous lectures of his career Poteat answered with a resounding yes to his question, *Can a Man Be a Christian To-day?*.[64] Poteat submitted himself as proof that a person could embrace modern ideas and also be a Christian but not without adjustment to Christianity. He cited the book of Genesis as "the capital example of the conflict between the

Bible and science."[65] But he argued that the conflict was merely superficial and was based on an outdated interpretation of the Bible that demanded more from the text than the text had to give. Poteat contended that the first two chapters of Genesis revealed only that creation was not instantaneous but progressive across a long expanse of time.[66] Genesis also refrained from specifics: "No process or method of creation is given; only the last terms, the finished products of the process are reported." Baptist minister L. Spurgeon Clark of Pennsylvania agreed and expressed Poteat's view well when he argued that science and religion did not inevitably conflict: "What has evolution to do with real religion? Nothing. Real religion throws open the prison doors of the mind. Real religion searches for truth, the truth of science, of art, of history, for all truth is one and comes from the great source. Evolution is God's way of making the universe."[67] Traditional Christians had required too much from Genesis: "The main point and purpose of the whole is to affirm the Divine Agency in the process from beginning to end. First and last, one may say that this is practically all the writer is concerned to say." This left ample space for science to discover the details of the origins of life. Instead of conflicting when "interpreted within the scope of its purpose, the first chapter of Genesis is in remarkable accord with modern science."[68] Poteat explained that Christians had always known that God created humanity, but science had revealed how he did so. As the creator God directed the entire process of evolution: "Finding out how God makes things does not dispense us from the necessity of having Him to make them. We are still dependent upon the Divine Will and Power to initiate and energize and guide the process of evolution through to its final products."[69] Poteat's formulation provided an example of a development that Gary Dorrien observed in liberal thought:

> The Darwinian-accommodating liberals gave religious meaning to evolution by interpreting divine reality as a creative, personalizing factor in the evolutionary process. Human beings are dually constituted as creatures of nature and children of God, they taught: finite spirits created in the image of the divine Spirit, but also evolutionary products of the lower organic forms of natural existence.[70]

Poteat stressed that the alternative of forcing "these primitive creation pictures" to agree with science would never work. And anyone who questioned the authority of modern science would be sentenced to endure the scorn of modern society.[71] Poteat resented that this scorn might reflect back on him and his fellow progressives who were eager to overcome the backward image of traditional Protestant faith and the stigma of Southern provincialism they faced in the eyes of America's elites.

Poteat and his fellow Southern elites were determined to have it their way, but common Southerners became equally determined to oppose the evolutionists. The conflict, both religious and political, was a clash of alternative visions for Southern society. An article in the *Biblical Recorder* gave an ominous warning to those who continued to teach evolution despite the popular protest against it:

> Those who have the management of the State institutions would just as well learn that this question is not settled and will not be, until freak and free-lance teachers, who disregard public sentiment, and trample the Constitution, are dismissed from the faculties. The masses of our people may be 'suspicious,' 'prejudiced,' and 'uninformed' but they are the sovereigns in this state and will not forever submit to evils against which they have thus far protested in vain.[72]

THE PATH TO THE POOLE BILL

The political conflicts that arose in the mid-1920s in North Carolina were a part of a national debate over public education.[73] The teaching of evolution became the central issue in the debate. Willard Gatewood rightly indicated that in this period Americans demonstrated fresh interest in using the power of legislation to reform society. Most prominent in the southeastern and southwestern United States, they marshaled "the coercive powers of the state" in a crusade against Darwinian evolution.[74] Suzanne Linder noted that "between 1921 and 1929, thirty-seven anti-evolution bills were introduced into twenty state legislatures."[75] In 1922 Kentucky lawmakers defeated an anti-evolution bill. In 1923 Texas lawmakers narrowly defeated one, but Oklahoma passed the first such bill. Tennessee followed Oklahoma and outlawed the teaching of evolution in tax-supported schools in 1925, and the Scopes trial of Dayton, Tennessee, became both a rallying point for and embarrassing stain on the respective sides of the debate. The next year Mississippi outlawed teaching evolution in public schools, and in 1928 Arkansas followed suit.[76] In North Carolina, state representative D. Scott Poole was elected on the promise that he would introduce legislation restricting the teaching of evolution in public schools. On January 8, 1925, he fulfilled his promise when he introduced House Resolution 10.[77]

POOLE BILL OF NORTH CAROLINA, 1925–27

In January 1925 D. Scott Poole of Hoke County, North Carolina, introduced a bill that challenged the teaching of evolution in North Carolina public schools.[78] The bill called for prohibiting "any official or teacher in the State, paid wholly or in part by taxation, to teach or permit to be taught, as a fact, either Darwinism or any other evolutionary hypothesis that links man in blood relationship with any lower form of life."[79] Poole's bill stated what many rank-and-file North Carolinians believed: The implications of evolution were "injurious to the welfare of the people of the State of North Carolina."[80] Poole, a former school teacher himself, argued that evolution led to the conclusion that the "world has no true code of morals."[81] Darwinian evolution undermined the religious views of many North Carolinians, he argued, and religious instruction belonged not to state institutions, including public colleges, but to parents and churches. The state should remain free from any religious affiliation: "Neither the Evolutionist, nor the Christian Fundamentalist has the right to teach his peculiar views at public expense." Poole allowed that evolutionists had the right to propagate their beliefs, but they should do so at their "own expense," because "it is not fair to taxpayers to defray the expense of teaching their own peculiar doctrine."[82]

The University of North Carolina loomed large in the political conflict.[83] Anti-evolutionists in North Carolina zeroed in on the University of North Carolina as the state's flagship university.[84] Poole's bill included all public schools, from elementary through college, but the institutions of higher education were the most likely places for students to encounter Darwinism. The University of North Carolina took the lead in resisting the bill.[85] President Harry W. Chase, university faculty, and alumni lobbied against the bill.[86] Chase argued that free speech hung in the balance. He referenced Galileo, whom he cited as a victim of persecution at the hands of the Roman Catholic Church. Galileo's discoveries were by then settled science, but during his lifetime the church "thought his doctrine to be worse than a denial of the incarnation [of Christ]."[87] Chase's point had rhetorical power but rested on a faulty knowledge of the historical episode.[88] Chase also cited the United States Constitution, which "guaranteed the free right of speech," and he asked rhetorically "if the constitution meant to say that everybody should have the right of free speech except school teachers."[89] James R. Pentuff of Concord, North Carolina, called Chase's appeal to free speech "fallacious." Appealing to free speech was "a favorite dodge of Evolutionists when asked to give a sensible argument for their theory."[90] Like the Baptists who argued that evolutionists were free to teach their ideas as long as they did so at schools not supported by Baptist money, Chase had to confront the argument that evolutionists could teach Darwinism as long as it was not at a school supported by taxpayer money.[91] Like Poteat's prominence in the religious conflicts, Chase's views became a symbol to both sides of this political debate, simultaneously praised and vilified by opposing sides. Chase told Poteat, "You have fought our battles long enough," and he reassured Poteat that "now we are going to do some fighting ourselves."[92] Southern cultural observer Edwin Mims praised Chase's contribution as "a shining example of bold public service."[93]

Frank P. Graham, a history professor at the University of North Carolina, argued that instruction in evolution was not a new phenomenon at the university: "Evolution was taught at the University by North Carolinians before President Chase was born." And this was true of "most of the colleges in every civilized nation in the world."[94] The Poole bill, Graham charged, was merely the most recent manifestation of the same old spirit of censorship: "The Poole Bill raises issues older than the State of North Carolina. The inquisition, the index, and the stake are the unclaimed ancestors of the Poole Bill." Like the brave persons of old who endured opposition for the sake of progress "the teachers and the youth of North Carolina today would revolt against this ancient tyranny in its latest form." Graham praised Poteat for his bold stand against intellectual bigotry: "May we also salute . . . President William Louis Poteat, who, by his stand at Wake Forest, has been, for all our colleges, the buffer state against unreason, the shock absorber of intolerance, and the first line trench against bigotry lo! these many years." President Chase was leading the fight, and Graham charged the university community to "close ranks solidly about him." Like Chase, Graham argued that academic freedom was the central concern. And he contended that the University of North Carolina was founded upon this very freedom.[95]

At the conclusion of an initial hearing for the bill on February 10, 1925, the North Carolina House Committee on Education voted in a tie, but the committee's chair, Henry G. Connor Jr., cast the deciding vote against the bill. However the bill's proponents crafted a minority report and introduced the bill on the House floor on February 19.[96] Baptist educator Richard T. Vann entered the fray and proposed an alternative bill that he hoped would draw support from both sides. It restricted teachers from criticizing the religious views of any citizen while not prohibiting modern scientific instruction, which included evolution.[97] Livingston Johnson of the Baptists' *Biblical Recorder* supported Vann's bill and argued that it contained the spirit of the Poole bill by protecting against aggressive secularism.[98] Legislators considered Vann's alternative bill, called the Connor bill after Henry G. Connor, who introduced it as a reasonable compromise. It might have passed if the staunchest proponents of Poole's bill had not voted against it in favor of seeking Poole's stronger restrictions.[99] Opponents of the Poole bill remained confident and awaited its defeat. After three days of deliberation and political maneuvering, the anti-evolution forces were dealt a blow when the bill was defeated in a vote of 67 to 46.[100] Opponents of the Poole bill called its defeat a victory for academic freedom and professional expertise. The media praised it as a sign of progress in North Carolina.[101] Chase returned to Chapel Hill to "an ovation from faculty and students."[102]

The anti-evolution forces did not surrender after their loss in 1925. For two years they labored for their cause although in a more decentralized fashion.[103] Victories against evolution in other states boosted their confidence to try again. In early 1927 Poole introduced another anti-evolution bill into the North Carolina legislature. Poole's second bill contained stronger language than the first. In addition to clear prohibitions against state-supported schools teaching "any doctrine or theory of evolution," the bill also specified penalties for breaking the law: "That any professor, teacher or instructor violating the provisions . . . of this Act shall be guilty of a misdemeanor and upon conviction shall be fined or imprisoned in the discretion of the Court, and in the discretion of the court may be disqualified from teaching in such schools, colleges or educational institutions."[104] As proof of popular support members of the North Carolina Bible League came to the state capital and delivered a petition of ten thousand signatures from North Carolinians who supported the bill. But the opponents to Poole's measures had also been active. In large part, they had worked to earn confidence from North Carolinians for the present state of tax-supported schools. Willard Gatewood argued that the Scopes trial in neighboring Tennessee, although technically a victory for anti-evolution forces, also provided Poole's opponents with a convenient reference point to demonstrate the public embarrassment that North Carolinians could expect if they approved a comparable law.[105] In this second attempt the Poole bill failed to make it to the House floor and went down in defeat with little effort by the opposition.[106] By 1927 public interest in the issue had waned in North Carolina. In addition to organizational failures by anti-evolutionists, the public sensationalism of outside organizers like Thomas T. Martin alienated even many sympathetic North Carolinians.[107] The anti-evolutionist movement in North Carolina went out with a whimper.

An Enduring Symbol

Progressive Southerners credited Poteat with helping to defeat the Poole bill, but Poteat made no direct contribution to its defeat. One admirer stated:

> Poteat rallied every force of honest liberalism in the state, and with President Chase, of the University of North Carolina, a man of equal mind and like courage, he defeated legislation that would have been a negation of everything that North Carolina has been striving to do in education since Aycock and Alderman and Brooks and McIver began the revolution.[108]

A generation later journalist George M. Bryan wrongly cited Poteat as a star opponent of the bill who forced its defeat.[109] He incorrectly claimed that Poteat "pleaded successfully against [the Poole bill] before the legislative committee itself. The article appeared as Hollywood released *Inherit the Wind*, which depicted Tennessee's 1925 Scopes trial, still a sore spot for progressive Southerners. Bryan said while "'Inherit the Wind' is embarrassing Tennessee and ridiculing the Protestant religion in the South, it is good to remind ourselves that it was a vigorous Protestant layman who almost single-handedly kept North Carolina from this nonsense." Bryan overstated his case, but he illustrated how Poteat remained a symbol of enlightenment and a favorite counterexample to the caricature of a backward South. Poteat belonged to "a vanguard of religious thinkers, which in the case of North Carolina, saved both the Baptists and the Legislature from making a monkey out of themselves over the 'monkey' business."[110]

Poteat did not lead the fight against the Poole bill, but he lent his influence. He attended the 1925 debates that were held by North Carolina's House Committee on Education, but he declined to speak, even when called upon with cheers and applause. It made sense that the leaders of the opposition should come from the institutions who would be directly affected by it. And Suzanne Linder seemed to be correct when she concluded that Poteat was careful not to involve himself unnecessarily and awaken further conflict among North Carolina Baptists. But Poteat was also confident that the Wake Forest alumni in the legislature would vote down the measure.[111] Randal Hall indicated that "eighteen of the twenty-one [legislators] who had attended Wake Forest voted against Poole's resolution, an indication of the liberalizing influence of Poteat among the college's alumni."[112] Linder reflected upon Poteat's influence on these alumni. She suggested that while they listened to the legislative debates "perhaps they recalled their biology classes under Dr. Poteat," who had both convinced them of the veracity of evolutionary theory and also reassured them that evolution did not threaten Christian faith.[113] Poteat had taught evolution in North Carolina for decades and shaped generations of leading North Carolinians. Even without Poteat's direct involvement Wake Forest alumni could lead their state into a more progressive future. Poteat's vision for the New South seemed to take hold among the graduates of Wake Forest College.

CONCLUSION

Poteat was a prophet of evolution, and he became a symbol of the enlightened elite and the power of professional expertise. Although opposition was fierce at times, Poteat's liberal vision for Southern society prevailed both through his own religious conflicts but also in the political debates surrounding the Poole bill. Both for what he achieved and for what he represented Edwin Mims praised Poteat as "the voice of the real South, the South of the future."[114] Mims's optimistic words certainly did not apply evenly across the South. But in Poteat's North Carolina, as in other regions that embraced the progressive ideals of the New South, the future that was emerging favored modern ideas. Southern elites achieved greater influence than their numbers would ever suggest, but those who maintained traditional ideas and instincts were not going anywhere.

Chapter Eight

RACE AND EUGENICS

William L. Poteat held the paternalistic and elitist ideals that characterized progressive White Southerners of the New South. Eugenics was one of those ideals. Poteat advocated it as a measure to improve society. As a member of the social elite, he proposed eugenics as a tangible solution to the alleged human degeneration as discovered by the new hereditary science of the era. The ideas of social Darwinism gave formative shape to this movement and so also to Poteat's mission to improve society.[1] As self-appointed leaders over society the elites claimed as their own the responsibility to determine what was best for the general public, even if it infringed upon human rights and human dignity. Poteat was also dedicated to improving race relations in the South. But the goal of his work was establishing order in society and not achieving racial equality or justice for the millions of African Americans who were pressed into an inferior status in modern America. Poteat's vision of the good society included maintaining White supremacy.

Poteat advocated eugenics and worked to improve the race problem in America as a part of his social vision to establish the kingdom of God on earth. In his vision of social redemption Poteat had exchanged the supernatural and otherworldly elements of the Christian theological tradition for a mission of building a more prosperous and peaceful society. Poteat argued that this work progressively transformed society into the kingdom of God by the renewal of the entire social order: politics, business, education, and culture. With other reformers of America's Progressive Era Poteat looked forward to the unfolding of a utopian society. But this would require brave leadership from the leaders of society, who best understood what was necessary to redeem American civilization. He concluded that progress could only be achieved at a sacrificial cost. He and other reformers determined to let the weaker members of society bear the burden of this sacrifice.

ENLIGHTENED WHITE SUPREMACY

Poteat's views on race were progressive for his time, and he made significant contributions to the movement for racial cooperation. But his views were predicated on assumptions of White supremacy. Poteat viewed African Americans in a paternalistic manner with kindness and personal affection. He regarded himself as a modern and enlightened man, but his capacity for forward-thinking had limits. His views on race were shaped in part by the Old South paternalism of his early childhood with a heavy dose of nostalgia. But Poteat also embraced a new kind of paternalism of the Progressive Era that could be benevolent in its outward form but ultimately utilitarian at its core.[2] Poteat maintained that achieving harmony between the races was necessary for the social progress that he and the reformers envisioned, and his theology of the kingdom energized the work for racial cooperation. The march toward kingdom utopia had to include a solution to the deplorable state of race relations in the New South.

Poteat's views on race were shaped by an early childhood in the Old South and by a family that cherished the ideals of the Southern gentry. The Poteat family's Forest Home was among the larger plantations of North Carolina's Piedmont region.[3] Poteat remembered fondly the enslaved persons who called his father "Marse Jim." He recalled Uncle Jerry the carriage driver and Uncle Isaac who was the plantation's blacksmith, as well as Uncle Morris the cooper, whom Poteat remembered as a pious man who often read the Bible. After the Civil War and emancipation Morris remained with the family and became their carriage driver.[4] But more than anyone else Poteat recounted the bond that he shared with Nat who was born around the same time as Poteat. He said that Nat was as "black as Egypt." Because Nat's mother died the two infants shared the same wet nurse: "He was admitted to the superb abundance of the same white fountain from which I drew my infant nourishment—my turn then Nat's." They were intimate friends.[5] Poteat preferred to play with Nat more than with his own siblings.[6] He called Nat the "closest companion of my childhood," and he recalled their warm friendship: "It is now many a year since I saw the genial smile of his shining black face, but I shall never forget our boyish sports in the oak grove of my country home, & how, when the fried chicken had been taken up, we sopped the gravy in the wide skillet on terms of perfect friendship & equality."[7] Poteat noted that his father was "solicitous for the godly comfort & religious needs of the slaves." The paternalism even survived emancipation. Poteat claimed, "When freedom came, many of them begged to stay on with him."[8]

Poteat viewed Southern slavery in an idealized fashion, and he expressed no regret about his father being a major slaveholder. He believed that slavery's demise was the work of the kingdom's leaven, but he also remembered the Old South nostalgically.[9] With pride he depicted their plantation as "a self-sufficient social unit." He said, "Whatever it needed it produced, food of course, but clothes including shoes as well. The only exception was hats."[10] In 1930 he visited his childhood home and reflected on the changes that the modern world had wrought: "But there can be no new world apart from the old. Forever the present is the child of the past."[11] The paternalism of the Old South remained with Poteat and it provided a contrast with a new form of racism that arose in the Jim Crow era. Poteat's nostalgia, however, also blinded him from acknowledging the deplorable nature of the race-based enslavement that he remembered so fondly.

With the rise of the New South came the rise of Jim Crow and new challenges of postemancipation race relations.[12] Historian Michael McGerr rightly argued that the roots of modern race relations lay in the Progressive Era when a social experiment was underway as White and Black persons were pressed together in the growing cities the New South. The Progressive Era saw "a fresh brand of racism, hysterical and harsh, proclaimed in legislatures, country stores, and newspaper columns." McGerr argued that the new manifestation of racism was especially pronounced among lower-class White people and among the younger generation: "The New South created a new people, too. The younger whites, who had not grown up with the paternalistic example of the old antebellum planter class, were less tolerant of blacks."[13] Historian William Link in *The Paradox of Southern Progressivism* recognized that paternalistic racism lived after the Civil War, but it took new shape within the social reforms of the Progressive Era. Southern elites feared that they were witnessing the growing instability of their social order, which implied White superiority, and some professed a sense of paranoia over a brewing race war. White leaders took White supremacy for granted, and they were determined to disfranchise African Americans and reestablish White rule. They pursued peace and order and also inequality.[14]

Poteat argued that Black and White persons were one common humanity, and he believed that one day they would overcome their antagonism.

In an address before the 1937 Baptist State Convention of North Carolina titled "Christ and Race," he urged Christian love as the basis for racial harmony in American society. He argued that both science and the Bible taught the biological unity of the human race: "The varied types of men . . . have developed from a common ancestor under varied isolated conditions. Their power of adaptation has established them in every region of the globe except the Antarctic Continent."[15] He defined three major races—White, Yellow, and Black—and from these all of the ethnicities of the world "are derivatives." Lengthy periods of isolation between the ethnic groups explained their differences, but he argued that the antagonism that often existed between them was learned rather than instinctive. In the modern world isolation became the exception when the races increasingly lived together, but this created new tensions: "Contacts are no longer occasional, but free and general. Anywhere throughout the world two or more races may be found occupying the same area, and New York or North Carolina has its race problem, California or Hawaii, India or South Africa." He cited the "universal indignation at Italy in Ethiopia and Japan in China." Poteat argued that ethnic hostility was not a Southern problem but rather a global phenomenon.

Poteat contended that Jesus was the solution to the hostility. He theorized that sometime in the distant future the human race might return to something closer to a single race, "becoming again one flock in physical feature, as our Lord proposes to make them one in moral relationship." But as it was, Christians needed to embrace the essential unity of the human race as Jesus did. Jesus cared for all people "without social or racial discrimination." Poteat declared that Jesus was the key to achieving racial harmony: "So the thing to do with our problem is to bring it to Him, not as a last resort, but as the first, and with assurance and great hope." Poteat was not envisioning the divine work of spiritual regeneration of the human heart, but on their own people should embrace the humility and love that Jesus demonstrated in the New Testament. He argued that Christianity was not ultimately doctrinal or institutional but was concerned with inspiring love and goodwill: "In other words, the religion of Jesus is love, not subscription to intellectual propositions or an external connection, but an inward attitude of love to God and fellowman controlling relationships." However Poteat did elevate two doctrinal points unequivocally: the spiritual fatherhood of God and the brotherhood of humanity. He said, "Love of one another and of a common Father, according to His own declaration, makes brothers of us all." This brotherhood could be the needed basis for mutual respect between the races. Putting theological convictions aside, Christians could rally together to advance the kingdom of God by spreading love and harmony: "The obligation of Christians to love one another as brothers and to cooperate in making the will of God prevail transcends theological barriers. We shall never agree in our opinions. Let the differences be." Poteat expressed optimism that "it is possible to be different in Christian philosophy and cooperate in Christian work." Demonstrating humility and charity Poteat encouraged White Americans to "be willing to judge the race by its best specimens." When White persons weighed the "quality and promise" of the African American community, they should judge it by "[Booker T.] Washington and [Robert R.] Moton and John Hope in education, by [W. E. B.] Du Bois, [Paul L.] Dunbar, and [Joseph S.] Cotter in letters, Pearce, Roman, and [George W.] Carver in science, [Harry] Burleigh in music." Christian charity, inspired by the spirit of Jesus, called for White Americans to consider "the vanguard of the race, not the rag-tag in the rear." White Americans would hope that others did the same for them rather than judging their racial group by their "millions of defectives, anti-social and [those] incapable of unsuperintended labor." Poteat presented a picture of White and Black Americans living peacefully in a shared land, "participating in its blessings, mutually respectful, mutually helpful and cooperant in advancing the common well-being."[16]

Poteat was committed to improving interracial cooperation to keep peace in Southern society, but he did not challenge White supremacy. He joined the Commission on Interracial Cooperation along with other key leaders: Robert R. Moton of Tuskegee Institute, George F. Peabody of New York, and Governor of Virginia Harry F. Byrd.[17] The organization opposed lynching and all forms of racial violence, and it promoted a more peaceful coexistence between Black and White Americans. One of the commission's officers, Robert B. Eleazer, explained that their work was "an adventure in good will" and "an adventure in faith—a gamble on the essential soundness of human nature."[18] Further revealing the optimism that characterized the organization's progressive and predominantly White leadership, Eleazer argued that the commission undertook "the stupendous task of establishing across the South thousands of points of interracial contact through which mutual understanding might be created and the facts discovered and acted upon." Eleazer attested that they had achieved early progress: "The leaders of the two groups [of both races] promptly came to terms, cast off their mutual distrust, and began to reestablish the relations of the races on the basis of friendly helpfulness." Although based in the South, the movement had support in the Northeast, Midwest, and as far away as South Africa.

The organization did not intend an "amalgamation of the races, but their amicable adjustment in mutual helpfulness." Their work centered around two goals: "1. The correction of interracial injustices and the betterment of conditions affecting Negros. 2. The improvement of those interracial attitudes out of which unfavorable conditions grow." Poteat especially sympathized with the goal of having the "best spirits of the two races . . . brought together to face their mutual problems and obligations." The commission claimed to encourage honest conversation: "The Negro members are encouraged to lay bare any injustices which they feel they are suffering, or any needs of which they are keenly sensible." They discussed what might be done "co-operatively to accomplish" their goals. The organization obtained resources for Black persons' education in excess of a million dollars and led health campaigns in every Southern state in addition to establishing hospitals. The organization also provided new public amenities for African American communities: sewers, water, lights, paved roads, and "other civic advantages have been secured." But Poteat and the commission seemed to avoid the root problem. As significant as these causes were, they were made necessary because governments in Southern states allocated nearly all their resources to White communities and institutions. The commission did forestall lynchings and in a few cases prosecuted lynch mobs. Its members published newspapers and magazines and taught courses on race relations in colleges across the South.[19] Progress had been made, but they recognized the long road ahead: "This should not be understood from the above that the race problem has been solved. There are still vast areas of prejudice that have scarcely been touched, vast realms of injustice that so far have proved impregnable." Poteat undoubtably shared Eleazer's assessment that most of the progress that they had made was among "the South's intelligent leadership . . . but the mass mind is still largely untouched." Edwin Mims likewise confined the movement's progress to "the intelligent white man and the intelligent Negro."[20] As one who elevated order, decency, and polite society, it was the mass mind that deeply troubled Poteat.[21]

Leaders in the interracial movement regarded Poteat as a crucial asset to their work. W. C. Jackson of the North Carolina Commission on Interracial Cooperation, the state affiliate of the Commission on Interracial Cooperation, recognized Poteat's standing and requested his help: "I am writing to ask whether or not you will be willing to present the matter of inter-racial cooperation to the Baptist Convention at its next session. I think that there's no argument on the question as to your preeminence for this presentation . . . you are universally known as the leader of thought in the state on inter-racial problems, and it would seem to me that you are the only person that could present this matter with certainty of success."[22] Poteat developed a reputation as a leading voice in race relations.

Poteat was interested in establishing order and peace in society more than in racial equality. Among White Southerners, both elites and populists accepted the ideology of White supremacy, but populists were more comfortable with the use of violence to preserve White rule. Poteat vocally opposed the Ku Klux Klan, and he deplored lynching and all types of mob violence, but his motives were less than altruistic.[23] Poteat was concerned with order and the public image of polite society. Historian Randal Hall argued that to Poteat the Klan "was antithetical to the carefully reconstructed Progressive community that mediated race relations" and it "endangered . . . social order."[24] The poor White people who stooped to lynching were an embarrassment to their race not because of their racism but because of their beastly methods. Every segment of White society in the South appealed to White supremacy but did so on different terms. Poteat lamented that "there are still a hundred lynchings a year. Nine-tenths of them occur in the South, and in four-fifths of them the victims are negroes."[25] Poteat argued that vigilante violence had no place in modern society, but his concern about racial violence stemmed from a desire to preserve social order. In *The Mind of the South,* Wilbur J. Cash argued that just because lynchings were decreasing in some regions did not mean that racism was diminishing. He rightly indicated that the New South boosters realized the woeful image that lynching made for the South, and they were determined to overcome it. As the South industrialized and urbanized, and especially in those areas in which urbanism progressed most, lynching decreased. Cash noted that North Carolina, which was among the most rapidly industrializing states, had witnessed a significant decrease in lynchings, whereas the most rural state, Mississippi, had the highest number.[26] Historian Bruce Clayton explained, "The machine, the love of money, the desire to maintain control over whites—these, not goodwill or even old-fashioned southern paternalism, led the ruling race to demand better race relations."[27] Historian Paul Harvey captured the point well: "Controlling race was the key to controlling society."[28]

Poteat did not intend for his work for racial harmony to open the door for the mixing of races. The work for racial cooperation did not challenge the status quo of Jim Crow, as Bruce Clayton noted.[29] Poteat expected a path to "permanent social peace [and] cooperation" along with "uncompromised racial integrity."[30] Randal Hall came to the same conclusion when he described the "sharp limits of the interracial movement's aims," and he recognized Poteat's determination to uphold his idea of racial purity.[31] Like most Southern reformers, Poteat approved of segregation to keep peace and good order in Southern society.[32] He argued that social reform would be incomplete without improving racial cooperation, but he did not envision a blending of the races: "We are here together, and if either soup is saved, both must be. The corn and beans of our succotash will remain distinct, but they are boiled in the same pot."[33] Black and White Americans could live together peacefully but to do so, they had to maintain separation.

Poteat seemed to be comfortable with the White supremacy that was commonplace in America. In his personal collection he preserved a poem titled "Rise, Mighty Anglo-Saxons" that well defined the racial assumptions White Americans widely held in this period. The poem called upon Anglo-Saxons to lead the way to a better society. The responsibility belonged to them as the superior race. It declared, "O mighty Anglo-Saxons! You assert with conscious pride the kingship of your race. Rise! Prove that kingship in a purblind world by your high likeness to the King of kings." It called the "mighty Anglo-Saxons" to "[rule] by right divine." Poteat also maintained a curious friendship with one of the most infamous agents for White supremacy in American history. Thomas Dixon Jr. was the author of *The Leopard's Spots* and *The Clansman,* which powerfully advanced the South's Lost Cause mythology and popularized it among White Americans. He valorized the Reconstruction-era Ku Klux Klan and exploited racist stereotypes of African Americans. In 1915 Dixon's work, initially a successful play, became the motion picture, *The Birth of a Nation,* which inspired the formation of a powerful new organization that was predicated on racial prejudice and took the name Knights of the Ku Klux Klan.[34] Poteat and Dixon's relationship began when Dixon was a student at Wake Forest during the early years of Poteat's teaching career.[35] They were friends. The two hunted together and discussed politics, and Poteat never revealed a sense of discomfort about Dixon's views.[36] Poteat opposed violence and the mean-spirited racism that swelled during the Jim Crow era, but he also opposed social equality. He acknowledged the biological unity of humanity and argued for a universal spiritual brotherhood, but he believed fully in White supremacy. For all his commitment to enlightenment and the advancement of God's kingdom, Poteat failed to recognize the larger implications of his theology of the fatherhood of God and the brotherhood of humanity.

THE "SCIENCE" OF PROGRESS

Poteat was part of a coalition of social reformers who advanced eugenics, an experimental movement that proposed new measures of social control to aid the forward march of civilization. Cherishing the advances of modern society many of America's social elites feared the loss of what had been gained. Further progress remained possible, but society showed signs that considerable obstacles stood in the way of advancement. The elites reassured themselves that those who were social leaders needed the resolve to make hard choices if they were necessary for the betterment of society. Equipped with the new authority of modern science social reformers embraced new theories of human heredity that perpetuated old prejudices and identified individuals who threatened the advancement of the human race: the feeble-minded, epileptics, criminals, alcoholics, and ethnic minorities. The eugenicists laid claim to a strategy that could overcome humanity's regression by selectively controlling human procreation. Liberal Protestants were among the leading advocates for eugenics. They embraced it as a new instrument for the kingdom work of social salvation.[37]

The scientific concept of hereditary degeneration formed the basic ideology of the eugenics movement. Since the nineteenth century experts in the fields of medicine, biology, and psychiatry advanced a theory of human degeneration that posited the human race's risk of biological regression if the so-called defectives of society were allowed to pass on their genes. They argued that the undesirable traits of the feebleminded, criminals, and others could be passed to their progeny to weaken the human race. The influential medical and scientific expert Eugene S. Talbot warned of "reversional heredity or atavism" and argued that in addition to physical qualities, moral qualities could also be passed on from one generation to the next.[38] Poor heredity along with the parallel influence of social factors put the future well-being of society at risk at a time when humanity had demonstrated such brilliant signs of potential.[39] Social reformers stoked fears of social and hereditary regression to gain traction for social policies that could forestall degeneration.[40] French psychiatrist Bénédict Morel had warned that the children of defective individuals might even deteriorate into a subhuman state.[41] Eugenicists argued that social control over procreation was the only solution to avoid degeneration and improve American society. Historian Christine Rosen rightly described their mindset: "So dire was the deteriorating state of human heredity . . . that its correction could no longer be left to the ad hoc efforts of amateurs."[42]

The idea of biological degeneration buttressed the well-established ideology of White supremacy.[43] The science of evolution too seemed to substantiate the classifications of fit and unfit persons. Eugenicists formulated a racial hierarchy and privileged select European ethnicities as the purest and most ideal stock for the progress of the human race in North America.[44] Although some inferior races would die out naturally eugenicists also proposed policies to root out races that they deemed inferior. Eugenicists used the rhetoric of degeneration to stoke fear in the minds of White Americans. If not monitored carefully African Americans and the growing wave of immigrants from southern and eastern Europe posed a threat to American civilization.[45] Poteat never seemed to endorse the racial component of eugenics, but it was an undeniable part of the eugenics movement that he enthusiastically promoted.

The ideology that undergirded eugenics took root in the South just as it did in the North. Historian Dan R. Frost argued that social Darwinism fit especially well within White Southerners' ideas of racial supremacy and Black inferiority.[46] New South elites like Edwin Mims supported eugenics. As an educator and cultural observer Mims longed for a more progressive South that would institute such bold measures as were necessary for progress: "And some day, when we have waked up to the importance of eugenics, [we will] have a workable sterilization law to supplement institutional care."[47]

Many liberal Protestants joined the eugenics movement and applied its ideology to the ministry of social reform that was born of their kingdom theology.[48] They recognized the explanatory power of modern science. They looked to scientific anthropology to provide answers to questions regarding what it meant to be human. They wove theological themes with biological and psychological arguments for eugenics, drawing on theological ideas like original sin and human depravity to support the theories of biological degeneracy.[49] Historian Dennis Durst correctly observed that "heredity and theology could find a common discursive frame of degeneration theory within the thinking of American Protestant elites.[50] Liberal ministers used religious rhetoric to support the drive for social control as a bold measure to advance American civilization and the human race. Thomas C. Leonard insightfully recognized that "the new discourses of eugenics and race science recast spiritual or moral failure as biological inferiority, making old prejudices newly respectable and lending scientific luster to [these] arguments."[51]

An exchange of cultural authority was underway in the early twentieth century as scientists became the sages of modern society. Many educated ministers rather than resisting the new authority appropriated science to empower their work to reform society for the kingdom.[52] Christine Rosen observed that "many religious leaders voiced an awareness of their own declining prestige—an expression of 'status anxiety.'"[53] Many Christian leaders, she argued, surrendered their potential for prophetic resistance to an immoral project in exchange for social relevance and the promise of social progress.[54] The outcome was the shameful policy of involuntary sterilization, marriage discrimination, and wrongful confinement to mental facilities and prisons filled with people who were deemed unfit for procreation and equal participation in society.[55]

POTEAT'S ADVOCACY OF EUGENICS

Poteat advocated eugenics to improve society through selective control over human procreation. He defined eugenics as the "science of race improvement through the control of heredity."[56] He argued that modern science had proven that poor breeding was degrading the human race. He concluded that society needed greater control to limit the procreation of unfit peoples—the feebleminded, alcoholics, criminals, epileptics, and other so-called defectives—before human degeneration grew to unmanageable proportions. Poteat concluded that he and other reformers could not accomplish this by a voluntary campaign. In order to achieve substantial reform, the state needed to enact laws of compulsion. Eugenics warranted whatever means necessary to accomplish its goals.

Randal Hall seemed to be correct when he argued that Poteat had followed the development of hereditary science since at least 1893. Poteat taught eugenics on several occasions during the 1910s and 1920s.[57] Poteat's state of North Carolina became one of the most active in the eugenics movement in the 1920s.[58] In 1929 North Carolina authorized state institutions to sterilize persons when they deemed it in the best interest of the individual and or society.[59] Poteat was gratified by the early progress, but he was determined to achieve more.

The base of Poteat's influence was with the students of Wake Forest College, and he used his influence to persuade students that eugenics presented a viable program to reform society. To convince them he furnished pamphlets that presented eugenics as the answer for a better society. Ezra S. Gosney, president of the Human Betterment Foundation, provided Poteat with a supply of pamphlets titled *Human Sterilization*.[60] In a letter to Poteat, Gosney seemed to be defensive about the subject and the materials that he supplied: "We request that you impress upon your students that these are composed of serious, scientific data based on an impartial study of the actual results on eugenic sterilization in practice." Gosney insisted that they were not merely "propaganda."[61] Upon sending more pamphlets on another occasion Gosney insisted that misinformation about eugenics was widespread: "Current literature contains so much that is erroneous, radical, and misleading on human sterilization, that there is a growing demand for the real facts."[62] The pamphlet argued that even a casual glance demonstrated that "intelligent, useful families are becoming smaller and smaller," while "diseased, defective parents, on the other hand" were producing more children than ever. Nothing less than the degeneration of the human race was the result. He argued that an urgent situation called society to action: "When families that send a child to an institution for the feebleminded average twice as large as families that send a child to the university, it is time for society to act."[63] It went into detail about the proposed remedy: "This measure is the sterilization, by a harmless surgical operation, of men and women who are so seriously defective, that, for the protection of themselves and their families, of society and of posterity, they should not bear and rear children." The pamphlet reassured readers that the procedure was minor and produced "no physical change . . . except in making parenthood impossible." Sterilization was not punishment but a form of protection for the individual and a cure for society.[64] The pamphlet implied that eugenics was in truth a "humanitarian program." The growing burden of caring for defectives showed no signs of slowing down: "The economic burden is tremendous and steadily growing worse."[65] Eugenics promised to "help reduce the burdens and increase the happiness and prosperity of the population in this and future generations."[66] Poteat had no question about the necessary course of action. The leaders of society should embrace the policies of eugenics for a healthier and more prosperous society.

Poteat outlined three factors that determined the state of humankind: environment, training, and heredity. Of the three, Poteat considered heredity to be the most important: "[Heredity] supplies the substance of life, the material upon which the other factors operate. It determines our nature, what we start life with, what are by virtue of our ancestry

. . . Heredity ordains our inborn gifts and capacities, limitations, weaknesses, defects." Poteat pointed out that "the individual once here is predetermined in important aspects of his nature. But coming individuals may be saved from hereditary defects and handicaps."[67] Society therefore needed to prioritize greater control over heredity. And because of past inaction, humanity was showing signs of hereditary degeneration to the point of "a social emergency."[68] Poteat argued that the modern world had advanced, but humanity itself had failed to keep pace: "Man's world has developed faster than man's capacities." Poteat lamented the "defeat which characterized our time." It was like "setting a cave man down on Fifth Avenue."[69] The reason that humanity had failed to progress was its emphasis on environment and training at the expense of heredity. Modern society needed to move beyond the failures of past generations and do what was necessary to redeem society. For too long society was content to treat hereditary problems rather than preventing them: "In cases where the human stock has been weak or degenerate, the treatment has been palliative, not remedial and preventative. Of course, betterment and relief are as noble as necessary, but they are costly and superficial as compared with the effort to forestall."[70] Poteat was convinced that human society would never achieve its potential, a utopian kingdom of heaven on earth, without earnestly addressing the issues of heredity. Whatever the cost, the end justified the means.

Sterilization was not the only course of action for eugenics. Poteat and Frank W. Hanft of the University of North Carolina discussed a North Carolina legislative proposal in which the state would place stronger restrictions on granting marriage licenses. Poteat argued that selectively prohibiting marriages was another way to limit defective offspring. The problem was simple: "Matings of defectives with defectives yield defective children; exceptions are negligible and doubtful. The defect may be feeble-mindedness, epilepsy, or insanity; in any case we look for some defect of the nervous system to appear in the children in the great majority." It was in society's best interest "that such a catastrophe . . . be forestalled, if it is at all possible." Poteat contended that the state had a vested interest in prohibiting marriages of unfit persons. This form of selective breeding would produce a healthier and stronger human stock for North Carolina.[71]

Birth control was an auxiliary to eugenics. In a letter to Poteat from the American Birth Control League the author advocated for a greater supply of birth control to be supplied for the poor, and he asked for Poteat to join the league in this work.[72] Poteat made his sentiment clear when he recorded a note in his diary about birth control: "We want better reasons for having children than not knowing how to prevent them."[73] The pamphlet that Poteat gave to his students helpfully distinguished between eugenics and birth control by noting that sterilization was applied by the power of the state whereas contraceptives were used voluntarily. In the end, eugenics represented a more aggressive measure and was not dependent on the choices of individuals. Once laws were established, individual compliance became a nonissue.[74] For the good of society the state should regulate human procreation as necessary.

Eugenicists included alcoholics among the degenerates, and prohibition became another form of social control. The scourge of alcoholism had plagued American society for generations, and Poteat laid much of the blame on heredity.[75] Dennis Durst noted that the reigning theory of degeneration held alcoholism to be hereditary so it needed to be addressed just as other defective traits.[76] The challenges of modern society called for new measures for reform. Poteat's concern with temperance was social rather than moral, but it was also theological as he worked to extend the kingdom of God by ridding society of vice with aggressive action.

Poteat considered America's "best blood" to be "the nation's most precious possession" and for this reason he opposed war. He lamented that the "best blood of the race has been wasted in ever-reoccurring wars."[77] Poteat was especially protective of his fellow North Carolinians. Referring to White North Carolinians, he made an optimistic assessment of their hereditary health and ethnic purity. With pride he argued that North Carolina's good environment had also contributed to the relative hereditary progress of its people when compared to the United States more broadly.[78] With the hope of progress for the eugenics movement in North Carolina he was optimistic about the state's future.

Poteat argued that so-called mental degenerates were the heaviest burden on society: "We have seen the peril of feeble-mindedness and insanity multiplying under the cloak of silence." He estimated that eight percent of the population was "a burden on the back of the rest of us."[79] Poteat warned that the "degeneracy of the [human] race" was a "dangerous possibility before which no social convention could stand." But he recognized that the broader public was reluctant to embrace the policies of eugenics especially positive eugenics or selective breeding for ideal procreation. He advised caution but he surmised that society might be more ready to institute negative eugenics: denying procreation by sterilization or institutionalization. His proposal was as callous as it was clear: "The feeble-minded, the insane, the epileptic, the inebriate, the congenital defective of any type, and the victim of chronic contagious diseases ought to be denied the opportunity of perpetuating their kind to the inevitable deterioration of the race."[80] Randal Hall recognized that because Poteat conceived of society as organically conjoined he "could not conceive of the right of those he considered inferior to exist independent of control."[81] The complexities of modern society called for brave leadership from the elites. Poteat contended that modern knowledge had provided the means to "save us from personal defeat and social catastrophe." The choice was "civilization vs barbarism."[82]

Although spirituality was always important for Poteat his advocacy of eugenics revealed something evident in his vision of social redemption more broadly: the imprint of a materialistic worldview. Eugenics as a solution to redeem society seemed justified only in a naturalistic worldview, in which humans are mere animals, to be bred like dogs or horses. Dennis Durst noted the callous manner in which elites sometimes spoke "of those on the ostensibly lower rungs of the social ladder." He explained that it "betook of a rhetoric that can be jarring to the reader's ear today."[83] Poteat may have been motivated by compassion and genuine concern as Christine Rosen argued about eugenicists more broadly.[84] Proponents of the movement argued that eugenics was a way to eliminate disease and alleviate suffering, and they promoted it as a path to human flourishing.[85] But it also implicitly denied the full humanity of a large number of people and subverted their natural human rights. This denial seems ironic when considering the fear that eugenicists expressed about the threat of human degeneration toward a subhuman state.

CONCLUSION

Poteat's views on race and eugenics demonstrated that liberalism in the broad sense of a movement for progressive thought, personal liberty, and enlightenment had its limits. As Thomas Leonard expressed it eugenics especially was a decidedly illiberal program.[86] For Poteat, who aimed to uphold a version of Christian morality and love, eugenics seemed to be unquestionably sub-Christian. On race Poteat demonstrated a level of benevolence and well-intended activism. But he fell short of proposing genuine equality for African Americans as fellow human beings. The White supremacy that dominated his social context made him content with the privileged status he enjoyed in American society. Even with his acknowledgement of the biological unity of humanity and his belief in universal spiritual brotherhood he somehow overlooked the implications that followed from the Bible's declaration that all humans carried the image of God. Poteat's convictions on these points were more informed by the ideals of social Darwinism than by Christianity. Poteat's blind spot on eugenics revealed the dark potential that looms beneath unchecked authority, which can be packaged in the language of progress and goodwill. The rhetoric of progress proved effective in North Carolina and elsewhere but at a disturbing cost. Science, a source of tremendous good in modern society, also produced evil when it has wielded authority without the checks of popular democracy or other forms of ethical oversight. In the case of eugenics social reformers preyed on the weaker members of society in an experiment to engineer a superior human race. It took the program of Nazi Germany to awaken Americans to what can occur when commitment to universal human dignity is lost.

CONCLUSION

William Louis Poteat redefined Christianity to appeal to the cultured people of the New South. As a leading religious figure and respected public intellectual, he aimed to harmonize Christianity with modern notions of authority, values, and sentiments, to provide a religion that suited the cosmopolitan image that the professional class of Southerners was cultivating for itself. Reaching these persons and especially the young among them was an urgent and vital task for Poteat after he went through his own spiritual crisis early in his career. Furthermore Poteat's revised faith was formed to preserve a social respectability that seemed to be in jeopardy in the more sophisticated age that reached the South in the late nineteenth century. As evangelist and apologist Poteat played a leading role in spreading liberalism among Southern Baptists. He also helped secure space for liberals to expand their influence for generations to come as they carried on his vision of seeking a more enlightened South.

Like the father of liberalism, Friedrich Schleiermacher, Poteat took upon himself an apologetic mission for the hearts and minds of the cultured despisers of his New South. Poteat believed that the younger generation whom he observed daily needed a faith that could pass the intellectual tests of modernity and also meet the cultural standards of the new bourgeoisie of Southern society. Poteat believed that the religion of common Southerners was destined to be brushed aside by the steady march of progress. It seemed that liberalism proceeded from a subtle but deep-seated insecurity that a failure to modernize religion would mean its decline and with it would come the decline of its leaders' social respectability. Poteat was determined to be both modern and religious without compromising the former. He seemed to be modern first and Christian second, which aligned with the posture of liberal Protestantism.

When Poteat reconceptualized Christianity, it was not a harmonious union of Christianity and modernity. He made Christianity fit with the higher revelations of modern science and the progressive spirit of the age.

He found himself compelled to do so by the power of science, modern criticism, and an age in which people resisted external forms of authority. Poteat felt this dilemma, but he rejected the possibility of maintaining a faith that he believed to be out of step with the modern age when the tailwinds of modernity were blowing so powerfully forward. Many educated leaders of the period embraced a similar approach to religion, and this approach became an important part of the story of American religious history through the end of the twentieth century.

At the heart of theological liberalism was a motivation to escape the ridicule of the modern world. Failure to embrace modern thought and the sensibilities of modern society was sure to jeopardize one's standing in enlightened society. In *Can a Man Be a Christian To-day?* Poteat expressed what he had concluded as a young professor and what compelled him to redefine his faith: "The attitude of resistance to the enlightenment of the world exposes itself to the ridicule of the world and can hardly hope to escape it."[1] Poteat was affected by what historian Christine Rosen called "status anxiety," which troubled educated ministers and other professionals in this period of American history: "Many religious leaders voiced an awareness of their own declining prestige . . . that led them to search for relevance and, as a result, cast off the more cumbersome elements of their theologies."[2] Poteat believed that it would be increasingly difficult to maintain the image of social respectability without accepting the unique authority of science and modern research over the realm of facts. Similarly the otherworldly gospel of evangelical Protestantism needed to be redefined to pursue more temporal concerns and particularly those that would appeal to the spirit of reform that characterized the Progressive Era. Those who vocally insisted upon holding onto an older form of Protestantism and its outdated modes of thought were labeled fundamentalists. The contempt that the fundamentalists faced and the prospect of their social marginalization were precisely what Poteat and other liberals were determined to escape. In large measure they succeeded and enjoyed the admiration of cultured people in American society throughout much of the twentieth century.

Poteat played a leading role in spreading theological liberalism among Southern Baptists. But historians have often overlooked the presence of liberalism in the South and have instead depicted liberalism as an exclusively Northern phenomenon. But not only did the South have a movement of theological liberalism its members achieved early institutional influence and demonstrated staying power that was greater than scholars have typically appreciated. Liberals moved with an impressive amount of freedom in the highest places of Southern Baptist life from the early 1900s to the 1930s in educational institutions, denominational leadership, and prominent churches. Conservative leaders often demonstrated little interest in the emergence of liberalism in their midst, and some offered more than tacit approval to liberal colleagues. Something else held together Baptist identity, or at least Baptist leadership. Controversy grew fierce at times in the 1920s. But the general trend was toward the tolerance of liberalism based upon the decision to privilege denominational cooperation over doctrinal accountability. Poteat proved that an outspoken liberal could thrive in the South. As an educator and public intellectual he influenced generations of Southerners with his plea that modernist Christianity was a viable option for addressing the challenges of the modern age. He prevailed against all opposition, and North Carolina Baptists vindicated him as a man of piety and forward thinking.

Theological liberalism was a national phenomenon in American Protestantism, but it was tied to particular environments. In the North and the South, it arose in the cities and institutions of higher education. And liberalism belonged to one cross-section of American society: It seemed to be inextricably linked to the American bourgeoisie. When conditions arose in the South that mirrored those of the urban and industrialized North liberalism arose in New South towns and cities among middle class Southerners who aspired to urbane sophistication and social respectability. The Southern bourgeoisie cheered Poteat for his commitment to elevating the South into greater respectability. But this disparity ensured that great distance would separate liberal leaders like Poteat from the majority of Southern Baptists.

So great was the disparity between liberal leaders like Poteat and rank-and-file Baptists that tension was inevitable. An uneasy relationship developed especially when the educated elite became noticeably out of touch with the grassroots membership. Over time the two groups grew content to move in their own spheres, which benefited the liberals who gained hegemony in many Southern Baptist colleges and eventually in the denomination's seminaries. And conservatives had to acknowledge that a growing number of progressive leaders were firmly established in the convention. From the 1930s to the early 1960s liberal Southern Baptists generally took a more discreet approach. But after sporadic episodes of controversy in the mid-twentieth century, a group of conservatives, labeled fundamentalists, began organizing in the late 1970s to challenge leaders they deemed out of step with traditional Baptist convictions. A tumultuous conflict or series of conflicts resulted in denominational fractures and a successful revolution by conservatives who gradually took control of every major entity owned by the national Southern Baptist Convention by the late 1990s. But the liberal Baptist tradition has lived on in the South in many of the same places that gave rise to its formation more than a century ago. Although few still know his name Poteat's legacy has survived. A religion that is fashioned to complement modern sensibilities and to pass the intellectual tests of modernity makes a liberal version of Christianity appealing to educated people who hope to maintain their own social respectability while also maintaining a vital role for religion. Poteat played an important role in establishing this third way as a viable option for educated Southerners.

Notes

CHAPTER ONE: A TRADITIONAL FAITH

1. Edward Grace, "The Place of Prayer in the Modern World-view," *Proceedings of the Baptist Congress: Twenty-Eighth Annual Session* (University of Chicago, 1911), 13.

2. For sources on the religious life of the Poteat family see Charles F. Hudson, "The Authorized Personal Interview of W. L. Poteat," Poteat Papers, box 4, folder 532, and First Baptist Church of Yanceyville, NC, Minutes, Z. Smith Reynolds Library Archives, Wake Forest University. For the religious background of Julia Poteat's family see the obituary of her father Hosea McNeill in "Lamented Deaths," *Biblical Recorder,* August 27, 1857. The article called him a longtime and active member of the local Beulah Baptist Association, which honored him at its meeting on account of his death. Julia attended Oxford Female College, which was a Baptist institution founded in 1850. The school closed in 1925. For a source on Oxford College, see William S. Powell, *Encyclopedia of North Carolina* (University of North Carolina, 2006), 861. When Julia Poteat died, Charlotte, North Carolina's, *News and Observer* noted her passing and said that she was "a woman of splendid Christian character, a member of the Baptist church, held in the highest esteem and regard." At the time of her death both of her sons were presidents of Baptist colleges, which would place her death some time between 1905 and 1918. Article, "Mrs. J. A. Poteat Dead," *News and Observer,* no date, clipping, Poteat Papers, box 10, folder 1176.

3. For background on James Poteat see Hudson, "The Authorized Personal Interview of W. L. Poteat," 1–2. For Poteat's baptism see "In Memoriam," *Biblical Recorder,* February 27, 1867. This article named the two sons who were baptized with their father James Poteat in the summer of 1858, but both died as casualties of the Civil War. About the two brothers it read, "From that period [after baptism] they ever sustained their Christian profession without reproach and were truly brethren beloved in the Lord." For a survey on the history of Caswell County see William S. Powell, *When the Past Refused to Die: A History of Caswell County, 1777–1977* (Moore Publishing, 1977). For secondary sources on the early religious life of the Poteat family see Randal Hall, *William Louis Poteat: A Leader of the Progressive-Era South* (University of Kentucky Press, 2000), 7–18, and Suzanne Linder, *William Louis Poteat: Prophet of Progress* (University of North Carolina, 1966), 3–22.

4. For James Poteat's leadership in Beulah Baptist Association and the Baptist State Convention of North Carolina see "Baptist State Convention of North Carolina," *Biblical Recorder,* June 5, 1867. See also the proceedings as published in *Biblical Recorder,* October 30, 1867. For his appointment as a trustee of Wake Forest College see Charles E. Taylor, *General Catalogue of Wake Forest College, North Carolina, 1834–5–1892–2* (Edwards & Broughton, 1892), 16. For background on the closure of the college during the Civil War

and the devastated state of the school afterward see George W. Paschal, *History of Wake Forest College, 1865–1905* (Edwards & Broughton, 1943), 2:3–22.

5. At one time James Poteat owned approximately two thousand acres, about twelve hundred of which were improved land for farming, and he owned more than 80 slaves. Randal Hall estimates that the number of slaves might have been as high as 105. Unlike in much of the Deep South, tobacco rather than cotton was his cash crop. But Hall rightly argued that the success of the Poteats' operation placed them "among the select few in the Old South for whom reality approached the later legends about antebellum prosperity and refinement." See Hall, *William Louis Poteat,* 6–7, and Linder, *William Louis Poteat,* 6–8. For William Poteat's personal reflections on his early life on the plantation see William L. Poteat, "Memories," 1928, Poteat Papers, box 3, Z. Smith Reynolds Library Archives, Wake Forest University; William L. Poteat, "An Intellectual Adventure," *The American Scholar* 5 (Summer 1936): 280–81; and Hudson, "The Authorized Personal Interview of W. L. Poteat," 1–2. Poteat estimated apparently incorrectly that the plantation was closer to three thousand acres, and although he was unable to recall an exact number of enslaved persons on the plantation, he remembered many by name and described various types of labor among them. For a helpful source on the economic history of the South see Susanna Delfino, Michele Gillespie, and Louis M. Kyriakoudes, eds., *Southern Society and Its Transformation, 1790–1860* (University of Missouri Press, 2011). For an intellectual history of the slaveholding class of Southerners see Elizabeth Fox-Genovese, and Eugene D. Genovese, *The Mind of the Master Class: History and Faith in the Southern Slaveholder's Worldview* (Cambridge University Press, 2005). Chapter 8 of this book addresses Poteat's views on race and his activism related to racial issues.

6. William Poteat was the oldest child of James and Julia Poteat, born in 1856. His sister Ida was born in 1859, and Edwin McNeill was born in 1861.

7. See Poteat, "Memories," 12–13; and Hudson, "The Authorized Personal Interview of W. L. Poteat," 1–2. Although North Carolina had supported public education in the form of common schools since 1839, one did not exist in Poteat's immediate region. Private education, such as the one Poteat received, was the only option available and only for those with substantial financial means. See Hall, *William Louis Poteat,* 11–12; and Powell, *When the Past Refused to Die,* 395. For the best work on the history of education in North Carolina see James L. Leloudis, *Schooling the New South: Pedagogy, Self, and Society in North Carolina, 1880–1920* (University of North Carolina Press, 1996). During Poteat's childhood great progress was made in free universal education in North Carolina. Leloudis traces this movement well, particularly focusing on the transition from common schools to graded schools. See Leloudis, *Schooling the New South,* xi–35. See also Glenda E. Gilmore, "Education Capital and Human Flourishing: North Carolina's Public Schools and Universities, 1865–2015," in Larry E. Tise and Jeffrey J. Crow, *New Voyages to North Carolina: Reinterpreting North Carolina History* (University of North Carolina Press, 2017), 194–216.

8. Linder, *William Louis Poteat,* 18.

9. For Poteat's portrayal of an idyllic childhood see Poteat, "Memories," 1–20. Poteat relished his rural upbringing: "Thank God I was reared in the country. . . . Country sights, country smells, and country sports occupied me and probably in a measure molded me." William L. Poteat, "An Intellectual Adventure: A Human Document," *American Scholar* 5, no. 3 (Summer 1936): 280. For the best source on the Civil War and Reconstruction see Allen C. Guelzo, *Fateful Lightning: A New History of the Civil War & Reconstruction* (Oxford University Press, 2012). For the difficult period of Reconstruction see Carole

Emberton, *Beyond Redemption: Race, Violence, and the American South after the Civil War* (University of Chicago Press, 2013).

10. See Hall, *William Louis Poteat*, 12–16. Holden, a Republican, was so despised for these actions that he was impeached and removed from office by the Democrats who successfully maneuvered for control of the state. For sources on Reconstruction in North Carolina see Richard L. Zuber, *North Carolina During Reconstruction* (Division of Archives and History, 1969); and Powell, *Encyclopedia of North Carolina*, 949–51. For sources on the Ku Klux Klan see Allen W. Trelease, *White Terror: The Ku Klux Klan Conspiracy and Southern Reconstruction* (Harper & Row, 1971); and Elaine Frantz Parsons, *Ku-Klux: The Birth of the Klan During Reconstruction* (University of North Carolina Press, 2015). Poteat never recorded his thoughts or experiences of these events, but it is almost certain that he knew of them.

11. Poteat, "An Intellectual Adventure," 280.

12. John Dagg's *Manual of Theology* (1857) and *Church Order* (1858) are representative of American Baptists' theology of conversion in this era. For a secondary source on Dagg see Paul A. Sanchez, "A Modern Analysis of John L. Dagg's *Manual of Theology*" (MA thesis, New Orleans Baptist Theological Seminary, 2012).

13. Poteat, "An Intellectual Adventure," 280. Poteat's second spiritual experience in college involved a deeper emotional response. See William L. Poteat, "Christianity and Enlightenment," 8–9, Address to North Carolina Baptist State Convention, Winston-Salem, North Carolina, December 13, 1922, Pamphlet published by North Carolina Baptist State Convention.

14. Poteat, "An Intellectual Adventure," 280; Minutes, Yanceyville Baptist Church.

15. Poteat, "An Intellectual Adventure," 280.

16. In Latin classes students read Cicero, Livy, Horace, and Virgil, and in Greek, they read Plato, Homer, and Herodotus, among others. See Paschal, *History of Wake Forest College* 2:131–37. For the best source on the history of higher education in the South see Joseph M. Stetar, "In Search of a Direction: Southern Higher Education after the Civil War," *History of Higher Education Quarterly* 25 (Fall 1985): 341–67. For a history of higher education in North Carolina focusing upon on the neighboring University of North Carolina see Leloudis, *Schooling the New South*, 37–72.

17. Minutes of Euzelian Society, April 5, 1873, January 31, 1873, December 19, 1874, March 20, 1875, September 18, 1875, Z. Smith Reynolds Library Archives, Wake Forest University, Winston-Salem, NC. See also *Greensboro Daily News*, March 27, 1938. For secondary sources see Linder, *William Louis Poteat*, 23–25, and Hall, *William Louis Poteat*, 16–21.

18. Paschal, *History of Wake Forest College* 2:140–43. North Carolina's *Biblical Recorder* announced the upcoming Wake Forest graduation and expected high quality from students' speeches based on previous addresses. See "The Next Commencement of Wake Forest College," *Biblical Recorder*, May 23, 1877. The following edition of the paper praised the speakers. Poteat's address was titled, "Ripples on the Sea of Life." See "Wake Forest College Commencement," *Biblical Recorder*, June 20, 1877. The valedictory address was given by E. E. Folk, who graduated with a master of arts. For the role that these exercises played in the image of Southern personhood see Leloudis, *Schooling the New South*, 47–49.

19. At that time Poteat was facing scrutiny from grassroots Southern Baptists due to his outspoken belief in evolution, and he had faced a public controversy two years earlier

led by evangelist Thomas T. Martin, who questioned Poteat's theological orthodoxy. For the theological controversy in 1920 see Thomas T. Martin, *Three Fatal Teachings* (n.p., 1920); and William L. Poteat, "Wherein Lies the Efficacy of Jesus' Work in the Reconciliation?" *Proceedings of the Baptist Congress: Eighteenth Annual Session* (Baptist Congress, 1900), 94–102. For a secondary source on both controversies see Willard B. Gatewood, *Preachers, Pedagogues, & Politicians: The Evolution Controversy in North Carolina, 1920–1927* (University of North Carolina Press, 1966).

20. Poteat, "Christianity and Enlightenment," 8.

21. Poteat, "Christianity and Enlightenment," 8–9. Randal Hall identified this as a reaffirmation of faith for Poteat, rather than his conversion. See Hall, *William Louis Poteat,* 18.

22. See William L. Poteat, "Why Do So Many Brilliant Men Reject Christianity," unpublished manuscript, no date, Poteat Papers, box 7. The essay was unfinished and seemed to be a reflection many years after the events discussed within.

23. The document ends abruptly in the middle of the sentence. Poteat, "Why Do So Many Brilliant Men Reject Christianity?"

24. For the best source on the New South see Edward L. Ayers, *The Promise of the New South: Life after Reconstruction,* 2nd ed. (Oxford University Press, 2007). For the classic work see C. Vann Woodward, *Origins of the New South, 1877–1913* (1951; repr., Louisiana State University Press, 1971). On the debate about the relative newness of New South ideas, Gavin Wright rightly argues that the New South did manifest a fundamentally new set of ideas. See Gavin Wright, *New South, Old South: Revolutions in the Southern Economy since the Civil War* (Basic Books, 1986). Ayers likewise argued that the New South represented a remarkably new vision for Southern society. See Ayers, *The Promise of the New South.* For an argument that emphasized the limits of change for the New South see Paul M. Gaston, *The New South Creed: A Study in Southern Myth Making* (Vintage Books, 1973). For the New South in North Carolina, particularly as related to education, see James L. Leloudis, *Schooling the New South.* Leloudis argued that the changes of the New South era called for new modes of education. A new model of teaching forged a new mindset of increased ambition, industry, and individualism. For a broader survey of New South North Carolina see William A. Link, *North Carolina: Change and Tradition in a Southern State,* 2nd ed. (Wiley-Blackwell, 2018), 239–342. The New South generated a generally progressive, forward-looking spirit but was neither synonymous with nor the only cause of the rise of theological liberalism in the South. However I argue that New South ideology bolstered the movement for liberal Christianity in the South.

25. North Carolina developed a reputation as a leading liberal state in the South. Henry L. Mencken largely credited Poteat for that legacy: "The fact that North Carolina is now the most intelligent of all the Southern States is largely due to him." *Charlotte News,* November 8, 1925, clipping, Poteat Papers, box 5, folder 554. For Mencken's classic and deeply critical assessment of the South see Henry L. Mencken, "The Sahara of the Bozart," in *The American Scene: A Reader,* ed. Huntington Cairns (Alfred A. Knopf, 1965). See also Virginius Dabney, *Liberalism in the South* (University of North Carolina Press, 1932), 275. Dabney argued, "Such a crusading liberal as Governor Aycock of North Carolina, for example, is a rarity among Southern public men. Aycock was one of the most progressive and far-seeing leaders of his generation and the South as a whole owes him a debt of gratitude for his fearless pioneering in the early years of the century." For the battles, both political and religious, over evolution in North Carolina see Gatewood, *Preachers, Pedagogues, &*

Politicians. Related was the rise of the Progressive Era. For progressivism in the South see Dewey W. Grantham, *Southern Progressivism: The Reconciliation of Progress and Tradition* (University of Tennessee Press, 1983); and William A. Link, *The Paradox of Southern Progressivism, 1880–1930* (University of North Carolina Press, 1992). For the national movement of Progressivism see Michael McGerr, *A Fierce Discontent: The Rise and Fall of the Progressive Movement in America* (Oxford University Press, 2003).

26. Wilbur J. Cash, *The Mind of the South* (Alfred A. Knopf, 1941), 327. For Cash's liberalizing experience at Wake Forest see Bruce Clayton, *W. J. Cash: A Life* (Louisiana State University Press, 1991), 33–40, 54, 78. See also Joseph L. Morrison, *W. J. Cash: Southern Prophet, A Biography and Reader* (Alfred A. Knopf, 1967).

27. William L. Poteat, *Youth and Culture* (Wake Forest College, 1938), 138. Poteat advised students as he did countless times during his career: "That happy issue is sure to follow if it shows them how to distinguish between religion and proposed explanations of religion, between the religious experience and the effort to account for it in terms of intellect." He proposed a subjective, experience-based religion: "You do not have to account for that inscrutable experience in the terms of any metaphysical system in order to be assured of its validity." Poteat, *Youth and Culture*, 139.

28. Poteat, "An Intellectual Adventure," 280–81. Historian Bradley Gundlach argued that Darwinism's effect was not immediately felt in the United States. It did not become a significant issue in America until about 1870, more than a decade after the publication of *Origin of Species*. These ideas were even slower to reach the South, which was still recovering from the Civil War and Reconstruction. See Bradley J. Gundlach, *Process and Providence: The Evolution Question at Princeton, 1845–1929* (Eerdmans, 2013), 50.

29. Randal Hall emphasized the Victorian ideals that shaped Poteat's worldview. See Hall, *William Louis Poteat*. Michael McGerr correctly argued that late-nineteenth-century middle-class values, which might rightly be called Victorian values, were essential to the Progressive movement in America. The values of refinement, public morality, thrift (in opposition to materialism), and polite society drove the progressive movement. See McGerr, *A Fierce Discontent*.

30. In this period of time Southern colleges commonly admitted students who lacked the foundational education that was necessary for college. See Hall, *William Louis Poteat*, 23. As a model for higher education, classical education, with the goal of forming cultured leaders for Southern society, continued after the Civil War. At schools like Wake Forest, educators reluctantly surrendered the classical model only gradually in the final years of the nineteenth century when strong utilitarian influences compelled them to do so. See Stetar, "In Search of a Direction: Southern Higher Education after the Civil War," 343–62. For background on Wake Forest College in particular see Paschal, *History of Wake Forest College*, vol. 1–2. For sources on other colleges in North Carolina see Earl W. Porter, *Trinity and Duke, 1892–1924: Foundations of Duke University* (Duke University Press,1964); and William D. Snider, *Light on the Hill: A History of the University of North Carolina* (University of North Carolina Press, 2004). Baltimore's Johns Hopkins University followed the German-influenced research model of higher education from its inception, and Nashville's Vanderbilt University adopted the research model relatively early in its history. For the history of higher education in America see John R. Thelin, *A History of American Higher Education*, 3rd ed. (Johns Hopkins University Press, 2019).

31. Hudson, "The Authorized Personal Interview of W. L. Poteat," 3–5; and Poteat, "My Intellectual Adventure," 281–82. In addition to instructing students in Greek and

Latin, Poteat took on minor administrative responsibilities like monitoring students' grades and attendance. Hall rightly noted that in this period it was not unusual to appoint a professor to a field in which he had no specialized training, but this began to change early in Poteat's career with the rise of professionalization and specialization. See Hall, *William Louis Poteat,* 23–4. See also Linder, *William Louis Poteat,* 34.

32. Stetar, "In Search of a Direction: Southern Higher Education after the Civil War," 341. Schools in the North and West experienced great growth after the Civil War, but most Southern colleges struggled simply to reopen after the war. Stetar argued, "Left virtually destitute by the War and lacking students, buildings and assets, [southern] college leaders clung more to romantic dreams and were unable to share in the bold expansion experienced by other regions." And he rightly depicted the precarious state of higher education in the South: "The region's colleges were all but destroyed, and their clientele and financial support lost. Colleges that prospered in the ante-bellum era entered the latter years of the 1860s with great apprehension and little cause for optimism. Endowments had disappeared, students and faculty were in disarray and facilities were often in ruins." See also chap. 3 of Thelin, *A History of American Higher Education.* For the precarious state of Wake Forest in the years after the Civil War see Paschal, *History of Wake Forest College, 1865–1905,* 2:3–22.

33. *Catalog, 1880–81,* Z. Smith Reynolds Library Archives, Wake Forest University, Winston-Salem, NC. For the emergence of science as a significant field of study in Southern colleges see Stetar, "In Search of a Direction: Southern Higher Education after the Civil War," 353–54.

34. Hudson, "The Authorized Personal Interview of W. L. Poteat," 3–4. See also *Wake Forest Student* 3 (September 1883): 33; and Edward S. Burgess to William L. Poteat, August 20, 1898, Poteat Papers, box 1, folder 44. For Poteat's account of acquiring a microscope and engaging in independent research see Poteat, "My Intellectual Adventure," 281–82. See also Linder, *William Louis Poteat,* 40; and Hall, *William Louis Poteat,* 24–25. The *Wake Forest Student* was the paper of the Euzelian Society.

35. Some of Poteat's specimens are preserved in his archival collection. See Poteat Papers, box 13, folders 1250–52. Included are "Spores of Equisetium Avuense," a perennial plant native to the region, and "Showing Elaters," which was another plant specimen. Both were dated April 28, 1883. Another specimen, "Spores of Small Mushroom and Its Liquid" does not have a legible date. For a collection of Poteat's detailed scientific notes see Poteat Papers, box 7, folders 720, 768–69, 774, 783, 838. One of Poteat's students, Rufus Weaver, recalled fondly their hunting for specimens in the woods near the campus in Wake Forest. Rufus Weaver to William L. Poteat, August 12, 1931, Poteat Papers, box 1, folder 21. See also Hall, *William Louis Poteat,* 25, 29.

36. Hall, *William Louis Poteat,* 28. See *Catalog, 1892–93,* 10, 36–7.

37. For the rise of professionalization in higher education see Bruce A. Kimball, *The "True Professional Ideal" in America: A History* (Rowman & Littlefield, 1996). See also Thelin, *A History of American Higher Education.* For scientific specialization in particular see Kimball, *The "True Professional Ideal" in America,* 270–72. For the growing expectations of a doctoral degree see Thelin, *A History of American Higher Education,* 359–61. Randal Hall rightly argued, "That other scientists, many with graduate degrees, readily accepted Poteat as a colleague despite his lack of credentials underscores the openness or fluidity of the early stages of professionalization within the region." Hall, *William Louis Poteat,* 33.

38. Poteat, "My Intellectual Adventure," 281. For his research on cell division see Poteat, "My Intellectual Adventure," 282.

39. Poteat and his companions had recently studied at Johns Hopkins University, a leading research university and the most important such institution for Southerners. Poteat had also visited Johns Hopkins, which was modeled on the University of Berlin, and this might have been one of the motivating factors to go to Berlin itself. For the importance of Johns Hopkins to the training of Southern educators see Stetar, "In Search of a Direction: Southern Higher Education after the Civil War," 360–62. Stetar argued that it was "the primary source of Southern doctorates by 1903." See also Woodward, *Origins of the New South*, 440–41. For Poteat's research in Berlin see *Wake Forest Student* 7 (June 1888): 378, and William L. Poteat, Notebook, June 21 to June 28, 1888, Poteat Papers, box 8, folder 937. See also Paschal, *History of Wake Forest College*, 3:456.

40. Although Poteat's time at the University of Berlin was minimal historian Willard Gatewood did not qualify his statement when he called Poteat "a University of Berlin-educated scientist." See Gatewood, *Preachers, Pedagogues, and Politicians*, 16. Some historians have incorrectly identified Poteat as a graduate of the university. William Link incorrectly called Poteat "a zoologist with a Ph.D. from the University of Berlin." See Link, *North Carolina: Change and Tradition in a Southern State*. Wayne Flynt noted that Poteat studied in Berlin and incorrectly claimed that he held a PhD in biology, without citing an institution. See Wayne Flynt, *Alabama Baptists: Southern Baptists in the Heart of Dixie* (University of Alabama, 1998), 275. Hall rightly noted the relatively minimal nature of Poteat's research in Germany and argued that he might have been there as few as eight days. See Hall, *William Louis Poteat*, 33–34. That he had exposure to the leading institution of scientific research in the world was substantial for the time and demonstrated Poteat's enthusiasm and dedication.

41. Hall, *William Louis Poteat*, 33–34.

42. His honorary degrees included the following: LLD, Baylor University, 1905; LLD, University of North Carolina, 1906; LLD, Brown University, 1927; LLD, Duke University, 1932; LittD, Mercer University, 1933. Poteat's doctoral hoods are preserved at the Z. Smith Reynolds Library Archives, Wake Forest University, Winston-Salem, NC.

CHAPTER TWO: THE PATH TO LIBERALISM

1. For a historical work that assesses the classic conflict thesis between science and religion in modern America see James C. Ungureanu, *Science and Religion and the Protestant Tradition: Retracing the Origins of Conflict* (University of Pittsburgh Press, 2019). For a work that explores this story with special attention to the reaction of conservative Christians see Ronald L. Numbers, *The Creationists: From Scientific Creationism to Intelligent Design* (Harvard University Press, 2006).

2. These modern ideas were the exclusive role of science to explain the natural world, the privacy of religion and an epistemology based in experience, and the denial of all external forms of authority for religion. Poteat was also confronted by the spirit of skepticism that had been in the air for American intellectuals since the eighteenth century. For sources on modern thought see Roger E. Olson, *The Journey of Modern Theology: From Reconstruction to Deconstruction* (InterVarsity, 2013); Gary Dorrien, *The Making of American Liberal Theology: Imagining Progressive Religion, 1805–1900* (Westminster John Knox, 2001); Gary Dorrien, *Kantian Reason and Hegelian Spirit: The Idealistic Logic of Modern Theology* (Wiley Blackwell); Michael A. Gillespie, *The Theological Origins of Modernity*

(University of Chicago, 2008); Steven B. Smith, *Modernity and Its Discontents: Making and Unmaking the Bourgeois from Machiavelli to Bellow* (Yale University Press, 2016).

3. For the published article see William L. Poteat, "An Intellectual Adventure: A Human Document," *American Scholar* 5, no. 3 (Summer 1936): 28086. An earlier draft version of this article exists in Poteat's collection at the Z. Smith Reynolds Library Archives. See William L. Poteat, "My Approach to Religion," manuscript, Poteat Papers, box 9, folder 961, Z. Smith Reynolds Library Archives, Wake Forest University, Winston-Salem, NC. A difference in tone is discernible in Poteat's published article when compared to its earlier draft form. The published article presented a more triumphant tone than the more somber and reflective tone found in the draft. For sources on the development of the article see letters from 1935 to and from Ruth E. Campbell, assistant editor at *The American Scholar,* Poteat Papers, box 1, folder 9. Poteat received wide appreciation for the published article. H. Shelton Smith, a professor at Duke University (formerly Trinity College), was so appreciative that he encouraged a more extensive article that would also include an account of Poteat's brother, Edwin McNeill Poteat, a liberal minister and educator. Smith said about reading the article, "It made me want to write an article on 'The Intellectual and Religious Pilgrimage of the Poteat Brothers.' I became more convinced than ever that this should be done. You and your brothers represent a period of progressive thinking in the South that has not been set forth." H. Shelton Smith to William L. Poteat, April 9, 1937, Poteat Papers. R. H. Pitt of Virginia's *Religious Herald* also praised the article and asked Poteat for permission to publish it in his paper for Virginia Baptists. See R. H. Pitt to William L. Poteat, July 1936, Poteat Papers, box 3, folder 329.

4. He had studied the basics of science and mathematics for his bachelor of arts degree, but it consisted only of recitations of the elementary principles of science. For a brief account of his course on chemistry see Poteat, "Why Do So Many Brilliant Men Reject Christianity." For the nature of scientific instruction at Wake Forest through the 1870s see Paschal, *History of Wake Forest College, 1865–1905,* 2:9–10. Paschal recorded that obtaining the BA degree required "ten recitations, each in Natural Philosophy, [and] Chemistry."

5. Poteat, "My Intellectual Adventure," 281.

6. He described the crisis as a "crisis of my religious [experience]." See Poteat, "My Approach to Religion," 3.

7. Poteat, "My Intellectual Adventure," 282.

8. Poteat, "My Intellectual Adventure," 282. Suzanne Linder also recognized the depth of Poteat's spiritual and intellectual crisis. See Linder, *William Louis Poteat,* 37–40.

9. He explained, "Back in the 70's a small Southern college was hardly aware of the opening phases of the biological revolution precipitated in England 15 or more years before by the publication of 'Origin of Species.' But called in the 80's to teach the biological sciences I passed into another crisis . . ." Poteat, "My Approach to Religion," 3.

10. Historian Jeffrey Straub has argued that a revised view of the Bible was foundational to liberal Christianity: "Essential to liberalism from the beginning was a radically different view of the Bible." Straub studied figures like Shailer Mathews, George B. Foster, and William Newton Clarke. See Jeffrey P. Straub, *The Making of Battle Royal: The Rise of Liberalism in Northern Baptist Life, 1870–1920* (Pickwick, 2018), 265–69. This was true in the South as it was in the North. Straub argued about Baptists in the late nineteenth century, "Baptist theology, henceforth, would necessarily wrestle with a sacred book that bore the marks of human hands. Just how future Baptists would handle the particular issue would ultimately determine to which party they belonged. [One group] viewed the Bible as

a book of human origin containing certain inevitable flaws would be identified as liberal and would usually show sympathy with modern scientific evolution, while at the same time, they would reject some aspects of historic biblical authority to which Baptists had long adhered." Straub, *The Making of Battle Royal*, 88–89.

11. Poteat, "My Intellectual Adventure," 282–83.

12. Poteat, "My Approach to Religion," 4.

13. Poteat, "My Intellectual Adventure," 283.

14. Poteat sketched in his draft, "[The] Bible [is] a book of religion, not astronomy, geology, or biology" and "[the] Bible handling, sci. material represents the level [of] intelligence [of] its time." Poteat, "My Approach to Religion," 4.

15. Poteat, "My Intellectual Adventure," 283. Poteat added, "I so think of them still."

16. For a source on how questions raised by modern science were addressed by theologians at Princeton University see Bradley J. Gundlach, *Process and Providence: The Evolution Question at Princeton, 1845–1929* (Eerdmans, 2013). B. B. Warfield, a leading proponent of "biblical inerrancy," a new term used by evangelicals in this period, argued that modern science and the Bible could be reconciled without modifying the traditional conception of the Bible. For a collection of essays by Warfield see Mark A. Noll and David N. Livingstone, eds., *Evolution, Science, and Scripture, Selected Writings* (Baker, 2000). Poteat also seemed unaware of approaches that had been offered throughout Christian history, including in the ancient church, some of which could be quite sophisticated and creative. See for example an exploration of Augustine's view of creation in Gavin Ortlund, *Retrieving Augustine's Doctrine of Creation: Ancient Wisdom for Current Controversy* (IVP Academic, 2020).

17. Poteat, "My Approach to Religion," 4.

18. Poteat, "My Intellectual Adventure," 283.

19. He characterized this tendency of classical Christianity saying, "In that case you are adjudged outside the pale and contaminate if you are unable to take this or that item of the speculation." Poteat, "My Intellectual Adventure," 283.

20. Poteat, "My Intellectual Adventure," 283.

21. Poteat, "My Approach to Religion," 4.

22. Poteat, "My Intellectual Adventure," 283.

23. Poteat, "My Intellectual Adventure," 283.

24. Gerald W. Johnson, "'The Future and Dr. Poteat': Memorial Address at the Wake Forest College Commencement," *Biblical Recorder*, June 28, 1938, 6, clipping, Poteat Papers, box 4.

25. Similar to Friedrich Schleiermacher, Poteat argued, "Apprehension here is immediate and untranslated. Not even does judgment or interpretation intervene." Poteat, "My Intellectual Adventure," 284. Schleiermacher, the father of liberal theology, argued that the divine encounter was precognitive and unmediated. In a subsequent section of this chapter, I explore Poteat's religious epistemology and its similarity to Schleiermacher's. For sources on Schleiermacher see Jacqueline Marina, ed., *The Cambridge Companion to Friedrich Schleiermacher* (Cambridge University Press, 2005); and Keith W. Clements, *Friedrich Schleiermacher: Pioneer of Modern Theology* (Collins, 1987). For the key sources see Friedrich Schleiermacher, *On Religion: Speeches to Its Cultured Despisers*, trans. Richard Crouter (1988; repr., Cambridge University Press, 2003), and Friedrich Schleiermacher, *The Christian Faith*, rev. ed., trans. H. R. Mackintosh and J. S. Stewart (T & T Clark, 1999).

26. Poteat, "My Intellectual Adventure," 284.

27. The limits of science formed a substantial theme in Poteat's corpus. For the early significance of this determination see Poteat, "My Intellectual Adventure," 284–86, and Poteat, "My Approach to Religion," 4.

28. Poteat, "My Approach to Religion," 4.

29. Christine Rosen, *Preaching Eugenics: Religious Leaders and the American Eugenics Movement* (Oxford University Press, 2004), 5.

30. Poteat, diary, November 8, 1896. Poteat Papers, box 4, folder 475.

31. William L. Poteat, personal Bible, Poteat Papers, box 11, folder 1213. The Bible is well worn but with relatively few markings inside. It was printed in 1875. A smaller New Testament volume in his collection is covered in notes, primarily with sermon notes and outlines, for instance on John 10:10, which he preached on several occasions. See *New Testament and Psalms,* Poteat Papers, box 11, folder 1211.

32. William L. Poteat, "Wherein Lies the Efficacy of Jesus' Work in the Reconciliation?," *Proceedings of the Baptist Congress: Eighteenth Annual Session* (Baptist Congress, 1900), 96. The Baptist Congress was an annual gathering of Baptist thinkers from across the United States, both ministers and academics, for substantive discussion on theological topics. This allowed Poteat significant interaction with leading liberals from the North, including Walter Rauschenbusch, Harry Emerson Fosdick, and Shailer Mathews.

33. Poteat, "Wherein Lies the Efficacy of Jesus' Work in the Reconciliation?," 96–97.

34. Poteat, "Wherein Lies the Efficacy of Jesus' Work in the Reconciliation?," 96–97.

35. William L. Poteat, *Laboratory and Pulpit: The Relation of Biology to the Preacher and His Message* (Griffith & Rowland, 1901), 14.

36. Poteat, *Laboratory and Pulpit,* 43.

37. Poteat, *Laboratory and Pulpit,* 47.

38. Poteat, *Laboratory and Pulpit,* 44.

39. Poteat, *Laboratory and Pulpit,* 69. He argued that men and women could find Christ in their own religious experience.

40. See Poteat, *Laboratory and Pulpit,* 83. Several years later he said, "What we need to observe is . . . Christianity has already dropped the antiquated view of the world and history, and has found its place in the new world of science." See Poteat, *A New Peace,* 121. The same kind of optimism characterized his 1925 book, *Can a Man Be a Christian To-day?*

41. For a concise summary of Romanticism see Michael Ferber, *Romanticism: A Very Short Introduction* (Oxford University Press, 2010). For a historical survey focused on the key German thinkers of Romanticism see Rüdiger Safrankski, *Romanticism: A German Affair,* trans. Robert E. Goodwin (Northwestern University Press, 2015).

42. Roger E. Olson, *The Journey of Modern Theology: From Reconstruction to Deconstruction* (InterVarsity, 2013), 109. Olson clarified that the Romanticists were not anti-reason—they were not irrational—but they challenged the idea that reason alone, especially given the very narrow definition of reason by Enlightenment thinkers, was the means to knowledge. See Olson, *The Journey of Modern Theology,* 110.

43. Roger Olson explained that Coleridge challenged the Enlightenment's "inflation of reason to the exclusion of feelings." Olson, *The Journey of Modern Theology,* 101. For sources on Coleridge see Gary Dorrien, *Kantian Reason and Hegelian Spirit: The Idealistic Logic of Modern Theology* (Wiley-Blackwell, 2012); Douglas Hedley, *Coleridge, Philosophy and Religion: Aids to Reflections and the Mirror of the Spirit* (Cambridge University Press, 2000); and Christopher W. Corbin, *The Evangelical Party and Samuel*

Taylor Coleridge's Return to the Church of England (Routledge, 2018). Dorrien argued that Coleridge launched English Romanticism with his book *Lyrical Ballads,* published in 1798. Coleridge's *Aids to Reflection* became deeply influential. See Dorrien, *Kantian Reason and Hegelian Spirit,* 119–45.

44. Olson, *The Journey of Modern Theology,* 111–12.

45. Dorrien, *Kantian Reason and Hegelian Spirit,* 139. Americans discovered Coleridge's *Aids to Reflection,* originally published in 1825, largely through James Marsh's 1829 edition, which included his lengthy introduction to the text. See Samuel Taylor Coleridge, *Aids to Reflection: With a Prelim. Essay,* ed. James Marsh (1829; repr., Kennikat Press, 1971). Poteat owned an 1883 edition of Coleridge's *Aids to Reflection.* See William L. Poteat, manuscript, "List of Books from the Library of Dr. William Louis Poteat Given to Wake Forest College," Poteat Papers, box 7, folder 727, Z. Smith Reynolds Library Archives, Wake Forest University, Winston-Salem, NC.

46. Coleridge, *Aids to Reflection,* 203.

47. Olson, *The Journey of Modern Theology,* 114, 124.

48. Olson, *The Journey of Modern Theology,* 113.

49. Poteat indicated Coleridge's influence when he inserted a quotation from Coleridge's *Aids to Reflection* as a prefatory note in chapter 3 of *Can a Man Be a Christian To-day?* in which he articulated his two-sphere philosophy of science and religion: "Our faith ought to be larger than our speculative reason, and take something into her heart that reason can never take into her eye." William L. Poteat, *Can a Man Be a Christian To-day?* (Oxford University Press and University of North Carolina Press, 1925), 82.

50. German Romantics contributed significantly to the philosophical and religious dimension of Romanticism. See Safrankski, *Romanticism: A German Affair,* and Manfred Frank, *The Philosophical Foundations of Early German Romanticism,* trans. Elizabeth Millan-Zaibert (SUNY Press, 2008). Gary Dorrien correctly identified Schleiermacher as belonging to "the same Romantic generation and atmosphere that shaped Schelling, Hegel, and Samuel Taylor Coleridge." Dorrien, *Kantian Reason and Hegelian Spirit,* 84. See also Richard Crouter, *Friedrich Schleiermacher: Between Enlightenment and Romanticism* (Cambridge University Press, 2005).

51. See Adams's exploration of Schleiermacher's religious epistemology: Robert M. Adams, "Faith and Religious Knowledge," in *The Cambridge Companion to Friedrich Schleiermacher,* ed. Jacqueline Marina (Cambridge University Press, 2005), 35–51.

52. For one of many identifications of Schleiermacher as the father of liberal theology see Jacqueline Marina, ed., *The Cambridge Companion to Friedrich Schleiermacher* (Cambridge University Press, 2005), 1. Keith Clements called Schleiermacher the "Pioneer of Modern Theology." Keith W. Clements, *Friedrich Schleiermacher: Pioneer of Modern Theology* (Collins, 1987). Although Poteat never cited Schleiermacher nor apparently owned any of Schleiermacher's works, his similarity to Schleiermacher is remarkable. Schleiermacher's ideas seem to have become a part of the landscape of liberal Christianity in America. For Poteat's library see William L. Poteat, manuscript, "List of Books from the Library of Dr. William Louis Poteat Given to Wake Forest College," Poteat Papers, box 7, folder 727.

53. See Dorrien, *Kantian Reason and Hegelian Spirit,* 90.

54. The first edition was published in 1799 and the second in 1806. However even in the first edition he considered the two as almost inseparable: "Intuition without feeling is nothing and can have neither the proper origin nor the proper force; feeling without

intuition is also nothing; both are therefore something only when and because they are originally one and unseparated." Friedrich Schleiermacher, *On Religion: Speeches to its Cultured Despisers,* trans. Richard Crouter (1988; repr., Cambridge University Press, 2003), 31.

55. Adams, "Faith and Religious Knowledge," in *The Cambridge Companion to Friedrich Schleiermacher,* 36.

56. Adams explained that Schleiermacher came to see intuition as outward looking whereas feeling looked inward. Adams, "Faith and Religious Knowledge," in *The Cambridge Companion to Friedrich Schleiermacher,* 36–37.

57. Friedrich Schleiermacher, *The Christian Faith,* rev. ed., trans. H. R. Mackintosh and J. S. Stewart (T & T Clark, 1999), 14. For his larger discussion on feeling see Schleiermacher, *The Christian Faith,* 12–18. Schleiermacher first published this work between 1821 and 1822. He published the revised edition in 1830 and 1831. Dorrien identified *The Christian Faith* as "the first full-orbed liberal theology, which surpassed in influence all the liberal theologies that followed it, and which eventually was recognized as the quintessential liberal theology." Dorrien, *Kantian Reason and Hegelian Spirit,* 105–6.

58. Dorrien explained that Gottfried W. Leibniz regarded feeling as a "confused and primitive form of knowledge." Immanuel Kant however disqualified it as a form of knowledge because it was an "emotive, noncognitive mode of consciousness that 'knew' no truth beyond psychological experience." Dorrien, *Kantian Reason and Hegelian Spirit,* 92.

59. See Dorrien, *Kantian Reason and Hegelian Spirit,* 85.

60. Schleiermacher, *The Christian Faith,* 18.

61. Schleiermacher, *The Christian Faith,* 76.

62. Schleiermacher, *The Christian Faith,* 83. See also Adams, "Faith and Religious Knowledge," in *The Cambridge Companion to Friedrich Schleiermacher,* 39.

63. Schleiermacher, *The Christian Faith,* 17.

64. Dorrien, *Kantian Reason and Hegelian Spirit,* 92.

65. Schleiermacher, *The Christian Faith,* 17.

66. Schleiermacher, *The Christian Faith,* 12–18.

67. Schleiermacher, *The Christian Faith,* 16–17.

68. Schleiermacher, *The Christian Faith,* 16.

69. Schleiermacher, *The Christian Faith,* 17.

70. Adams, "Faith and Religious Knowledge," in *The Cambridge Companion to Friedrich Schleiermacher,* 35–37.

71. This was likewise the case for Immanuel Kant's basis of morality.

72. Schleiermacher, *On Religion,* 17.

73. Adams, "Faith and Religious Knowledge," in *The Cambridge Companion to Friedrich Schleiermacher,* 35.

74. Poteat was closer to Schleiermacher than to subsequent shapers of liberal theology like Albrecht Ritschl. For a source on Ritschl see Olson, *The Journey of Modern Theology,* 147–63. Wilhelm Herrmann, after Ritschl, in part reemphasized Schleiermacher's distinctive approach by giving greater weight to religious experience. Like Ritschl, Herrmann was interested in history, but experience ultimately trumped what might be known historically. For instance one cannot know historically whether Jesus actually rose from death, but he or she can indeed know that Jesus still lived through personal encounter with the living Christ. One did not need to make a historical judgment about Christ's resurrection: Experience offered sufficient grounds for faith. See Wilhelm Herrmann, *Systematic Theology* (Macmillan, 1927), 125–29.

75. Manfred Frank argued similarly that Schleiermacher did not have a metaphysics, meaning he did not have a foundational philosophical doctrine. He argued that Schleiermacher "was not convinced that metaphysics could grasp the highest object of the human mind." See Manfred Frank, "Metaphysical Foundations: A Look at Schleiermacher's *Dialectic*," in *The Cambridge Companion to Friedrich Schleiermacher,* ed. Jacqueline Marina (Cambridge University Press, 2005), 15. Randal Hall came to a similar conclusion: "Poteat's denigration of rational theology left him comfortable with the irresolution of many . . . intellectual contradictions. He was not a systematic thinker and had no compulsion to analyze himself or the world in a rigorously logical way." Randal L. Hall, *William Louis Poteat: A Leader of the Progressive-Era South* (University of Kentucky Press), 197.

76. William L. Poteat, *The New Peace: Lectures on Science and Religion* (Gorham Press, 1915), 32–36. He gave these lectures at Hamilton Theological Seminary of Colgate University in May 1905, then October and November 1905 at Crozer Theological Seminary, Newton Theological Institution, Rochester Theological Institution, and the Divinity School of the University of Chicago. See "Prefatory Note" in *The New Peace.*

77. Poteat, *The New Peace,* 32–33.

78. Edgar Y. Mullins, *Axioms of Religion* (1908; repr., Mercer University Press, 2010), 144. Mullins, like Poteat, made experience the center of Christian spirituality: "Let religion take its proper form of personal experience. Art is the response of man's soul to beauty. Science is his response to truth. Religion is the response of the soul of man to God and righteousness."

79. Poteat recognized that science and philosophy had been more closely identified historically: "In the seventeenth and eighteenth centuries philosophy was often used as the equivalent of what we now mean by science." Poteat, *The New Peace,* 33. Poteat noted that because science was limited to explaining the natural world scientists regularly used philosophy for its deeper explanatory power. He explained that "scientific inquiry [moved] so easily into philosophy, passing unconsciously from the cognitive process and the investigation of phenomenal reality over into speculation about the ultimate reality, which is the special note of philosophy." Poteat, *The New Peace,* 34.

80. Poteat, *The New Peace,* 34.

81. He said, "Theology is concerned with things not on their own account, but only because of their relation to God. Science is concerned with things for their own sake, and only thinks of their relation to God when, rising into philosophy, it seeks their ultimate explanation." Poteat, *The New Peace,* 35.

82. Poteat, *The New Peace,* 35–36.

83. Poteat, *The New Peace,* 35–36. Friedrich Schleiermacher and others had made this argument to propose apologetic grounding for their highly spiritualized form of Christianity, in which a personal encounter with God and private illumination formed the center of religious epistemology. See Carl F. H. Henry, *God, Revelation, and Authority* (1976; repr., Crossway, 1999) 1:77–82.

84. Mullins made the same argument, also in 1905, but like Poteat he later stressed greater distance between the two and relinquished the argument for an empirical quality for religious experience. See Edgar Y. Mullins, "The Theological Trend," *Review & Expositor* 2 (October 1905): 506–21, and his later systematic theology, Mullins, *The Christian Religion in Its Doctrinal Expression* (1917; repr., Wipf & Stock). As with Poteat, the benefits of a sharper separation outweighed the benefit of proposing empirical legitimacy for religious experience.

85. William L. Poteat, "The Place of Prayer in the Modern Worldview," *Proceedings of the Baptist Congress: Twenty-Eighth Annual Session* (University of Chicago Press 1911), 42.

86. Poteat, "The Place of Prayer in the Modern Worldview," 42.

87. The lectures were published as William L. Poteat, *Can a Man Be a Christian To-day?* (University of North Carolina Press, 1925).

88. Poteat, *Can a Man Be a Christian To-day?*, 59.

89. Poteat, *Can a Man Be a Christian To-day?*, 59–60. For sources on the rise of modern science and its conflict with religion see Peter Bowler, *Evolution: The History of an Idea* (University of California Press, 2009); and Ronald L. Numbers, *The Creationists: From Scientific Creationism to Intelligent Design* (Harvard University Press, 2006).

90. Poteat, *Can a Man Be a Christian To-day?*, 69, 77.

91. He argued that a scientific analysis of Genesis revealed that it plainly could not be harmonized with modern science: "[To] say that the light created on the first day was cosmic light produced by collision of the molecules of the primal nebula, leaves unanswered the question: How were the first and second days marked before the creation of the sun and moon for that function? And the firmament or vault of heaven, solid and rigid enough to support an ocean of waters above it? And green plants growing on earth before the sun on which they depend, is set in the heavens? And birds which are a higher type than reptiles and appear later in geological time precede them in the order of creation." Poteat, *Can a Man Be a Christian To-day?*, 77–78. However some conservatives did find thoughtful ways to harmonize the biblical creation account and science. I explore some examples in chapter 7.

92. Poteat, *Can a Man Be a Christian To-day?*, 77–79.

93. Matt. 10:24–25.

94. Poteat, *Can a Man Be a Christian To-day?*, 70–71. For the South's new cultured middle class see chapter 3.

95. Poteat, *Can a Man Be a Christian To-day?*, 83.

96. Poteat, *Can a Man Be a Christian To-day?*, 85.

97. Mullins, *Christian Religion in Its Doctrinal Expression*, 83.

98. Poteat, *Can a Man Be a Christian To-day?*, 85.

99. Poteat, *Can a Man Be a Christian To-day?*, 85.

100. Eugene Lankford to William L. Poteat, January 14, 1929, Poteat Papers, box 2, folder 225.

101. Poteat, *Can a Man Be a Christian To-day?*, 83.

102. Poteat, *Can a Man Be a Christian To-day?*, 87–89. Poteat reflected on his initial exposure to science and the joy that it provided him. For a survey of Poteat's career as a scientist and educator see Hall, *William Louis Poteat*, 22–59.

103. Poteat, *Can a Man Be a Christian To-day?*, 90–91.

104. Poteat, *Can a Man Be a Christian To-day?*, 96. Randal Hall offered a compelling account of Poteat's gradual adoption of evolutionary ideas from cautious assent to bold affirmation. See Hall, *William Louis Poteat*, 47–51.

105. Poteat, *Can a Man Be a Christian To-day?*, 97.

106. Poteat, *Can a Man Be a Christian To-day?*, 97–98.

107. The analogy of accumulated baggage is the center of chapter 2 of *Can a Man Be a Christian To-day?*. He argued that the traveler—the Christian—cannot "get through the scientific gateway of the modern world with all the load he carries." When the baggage is stripped away, the pure essence of Christianity as religious experience remained: "From that

point springs the new life in Christ. I venture to think it the essence of Christianity." See *Can a Man Be a Christian To-day?*, 46–47, 98.

108. William L. Poteat, "Religion in Science," *Biblical Recorder,* May 9, 1888.

109. Mullins, *Christian Religion in Its Doctrinal Expression,* 40. Mullins was not thoroughly anticreedal and had a more appreciative view of the role of doctrine for religion than did Poteat, but he concluded that "religious knowledge does not arise primarily by subscription to creeds" but came "through the presence of God in the soul." As with Poteat, he felt that experience was the basis for religious knowledge: "Men learn of God through experience of God." In *Christian Religion in Its Doctrinal Expression,* Mullins denied that the Bible was the supreme source for religious knowledge in favor of experience. The Bible is the supreme "*literary* source of the revelation of God" but "God [himself] thus becomes our supreme authority, and the Bible is recognized as the authoritative *record* of his supreme revelation" and "God's revelation of himself to us comes through his direct action upon our spirits" (emphasis mine). Mullins, *The Christian Religion in Its Doctrinal Expression,* 41.

110. Poteat, *Can a Man Be a Christian To-day?*, 98.

111. Poteat, *Can a Man Be a Christian To-day?*, 99.

112. Poteat, *Can a Man Be a Christian To-day?*, 100.

113. Poteat, *Can a Man Be a Christian To-day?*, 100. Reason, he argued, functioned within the scientific sphere.

114. Poteat, *Can a Man Be a Christian To-day?*, 101.

115. For example see John 20–21.

116. Poteat would have stressed the social dimensions of religion in terms of public morality and social renewal, that is, the work to further the kingdom of God on earth.

117. Olson, *The Journey of Modern Theology,* 26. Olson argued that the theme that ran through each of the various responses to modernity—liberal and conservative—was "a desire to reconstruct Christianity to make it immune from the acids of modernity and especially science." Olson, *The Journey of Modern Theology,* 28.

118. As a scientist it would not be accurate to conclude that Poteat was intimidated by science, but he knew its power firsthand and sensed the threat it represented if it were allowed authority in religious matters.

119. He concluded, "Knowledge was handed over to the so-called hard sciences so that what was left to theology was opinion and value judgments only." Olson, *The Journey of Modern Theology,* 712.

120. Poteat detailed his crisis and subsequent religious evolution with striking transparency in an unpublished manuscript as well as a published article. See William L. Poteat, manuscript, "My Approach to Religion," Poteat Papers, box 9, folder 961; and William L. Poteat, "An Intellectual Adventure: A Human Document," *American Scholar* 5, no. 3 (Summer 1936): 280–86.

121. Poteat, *Can a Man Be a Christian To-day?*, 59.

122. Poteat, *Can a Man Be a Christian To-day?*, 47.

123. Poteat, *Can a Man Be a Christian To-day?*, 108.

124. Poteat, *Can a Man Be a Christian To-day?*, 47.

125. Poteat, *Can a Man Be a Christian To-day?*, 108.

126. Poteat, *Can a Man Be a Christian To-day?*, 64.

127. Poteat, *Can a Man Be a Christian To-day?*, 64.

128. Poteat, *Can a Man Be a Christian To-day?*, 109.

129. Poteat, *Can a Man Be a Christian To-day?*, 47.

130. For the tradition of conversionism in evangelicalism see David W. Bebbington, *Evangelicalism in Modern Britain: A History from the 1730s to the 1980s* (Routledge, 1989), 14–16.

131. For the theology of the priesthood of the believer see Timothy George, "The Priesthood of All Believers," in *The People of God: Essays on the Believers' Church*, eds. Paul Basden and David S. Dockery (Broadman Press, 1991).

132. For a source on the history of church structure and accountability in the South see Gregory A. Wills, *Democratic Religion: Freedom, Authority, and Church Discipline in the Baptist South, 1785–1900* (Oxford University Press, 1997).

133. When Poteat referred to the "rabbis" he likened conservative theologians and ministers to the religious teachers in the New Testament who, as he interpreted it, opposed Jesus's pure spiritual religion in exchange for the Jewish institutional religion of law, tradition, and authority.

134. Richard T. Vann, "What Have Baptist Colleges to do with Fundamentalism and Modernism?," 15, pamphlet, Address to Southern Baptist Educational Conference, Memphis, TN, February 4, 1925, James P. Boyce Library Archives, Southern Baptist Theological Seminary, Louisville, KY.

135. Poteat, *Can a Man Be a Christian To-day?*, 109–10.

136. For a source on soul competency in the Baptist tradition see George, "The Priesthood of All Believers," in *The People of God: Essays on the Believers' Church.*

137. Edgar Y. Mullins, *Axioms of Religion* (1908; repr., Mercer University, 2010) 64.

138. Mullins, *Axioms of Religion*, 64. For a recent treatment of the legacy of Mullins's theology of religious experience and soul competency see Curtis W. Freeman, "E. Y. Mullins and the Siren Songs of Modernity," in *Through a Glass Darkly: Contested Notions of Baptist Identity* ed. Keith Harper (University of Alabama Press, 2012), 84–111. Freeman rightly situated Mullins in the context of theological modernism, although Mullins stayed cautiously on the conservative side of the spectrum of modernism. However David Bebbington was also correct when he concluded: "Although the Bible was far from forgotten, soul competency became the supreme Baptist value. Mullins reoriented the way in which Baptist principles were presented." David W. Bebbington, *Baptists Through the Centuries: A History of Global People* (Baylor University Press, 2010), 260.

139. Mullins argued that "the principle of competency assumes that man is made in God's image, and God is a person able to reveal himself to man . . . Man has capacity for God, and God can communicate with man." Mullins, *Axioms of Religion*, 67. Timothy George defined Mullins's soul competency well: "Soul competency . . . is based on the premise that all persons have an inalienable right of access to God. Put otherwise, all persons created in the image of God stand in a unique and inviolable relation to their Creator and, when quickened by divine grace, are fully 'competent' or capable of responding to God directly." George, "The Priesthood of All Believers," in *The People of God*, 85–86.

140. Poteat referenced the KJV, but I have cited the ESV. See Poteat, *Can a Man Be a Christian To-day?*, 106.

141. Poteat, *Can a Man Be a Christian To-day?*, 106–7.

142. Poteat, *Can a Man Be a Christian To-day?*, 49.

143. Poteat, *Can a Man Be a Christian To-day?*, 49. Poteat was pessimistic regarding the value of theology in general. He argued that dogma was a fruitless pursuit and that revealed religion and doctrinal orthodoxy constricted religion's ability to evolve and thus inhibited its hope for vitality in the modern world. See William L. Poteat, *Laboratory and*

Pulpit: The Relation of Biology to the Preacher and His Message (Griffith & Rowland, 1901), 47–49.

144. Poteat, *Can a Man Be a Christian To-day?*, 48.

145. Poteat, *Can a Man Be a Christian To-day?*, 66.

146. Poteat, *Can a Man Be a Christian To-day?*, 47.

147. Edwin M. Poteat, "The Essence of Christianity," *Review and Expositor* 2 (August 1906): 349–52.

148. Mullins, *The Christian Religion in Its Doctrinal Expression*, 3.

149. Poteat, *Can a Man Be a Christian To-day?*, 105.

150. Poteat, *Can a Man Be a Christian To-day?*, 105.

151. Poteat, *Can a Man Be a Christian To-day?*, 106–7.

152. Alfred J. Dickinson, *Alabama Baptist*, May 29, 1907, 2.

153. Poteat, *Can a Man Be a Christian To-day?*, 53.

154. Archibald T. Robertson to William L. Poteat, April 1929, Poteat Papers, box 2, folder 225. Poteat responded to Robertson with thanks. The two evidenced a warm friendship. See William L. Poteat to Archibald T. Robertson, September 24, 1930, Poteat Papers, box 2, folder 225.

155. Alfred J. Dickinson, "The Religion of the Risen Lord." Convention Sermons, May 1907, Richmond, VA, Southern Baptist Historical Library and Archives, Nashville, TN.

156. Poteat, *Can a Man Be a Christian To-day?*, 103.

157. Poteat, *Can a Man Be a Christian To-day?*, 51. However Poteat regretted that this led to the growth of institutionalism.

158. Although this work focuses on Poteat's religious life Poteat was involved in an impressive number of other areas of service during the Progressive Era: education, sanitation, temperance, interracial cooperation, and politics. Randal Hall's biography focused on Poteat as a leader of Southern progressivism. See Hall, *William Louis Poteat.* Suzanne Linder also explored his social contribution: Suzanne C. Linder, *William Louis Poteat: Prophet of Progress* (University of North Carolina Press, 1966). However Poteat's social activism also included eugenics, which I address in chapter 8 of this book.

159. Edwin M. Poteat to James M. Frost, April 6, 1910. Frost Papers, Southern Baptist Historical Library and Archives, Nashville, TN. Interestingly when Edwin Poteat died in 1937 John Sampey, president of Southern Seminary in Louisville, Kentucky, wrote a moving letter about Edwin Poteat's passing. The two had been close and had been classmates at Southern Seminary in the 1880s. Regardless of Edwin Poteat's outspoken liberalism Sampey regarded him as a brother in the faith. Sampey wrote, "It is a great satisfaction to know that he was ready for the rendezvous with death" and "I shall always cherish his memory and hope in the near future to greet him in the father's house." See John R. Sampey to William L. Poteat, June 29, 1937. Poteat Papers, box 3. For a source in which Edwin Poteat articulated his expression of liberal theology see Edwin M. Poteat Sr., *The Scandal of the Cross: Studies in the Death of Jesus* (Harper & Brothers, 1928).

160. Hall, *William Louis Poteat*, 51. See also Hall, *William Louis Poteat*, 4.

161. The social gospel was not identical with theological liberalism. For instance social gospel Christianity did not have a contemporary counterpart in Europe, which became one of the criticisms against German liberalism. In the United States the rise of the social gospel under its early figures like Washington Gladden and later with Walter Rauschenbusch became a new stream within American Protestantism, which drew from theological liberalism and largely embraced its modern revisions of Christianity. But one could be a bona fide

theological liberal without embracing the social mission of the social gospel. For the best source on Rauschenbusch see Christopher H. Evans, *The Kingdom Is Always But Coming: A Life of Walter Rauschenbusch* (Eerdmans, 2004). See also Olson, *The Journey of Modern Theology*; and Gary Dorrien, *The Making of American Liberal Theology: Idealism, Realism, & Modernity, 1900–1950* (Westminster John Knox, 2003).

162. Historians have assumed that the South was essentially void of theological liberalism in the early twentieth century. Liberals who did reside in the South have been presumed to have embraced only a more moderate form of liberalism—adopting some progressive elements but retaining an otherwise traditional orthodox theology. C. Vann Woodward argued that "one searches vainly" for liberal religion in the early twentieth-century South. See Woodward's classic work, C. Vann Woodward, *Origins of the New South, 1877–1913* (1951; repr., Louisiana State University Press, 1971), 450. The standard works on liberal theology completely overlook the Southern scene. In his impressive work on the history of theological liberalism in the United States Gary Dorrien ignored the South, implying that liberalism was a Northern phenomenon. He even overlooked that the first professor in America to be fired for liberal views was Crawford Toy, a Southerner and professor at Southern Baptist Theological Seminary in Louisville, Kentucky. Charles Briggs of Union Theological Seminary in New York, whom Dorrien does discuss in detail, recognized Toy's significance in this regard. For Briggs's comments see Charles A. Briggs, *General Introduction to the Study of Holy Scripture* (Scribner's, 1899), 286. For Dorrien see Gary Dorrien, *The Making* of *American Liberal Theology: Imagining Progressive Religion, 1805–1900* (Westminster John Knox, 2001), and Dorrien, *The Making of American Liberal Theology: Idealism, Realism, & Modernity, 1900–1950* (Westminster John Knox, 2003). Roger Olson likewise overlooked the South in his work *The Journey of Modern Theology: From Reconstruction to Deconstruction* (InterVarsity, 2013). However Wayne Flynt has recognized that liberalism did take root in the South, although it did not became mainstream. See Wayne Flynt, *Alabama Baptists: Southern Baptists in the Heart of Dixie* (University of Alabama Press, 1998). Flynt's student Jeffrey Walters likewise recognized the growth of liberalism among Southern Baptists. See Jeffrey K. Walters, "'Though the Heavens Fall': Liberal Theology and the Southern Baptist Theological Seminary, 1894–1925" (MA thesis, Auburn University Press, 1992). Several of Poteat's contemporaries recognized the rise of liberalism. See for example Virginius Dabney, *Liberalism in the South* (University of North Carolina Press, 1932); and Edwin Mims, *The Advancing South* (Doubleday, Page & Company, 1926).

163. See Grant Wacker, *Augustus H. Strong and the Dilemma of Historical Consciousness* (1985; repr., Baylor University Press, 2018) 134. For Wacker's larger assessment of Strong's influences and motivations see 134–37. Strong provides a fascinating comparison to Poteat. Strong faced essentially the same intellectual challenges as Poteat, and although he seemed to embrace some elements of liberal theology, he carefully tried to nuance them and aimed to remain generally orthodox in his beliefs.

164. Gary Dorrien said, "Schleiermacher knew that his [skeptical] friends were wrong about religion because the thing they spurned had nothing to do with the thing he knew best, his own spiritual wellspring, piety." Dorrien, *Kantian Reason and Hegelian Spirit*, 90.

CHAPTER THREE: A NEW RELIGION FOR THE NEW SOUTH

1. For a work on the social turmoil that arose after the Civil War see Carole Emberton, *Beyond Redemption: Race, Violence, and the American South after the Civil War* (University of Chicago, 2013). For the best single volume on the Civil War and Reconstruction

see Allen C. Guelzo, *Fateful Lightning: A New History of the Civil War and Reconstruction* (Oxford University Press, 2012). For a concise work on Reconstruction see Allen C. Guelzo, *Reconstruction: A Concise History* (Oxford University Press, 2018). For Reconstruction in North Carolina in particular see Richard L. Zuber, *North Carolina During Reconstruction* (North Carolina Department of Cultural Resources, 1969).

2. Paul M. Gaston, *New South Creed: A Study in Southern Mythmaking*, new ed. (NewSouth Books, 2002), 28. Gaston's classic work, which was originally published in 1970 by Alfred A. Knopf, has stood the test of time and continues to provide a robust intellectual analysis of the New South. For an updated evaluation of the place of Gaston's work in contemporary historiography see Robert J. Norrell's introduction to the new edition: Gaston, *New South Creed*, 13–20. For the depressed state of the South fifteen years after the Civil War and the lengths that were necessary for the South to compete with the industrial Northeast see C. Vann Woodward, *The Origins of the New South, 1877–1913* (1951; repr., Louisiana State University Press, 1971), 107–41.

3. Edward L. Ayers, *The Promise of the New South: Life After Reconstruction*, new ed. (Oxford University, 2007), 3.

4. Gaston, *New South Creed*, 28.

5. For an extensive collection of Grady's writings and speeches see Joel Chandler Harris, ed., *Life of Henry W. Grady, Including His Speeches and Writings* (Cassell Publishing, 1890). For Grady's most important works see Mills Lane, ed. *The New South: Writings and Speeches of Henry Grady* (Beehive Press, 1971). For secondary sources on Grady see Harold E. Davis, *Henry Grady's New South Atlanta, A Brave & Beautiful City* (University of Alabama Press, 1990); and Ferald J. Bryan, *Henry Grady or Tom Watson?: The Rhetorical Struggle for the New South, 1880–1890* (Mercer University Press, 1994).

6. Harold Davis and others have made this point. See Davis, *Henry Grady's New South Atlanta, A Brave & Beautiful City*, 175.

7. Lane, ed. *The New South*, 3. Grady claimed to be quoting Benjamin H. Hill (1823–82), a Georgia politician. For a secondary source see Bryan, *Henry Grady or Tom Watson?*, 45. Harold Davis raised suspicion about the source of these words and argued that no record exists that the quotation belonged to Hill. See Davis, *Henry Grady's New South Atlanta, A Brave & Beautiful City*, 179.

8. Lane, ed., *The New South*, 7–8.

9. Lane, ed., *The New South*, 8–9.

10. Gaston, *The New South Creed*, 37. Although Grady's role was central, Gaston rightly noted that Henry Watterson's Louisville *Courier Journal* grew to rival Grady's *Constitution* as a voice for the New South. See Gaston, *New South Creed*, 56, 72. Watterson embodied the New South image and exerted a powerful influence for sectional reconciliation and economic development. As a former officer in the Confederate Army he reverenced the Old South, and he dressed as a Southern colonel with a bushy mustache and distinctively long soul patch, and he carried a cane. And Watterson's city personified the New South move toward industrialization and urbanization. For the best source on Watterson see Daniel S. Margolies, *Henry Watterson and the New South: The Politics of Empire, Free Trade, and Globalization* (University of Kentucky Press, 2006). Richard H. Edmonds was another leading voice for the New South and enjoyed a much longer career than Grady. Like Grady and Watterson, he was a journalist. He founded the *Manufacturers' Record* in 1881, and it became the South's leading industrial periodical. See Richard H. Edmonds, *The South's Redemption: From Poverty to Prosperity* (The Manufacture's Record, 1890); and Richard H.

Edmonds, *Facts About the South* (Fleet, McGinley, and Co., 1895). For a secondary source see Boyce M. Robbins, "Richard Hathaway Edmonds and the New South." (MA thesis, University of North Carolina, 1970). Isaac T. Tichenor is lesser known, but he was a significant figure as an industrialist, educator, and religious leader. See Michael E. Williams, *Isaac Taylor Tichenor: The Creation of the Baptist New South* (University of Alabama Press, 2005). For Gaston's robust account of the intellectual development of a New South vision see Gaston, *The New South Creed*, 38–82. See especially Gaston, *The New South Creed*, 60–61. Edward Ayers pointed out that in addition to men like Grady, Watterson, and Edmonds, "hundreds of lesser counterparts in remote corners of the South did the same." See Ayers, *The Promise of the New South*, 20. After Grady's death in 1889, the national press praised his contribution to Southern society and identified him as the foremost leader of the New South movement. For several articles from the nation's leading newspapers, including the New York *Times* see Harris, ed., *Life of Henry W. Grady, Including His Writings and Speeches*, 443–49.

11. Paul Gaston used the language of myth to refer to the set of ideas used by the leaders of the New South to shape their vision for the future. Gaston argued that the passing of civilizations then was more ideological than actual. Although his point is important and warranted, I argue that the transition of Southern society in the late nineteenth century truly was remarkable. Gaston was correct when he argued that the stain of social inequality continued into the New South era. But even on the topic of race the situation became strikingly different in the new era, for instance with the rise of Jim Crow, which was a product of the social changes that occurred in the New South. See Gaston, *New South Creed*, 25–27. For the idealization of the Old South see Gaston, *New South Creed*, 27–30, and the essential work on the Lost Cause mythology: Charles R. Wilson, *Baptized in Blood: The Religion of the Lost Cause, 1865–1920*, new ed. (University of Georgia Press, 2009).

12. For a survey of the place of agriculture in the New South vision see Davis, *Henry Grady's New South Atlanta, A Brave & Beautiful City*, 111–32. Davis rightly argued that nearly "every spokesman for the New South Movement had an agricultural component in his plan." For a survey on the history of Southern agriculture see Gilbert C. Fite, *Cotton Fields No More: Southern Agriculture, 1865–1980* (University of Kentucky Press, 1984). See also Sven Beckert, *Empire of Cotton: A Global History* (Vintage Books, 2014).

13. For Grady's address about agricultural reform see "The Farmer and the Cities," in Lane, ed., *The New South*, 64–86. See also Ayers, *The Promise of the New South*, 3–33, 187–213.

14. Richard H. Edmonds, *The South's Redemption: From Poverty to Prosperity* (The Manufacture's Record, 1890), 3. He argued that when the South's resources were considered together its advantages were unmatched: "No one can carefully study the remarkable combination of resources which the South enjoys without being convinced that, in natural advantages, this section stands far ahead of any other country in the world."

15. Paul Gaston rightly indicated the prejudice that existed when New South leaders like Grady and Edmonds were eager for immigration but were decidedly selective and preferred "Anglo-Saxon stock." The mass of immigration in Northern cities of the era came from southern Europe, but Grady and other boosters were uninterested in immigration if it meant this sort. See Gaston, *The New South Creed*, 92–94. See also Woodward, *Origins of the New South*, 297–99.

16. Edmonds, *The South's Redemption: From Poverty to Prosperity*, 5.

17. Gaston, *The New South Creed*, 65.

18. Gaston, *The New South Creed*, 94.

19. In chapter 4 I explore Poteat's philosophy of education and his vision of a cultured and enlightened society in contrast to the more utilitarian model of education that became an adversarial force throughout his career as president of Wake Forest College.

20. See Woodward, *Origins of the New South*, 1–22; and Ayers, *The Promise of the New South*, 8–9. Woodward argued that the redeemers did not merely restore an old order in the South but opened a new phase of Southern political rule. For the end of reconstruction and Southern "redemption" see Woodward, *Origins of the New South*, 23–74. For a work on reconstruction and redemption see Emberton, *Beyond Redemption*. For a concise work on the Reconstruction era see Guelzo, *Reconstruction*. For Southern political history see Michael Perman, *Pursuit of Unity: A Political History of the American South* (University of North Carolina Press, 2009).

21. Woodward, *Origins of the New South*, 456–81. With Wilson's election a significant shift occurred. Woodward rightly argued, "The change in the atmosphere in Washington represented a revolution in the geographical distribution of power. For the contrast between the South's position in 1913 and the humble place it had occupied during the previous half century was almost as marked as the contrast between the South of the ante-bellum period and the South of the era that followed." Woodward, *Origins of the New South*, 481.

22. For Ayers's study of the South's urban growth see Ayers, 18–20, 55–80. For the best source on urbanization in the South see Don H. Doyle, "The Urbanization of Dixie," in *New Men, New Cities, New South* (University of North Carolina Press, 1990), 1–21. See also Blaine A. Brownell and David R. Goldfield, eds. *The City in Southern History: The Growth of Urban Civilization in the South* (Kennikat Press, 1977).

23. For the best source on Atlanta as a New South city see William A. Link, *Cradle of the New South: Race & Remembering in the Civil War's Aftermath* (University of North Carolina Press, 2013). For an account of the newness or distinctiveness of a New South city from older Southern cities see Carl Carmer's contemporary reflections on a New South city: Carl Carmer, *Stars Fell On Alabama* (Blue Ribbon Books, 1934), 79–81. Carmer argued "Birmingham is the *nouveau riche* of Alabama cities . . . Hardly a half-century ago she was the little crossroads town of Jones Valley. Now she numbers her population in hundreds of thousands. She has no traditions. She is the New South." He described the Yankee capitalists who helped build the city and the idol of industry that drove its ambition. He argued, "Birmingham is not like the rest of the state. It is an industrial monster sprung up in the midst of a slow-moving pastoral. . . . Birmingham is a new city in an old land."

24. Ayers, *The Promise of the New South*, 55–56. For the importance of railroads see Scott Reynolds Nelson, *Iron Confederacies: Southern Railways, Klan Violence, and Reconstruction* (University of North Carolina Press, 1999); and Maury Klein, *History of the Louisville & Nashville Railroad* (1972; repr., University of Kentucky Press, 2003).

25. C. Vann Woodward rightly argued that many from the old order, the planter class, made their way into the new class of professionals. They especially did so as merchants. See Woodward, *Origins of the New South*, 21. Don Doyle demonstrated that the new class of professionals was not entirely without precedent: "To be sure, this class had antecedents in the antebellum towns and cities. But its incarnation in the New South era was far more imposing in scale, in geographic breadth, and in ideological vigor." Doyle, *New Men, New Cities, New South*, 87. See also Frank J. Bryne, *Becoming Bourgeois: Merchant Culture in the South, 1820–1865* (University of Kentucky Press, 2006). For the middle class in the

history of the South see Jonathan D. Wells and Jennifer R. Green, *The Southern Middle Class in the Long Nineteenth Century* (Louisiana State University Press, 2011). See also Jonathan M. Wiener, ed. *Social Origins of the New South: Alabama, 1860–1885* (Louisiana State University Press, 1978).

26. See Ayers, *The Promise of the New South*, 64–67, 97. Ayers argued that the newer and less-rooted cities like Atlanta, Nashville, Greensboro, Birmingham, and Roanoke demonstrated greater openness to people without the traditional connections of Southern society, such as local familial ties or ties to the old planter class. Older port cities like Charleston and Mobile demonstrated some aversion to New South progress. See Ayers, *The Promise of the New South*, 109. Similarly Don Doyle contrasted the key New South centers of Atlanta and Nashville with two more conservative cities, Charleston and Mobile, which resisted New South ideals and remained somewhat stagnant in the late nineteenth century. See Don Doyle, *New Men, New Cities, New South*. Doyle argued that towns and cities are "the wellsprings of any bourgeois society . . . In turn, the cities were the nerve centers of a changing economy and culture that penetrated the rural hinterland and remade the South in the decades following the Civil War." Doyle, *New Men, New Cities, New South*, xiii. For the movement toward the towns and cities and the rise of the middle class see also Ayers, *The Promise of the New South*, 187–213.

27. In chapter 4 I explore the relationship between the culture of refinement and middle-class respectability and the emergence of liberal Christianity.

28. Gaston, *The New South Creed*, 120. For a helpful source on education in the post-bellum South see Joseph M. Stetar, "In Search of a Direction: Southern Higher Education after the Civil War," *History of Education Quarterly* 24, no. 3 (Autumn 1985): 341–67.

29. Dan R. Frost, *Thinking Confederates: Academia and the Idea of Progress in the New South* (University of Tennessee Press, 2000), xi. With his argument Frost challenged the prevailing idea that older Southerners, especially those who had been committed to the Confederate cause, were starkly resistant to innovation, including in the area of education. Frost demonstrated that a significant number of persons from the old order embraced a progressive outlook in the area of education and transitioned from the classical model toward an emphasis upon the sciences and technology with the hope of advancing the South.

30. Williams, *Isaac Taylor Tichenor*, 79. For Tichenor's early biography see Jacob S. Dill, *Isaac Taylor Tichenor: Home Mission Board Statesman* (Sunday School Board, 1908).

31. William L. Poteat, "The Educated Person: Characteristics and Functions," Address to Shaw University, Raleigh, NC, May 15, 1896, manuscript in notebook, Poteat Papers, box 8, folder 853, Z. Smith Reynolds Library Archives, Wake Forest University, Winston-Salem, NC.

32. Randal Hall offered a substantial exploration of Poteat's philosophy of education and Poteat's resistance to the utilitarian spirit of the New South. See Hall, *William Louis Poteat*, 103–28. Hall rightly argued that the ostensible progress of Wake Forest College (the growth of the student body, physical plant, and curricular upgrades) compelled Poteat to gradually surrender his vision for education as an instrument to produce a cultured class to be characterized by high morals, a deep religious life, and leaders for the progress of society, which would gradually give way to the kingdom of God on earth.

33. See Ayers, *The Promise of the New South*, 67–71, 132–59; and Gaston, *The New South Creed*, 131–60. See also Woodward, *Origins of the New South, 1877–1913*, 205–43. See Grady's address, Grady, "The Race Problem in the South," in Lane, ed., *The New South*, 87–105.

34. Grady, "The Race Problem in the South," in Lane, ed., *The New South*, 91. Harold Davis recognized Grady's paternalistic racism in Davis, *Henry Grady's New South Atlanta, A Brave & Beautiful City.*

35. Doyle, *New Men, New Cities, New South*, 316. Doyle rightly concluded, "Despite lip service by reformers, though, public policy affecting the health, education, and welfare of blacks in the cities at best only partially lived up to the principles of the 'new paternalism.'" For the racist paternalism that drove the New South racial program see also Ayers, *The Promise of the New South*, 283–309, 427.

36. For the development of systems of legal segregation see Ayers, *The Promise of the New South*, 16–18; C. Vann Woodward, *The Strange Career of Jim Crow*, 3rd ed. (New York, 1971); Howard N. Rabinowitz, *Race Relations in the Urban South, 1865–1890* (New York, 1978); and Doyle, *New Men, New Cities, New South*, 260–312. See also Henry L. Gates Jr., *Stony the Road: Reconstruction, White Supremacy, and the Rise of Jim Crow* (Penguin Press, 2019).

37. See Ayers, *The Promise of the New South*, 326–29.

38. Doyle, *New Men, New Cities, New South*, 260. Similarly Paul Gaston's central argument in *New South Creed* was that the vision of a prosperous and powerful New South partially obscured the deep racism that continued into the New South era. See Gaston, *New South Creed.*

39. Chapter 8 of this book examines Poteat's work for racial cooperation.

40. See William S. Powell, *North Carolina through Four Centuries* (University of North Carolina, 1989), 245, 308–11. Powell demonstrated that North Carolina had made substantial gains leading up to the Civil War, but like most Southern states also regressed in the years immediately following the war. For a source on the perception of economic sluggishness in nineteenth-century North Carolina see Jack Clairborne and William Price, eds. *Discovering North Carolina: A Tar Heel Reader* (University of North Carolina, 1991), 25–30.

41. See C. Vann Woodward's work on the growth of Southern towns and cities from 1870 to 1900: Woodward, *The Origins of the New South*, 136–41. For a work on the New South-inspired growth of North Carolina see William A. Link, *North Carolina: Change and Tradition in a Southern State*, 2nd ed. (Wiley-Blackwell, 2018), 260–78.

42. Woodward, *Origins of the New South*, 139.

43. See Woodward's account of the rise of the tobacco industry in North Carolina: Woodward, *Origins of the New South*, 129–31. Tobacco was the South's oldest staple crop, and Woodward covered well how North Carolinians exploited the renewed industry and surpassed Virginia, the traditional leader in tobacco production. Other states like Kentucky and Florida also rapidly expanded their production of tobacco in the late nineteenth century. See also Ayers, *The Promise of the New South*, 105–8.

44. For Woodward's account of the cotton mill industry see Woodward, *Origins of the New South*, 131–33. For the general rise of North Carolina's industry see Phillip J. Wood, *Southern Capitalism: The Political Economy of North Carolina, 1880–1980* (Duke University Press, 1986). For the role of cotton mills in the transformation of the South see Jacquelyn D. Hall, James Leloudis, Robert Korstad, Mary Murphy, Lu Ann Jones, and Christopher B. Daly, *Like a Family: The Making of a Southern Cotton Mill World*, new ed. (University of North Carolina Press, 1987). See also North Carolina's furniture industry and the production of building materials like bricks and tile in Ayers, *The Promise of the New South*, 107–8.

45. See Woodward, *Origins of the New South*, 399–406. Woodward noted that Louisiana had the second highest rate of illiteracy among White persons at 17.3, then Alabama at 14.8, and Tennessee with 14.2 percent. Illiteracy among Black persons was approximately 75 percent in 1880 and decreased to 50 percent by 1900.

46. For the best work on New South-era education in North Carolina see James L. Leloudis, *Schooling the New South: Pedagogy, Self, and Society in North Carolina, 1880–1920* (University of North Carolina Press, 1996).

47. Leloudis, *Schooling the New South*, xii.

48. Leloudis, *Schooling the New South*, 1–35.

49. Gaston, *The New South Creed*, 119. For early sources on Page see Button J. Hendrick, *The Life and Letters of Walter H. Page*, vol. 1–3 (Doubleday, Page, and Co., 1923–1925); and Edwin Mims, *The Advancing South: Stories of Progress and Reaction* (Doubleday, Page, and Co., 1926), 23–49. See also John M. Cooper Jr., *Walter Hines Page: The Southerner as American, 1855–1918* (University of North Carolina Press, 1977). Page's so-called Mummy Letters, which he published from February through March of 1886 as a call for progress in politics, education, and economics, solidified his reputation as a liberal reformer in North Carolina. See William S. Powell, *Encyclopedia of North Carolina*, 772–73. But Page, irritated by the stubbornness of Southern tradition and the slowness of progress, left the South for New York, and later became a US diplomat to the United Kingdom.

50. Ayers, *The Promise of the New South*, 22.

51. See Woodward, *Origins of the New South*, 139. He rightly argued that the "Southern people remained, throughout the rise of the 'New South,' overwhelmingly a country people, by far the most rural section of the Union."

52. Ayers, *The Promise of the New South*, 105.

53. Gerald W. Johnson, "Billy with a Red Necktie," *Virginia Quarterly Review* 19 (Autumn 1943): 10.

54. C. Vann Woodward used religious language by calling the New South boosters "Southern apostles," referring to their pioneering role in shaping the modern South. See Woodward, *Origins of the New South,* 144. James Leloudis similarly described the leaders of New South education as New South apostles. See Leloudis, *Schooling the New South*, 37. Historians have also used other religious language like "prophets" to describe the leaders of the New South. See for example Gaston, *New South Creed*. However historians have often overlooked liberal religion in the South. One of the preeminent Southern historians, C. Vann Woodward, has widely been taken at his word when he famously argued that "one searches vainly for important manifestations of any one of these [liberal] tendencies in the annals of Southern Christendom." See Woodward, *Origins of the New South*, 450. But Edward Ayers recognized the early presence of liberal Christianity in the South and treated it briefly in Ayers, *The Promise of the New South*, 29–30.

55. James Leloudis well defined the significance given to the generational effect on the New South leaders. See Leloudis, *Schooling the New South*, 37. Don Doyle likewise defined the image of the New South generation that came of age after the Civil War who developed a "fresh vision of economic and social progress for the region." See Doyle, *New Men, New Cities, New South*, 88–90. Doyle indicated however that this could be exaggerated. He argued that many of the leading people of New South were actually older than the common rhetoric claimed. Paul Gaston had argued that nearly all of the leading spokespersons for the New South were born in the 1850s. See Gaston, *The New South Creed*, 67. In the

end it seems that there was some amount of diversity among New South leaders in terms of age, but many were born in the 1850s, and the generational element seemed to have a substantial impact. For the sense of glory of the war and the nostalgia of the Old South see Wilson, *Baptized in Blood.* For Poteat's older half brothers who fought in the war see "In Memoriam," *Biblical Recorder,* February 27, 1867. Both died as casualties of the Civil War. Many historians have explored the question of a Southern inferiority complex and the role that this has had in Southern history. For a survey of historiography on this topic see Angie Maxwell, *The Indicted South: Public Criticism, Southern Inferiority, and the Politics of Whiteness* (University of North Carolina Press, 2014), 1–26. See also George Tindall, "The Benighted South: Origins of a Modern Image," *Virginia Quarterly Review* 40, no. 2 (Spring 1964): 281–94; and Woodward, *Origins of the New South,* 149–50.

56. Unlike in much of the Deep South tobacco rather than cotton was his cash crop. But Hall rightly argued that the success of the Poteats' operation placed them "among the select few in the Old South for whom reality approached the later legends about antebellum prosperity and refinement." See Hall, *William Louis Poteat,* 6–7. For William Poteat's personal reflections on his early life on the plantation see William L. Poteat, "Memories," 1928, Poteat Papers, box 3, Z. Smith Reynolds Library Archives, Wake Forest University, Winston-Salem, NC; and William L. Poteat, "An Intellectual Adventure," *The American Scholar* 5 (Summer 1936): 280–81. For secondary sources on the Poteat family see Hall, *William Louis Poteat,* 7–1;8 and Suzanne Linder, *William Louis Poteat: Prophet of Progress* (University of North Carolina Press, 1966), 3–22.

57. For Poteat's graduation see "Wake Forest College Commencement," *Biblical Recorder,* June 20, 1877. Leloudis argued that the bachelor of arts degree was the "prestigious" degree for college education, particularly in comparison to the newer bachelor of science degree that initially struggled to attract students. Many other students attended college for a period of time but did not complete their degrees. See Leloudis, *Schooling the New South,* 50–51.

58. For the best source on Poteat's fondness for his early plantation upbringing see Poteat, "Memories."

59. For the most important works about Poteat's religious thought see William L. Poteat, *Laboratory and Pulpit* (Griffith & Rowland Press, 1901); William L. Poteat, *Can a Man Be a Christian To-day?* (University of North Carolina, 1925); and William L. Poteat, *The Way of Victory* (University of North Carolina, 1929). I survey these and other works later in this chapter.

60. William Newton Clarke, *An Outline of Christian Theology* (John Wilson and Son, 1894), 20. For Clarke's journey to liberal theology see William Newton Clarke, *Sixty Years with the Bible: A Record of Experience* (Charles Scribner's Sons, 1909).

61. Shailer Mathews, *The Faith of Modernism* (Macmillan Company, 1925), 171, 179. Mathews clarified that modernists did have beliefs, but they were more like a general spirit than settled doctrines. For a summary for Mathews and Clarke and of Baptist liberalism more generally see Tom Nettles, *The Baptists,* (Christian Focus Publications, 2007), 3:117–95.

62. Gary Dorrien, *The Making of American Liberal Theology: Imagining Progressive Religion, 1805–1900* (Westminster John Knox, 2001), 407.

63. Thomas T. Martin, *Three Fatal Teachings* (n.p., 1920), 18. The University of Chicago developed a reputation as a headquarters for liberal theology, and it became a key institution for the story of liberalism in the North, especially among Baptists.

64. Henry L. Mencken famously gave expression to the stereotype of Southern backwardness in the postbellum period. In one article, "Hiring a Hall," he argued that wealthy Northerners, instead of investing in more art museums and hospitals in the North, should invest their resources in "civilizing one of the more backward of our great and puissant States" of the South. See Henry L. Mencken, "Hiring a Hall," *The World,* January 24, 1926, clipping, Poteat Papers, box 4, Z. Smith Reynolds Library Archives, Wake Forest University, Winston-Salem, NC. For his most famous criticism of the South see Henry L. Mencken, "The Sahara of the Bozart," in *The American Scene: A Reader,* ed. Huntington Cairns (Alfred A. Knopf, 1977), 157–68. For a secondary source see Fred Hobson, *Serpent in Eden: H. L. Mencken and the South* (Louisiana State University Press, 1978). Edwin Mims, a professor at Vanderbilt University in Nashville, named Mencken along with several others who criticized the lack of modern progress in Southern society and contributed to the negative stereotypes of the South. See Mims, *The Advancing South*, 9–10, 17–18.

65. Unknown author, "A Man Who Made It Easier to Think in the South," unknown source, 1929?, clipping, Poteat Papers, box 3, Z. Smith Reynolds Library Archives, Wake Forest University, Winston-Salem, NC.

66. Unknown author, "A Man Who Made It Easier to Think in the South."

67. Virginius Dabney to William L. Poteat, May 19, 1931. See Virginius Dabney, *Liberalism in the South* (University of North Carolina Press, 1932). Dabney accurately described his project as a study of "liberalizing" movements "in the fields of politics, religion, education, industry, literature, journalism, and race relations."

68. Poteat obliged and gave names: "Certain Baptist pastors are to be remembered here, Dr. John E. White so long of Atlanta, now of Savannah, Dr. Ashby Jones so long of Atlanta, now of St. Louis, Dr. Edwin M. Poteat fifteen years president of Furman University, Dr. R. T. Vann of Raleigh." He also named Baptist papers that had been instrumental: *Religious Herald*, *Biblical Recorder*, *Baptist Courier*, and the *Christian Index*. See William L. Poteat to Virginius Dabney, June 15, 1931, Poteat Papers, box 1. In his book Dabney did explore the figures that Poteat referenced, as well as others like W. D. Weatherford of Nashville. He also criticized those progressive Baptists who were too willing to appease the conservative forces in the Southern Baptist Convention, namely Edgar Y. Mullins. See Dabney, *Liberalism in the South*, 300–302.

69. Dabney, *Liberalism in the South*, 300.

70. Johnson, "Billy with the Red Necktie," 9–10.

71. H. Shelton Smith to William L. Poteat, April 9, 1937, Poteat Papers, box 3. Smith was referring to William Poteat and to his brother Edwin McNeill Poteat, who was similarly known as a proponent of liberal Christianity. Smith was interested in writing an article on the Poteat brothers as liberal pioneers after reading William Poteat's article in *The American Scholar* that recounted his journey toward theological liberalism. See Poteat, "An Intellectual Adventure," 280–86.

72. For the burden of overcoming Southern traditionalism to achieve the New South vision of progress see Gaston, *The New South Creed*, 73–76, and Ayers, *The Promise of the New South*, 20–21. Many progressive Southerners like Walter H. Page, who left the South for New York, grew weary of the slowness of progress in the South. For Page see Cooper, *Walter Hines Page: The Southerner as American.* For a source on Southerners who left the South for the more progressive atmosphere of the North see Mims, *The Advancing South*, 19–20, 312–16. Mims lamented those who left the South: "What the nation has gained, the South has lost." Mims, *The Advancing South*, 312.

73. William L. Poteat, *Laboratory and Pulpit: The Relation of Biology to the Preacher and His Message* (Griffith & Rowland, 1901), "Note."

74. Poteat, *Laboratory and Pulpit,* 54.

75. Poteat, *Laboratory and Pulpit,* 52.

76. William L. Poteat, *The New Peace: Lectures on Science and Religion* (Gorham, 1915). Poteat wrote this "Prefatory Note" on February 22, 1915.

77. The McNair Lectures were established to explore the relationship between science and religion. The first lectures were given in 1906. Previous lectures were usually filled by Northerners, including men like Shailer Matthews of the University of Chicago. Poteat's status as a Southerner and native North Carolinian added to the interest in the lectures. See Poteat, *Can a Man Be a Christian To-day?*, "The McNair Lectures"; and Gatewood, *Preachers, Pedagogues, and Politicians*, 111. For a contemporary source on *Can a Man Be a Christian To-day?* see Edwin Mims, *The Advancing South: Stories of Progress and Reaction* (Doubleday, Page, & Co., 1926), 306–10. Mims concluded his study of liberalizing movements in the South with Poteat, using him as an example of the best hope of progress for the South.

78. Poteat faced his first public controversy in 1920 when Thomas T. Martin and D. F. King publicly challenged Poteat's theology of the atonement and his advocacy of evolution. Poteat's theistic evolution became the center of another attack in 1922 when the controversy reached the floor of the North Carolina Baptist Convention. I explore the 1920 controversy in chapter 5 of this book and the controversies of 1922 and 1925 in chapter 6. For the controversy that resulted from Poteat's lectures see Gatewood, *Preachers, Pedagogues, and Politicians*, 111–14. For Randal Hall's on the McNair Lectures see Hall, *William Louis Poteat*, 149–54. For the fundamentalist-modernist controversy see Mardsen, *Fundamentalism and American Culture.*

79. Willard Gatewood curiously called Poteat's lectures "moderate in tone." See Gatewood, *Preachers, Pedagogues, and Politicians*, 113. Randal Hall rightly argued that "Poteat presented his ideas with unusual aggressiveness." See Hall, *William Louis Poteat,* 149. By this time Poteat felt secure in his position, having been soundly vindicated through two public controversies. Poteat similarly felt confident that North Carolina would not follow Tennessee in passing anti-evolution legislation after the recent defeat of the Poole bill. See Powell, "Teaching of Evolution," in *Encyclopedia of North Carolina*, 404–5. Hall also agreed that these lectures represented "a summary statement of his brand of religious liberalism." Hall, *William Louis Poteat*, 150. However Hall concluded that Poteat's brand of modernism was a more moderate example of liberalism. Ultimately Hall unhelpfully seemed to evaluate theological liberalism alongside national movements toward secular and humanistic thought and a more aggressively naturalistic and secular vision for American society, which Poteat decidedly stood against. Hall seemed to miss the defining mark of theological liberalism as a third way, which could seem to be too religious for more radical, agnostic materialists and simultaneously too revisionist and dismissive of traditional Protestant Christianity for grassroots evangelicals. I argue that Poteat's religious liberalism paralleled that of the major proponents of liberalism in the North, who were themselves fixed within the uncomfortable middle position that defined the movement in the early twentieth century. See Hall, *William Louis Poteat*, 156.

80. See Gerald W. Johnson, "Men Are Fighting Over Baggage," *Alumni Review*, June 1925, Poteat Papers, box 5. Johnson graduated from Wake Forest College in 1910 and established himself as a respected journalist in North Carolina, first in Thomasville and

Lexington, North Carolina, and eventually at the *Greensboro Daily News* from approximately 1913 to 1924. Thereafter he became a professor of journalism at the University of North Carolina. Johnson later left North Carolina for Baltimore, Maryland, to work for the *Baltimore Evening Sun* and the *Baltimore Sun*, where he worked alongside Henry L. Mencken. For Johnson's relationship with Mencken see Johnson's foreword to Fred Hobson, *Serpent in Eden: H. L. Mencken and the South* (Louisiana State University, 1978). For the best secondary source on Johnson see Vincent Fitzpatrick, *Gerald W. Johnson: From Southern Liberal to National Conscience* (Louisiana State University Press, 2002).

81. Johnson was one of the many Wake Forest alumni who essentially idolized Poteat, so one might expect some embellishment in his account. But Johnson also had a reputation for journalistic integrity. Although Johnson used exuberant language the details of his account seem to be reliable. For the best example of Johnson's admiration of Poteat see Johnson, "Billy With the Red Necktie."

82. Poteat, "The McNair Lectures University of North Carolina May, 1925," Notebook, Poteat Papers, box 8, folder 944.

83. Johnson, "Men Are Fighting Over Baggage."

84. Johnson, "Men Are Fighting Over Baggage."

85. Johnson, "Men Are Fighting Over Baggage." See also Poteat, *Can a Man Be a Christian To-day?*, 35–36, 59–62.

86. Johnson, "Men Are Fighting Over Baggage." Edwin Mims also recognized the apologetic motivation behind Poteat's work. See Mims, *The Advancing South*, 308–9.

87. Johnson, "Men Are Fighting Over Baggage." See also Poteat, *Can a Man Be a Christian To-day?*, 4.

88. See William T. Couch to William L. Poteat, August 25 and December 9, 1925, Poteat Papers, Box 5, folder 551. A receipt from April 25, 1933, read that the book had sold 3,368 copies by March 31, 1933. See Receipt, "Report of Sales and Free Copies, Poteat: Can a Man Be a Christian Today," April 25, 1933, Poteat Papers, box 5. See also Hall, *William Louis Poteat*, 151. Hall argued that conservative opposition hindered Couch from publishing a second edition as he had desired.

89. *Biblical Recorder*, July 1, 15, 29, and August 5, 1925.

90. Joseph Alling to William L. Poteat, February 28, 1935, Poteat Papers, box 1.

91. Alling to Poteat, February 28, 1935, Poteat Papers, box 1. Alling quoted *Can a Man Be a Christian To-day?*, 70–71.

92. See "Note" in Poteat, *The Way of Victory*. For Hall's analysis of this work see Hall, *William Louis Poteat*, 172–73.

93. See especially Poteat, *Way of Victory*, 34–36.

94. See especially, Poteat *Way of Victory*, 38–41.

95. I explore Poteat's theology of social redemption later in this chapter and more extensively in chapter 5.

96. The theme of kingdom was prominent in the Bible and consequently held a noteworthy position in theological reflection throughout Christian history. However from the 1880s through 1930s theological liberals in America took a heightened interest in the theology of the kingdom as social gospel impulses infused liberal Protestantism and to some extent American Protestantism generally.

97. "Eschaton," in Christian theology, refers to the end of this present world. For background on the kingdom impulse of early evangelicalism in America see Thomas S. Kidd, *The Great Awakening: The Roots of Evangelical Christianity in Colonial America*

(Yale University Press, 2007); and Thomas S. Kidd, *George Whitefield: America's Spiritual Founding Father* (Yale University Press, 2014). The postmillennial kingdom impulse of the Puritans, the forerunners of evangelicalism, is well known, but as traditional postmillennialists they expected a supernatural work of God to consummate the kingdom and establish the eternal new heavens and new earth. See David D. Hall, *A Reforming People: Puritanism and the Transformation of Public Life in New England* (Alfred A. Knopf, 2011).

98. For a source on America's Progressive Era see Michael McGerr, *A Fierce Discontent: The Rise and Fall of the Progressive Movement in America* (Oxford University Press, 2003). For progressivism in the South see Dewey W. Grantham, *Southern Progressivism: The Reconciliation of Progress and Tradition* (University of Tennessee Press, 1983); and William A. Link, *The Paradox of Southern Progressivism, 1880–1930* (University of North Carolina Press, 1992). For Poteat as a progressive reformer see Hall, *William Louis Poteat.* Hall rightly concluded, "As historians have belatedly acknowledged, the American South participated actively in all aspects of the Progressive movement during the late nineteenth and early twentieth centuries." And he cited Poteat's North Carolina as "one of the states most involved in reform activities." See Hall, *William Louis Poteat,* 60.

99. Albrecht Ritschl defined the kingdom as "the uninterrupted reciprocation of action springing from the motive of love—a Kingdom in which all are knit together in union with everyone who can show the marks of a neighbor; further, it is that union of men in which all goods are appropriated in their proper subordination to the highest good." Ritschl, *The Christian Doctrine of Justification and Reconciliation*, 334–35.

100. William L. Poteat, "Putting the Kingdom First," 7–8, Pamphlet, Address to Southern Baptist Laymen's Convention, Chattanooga, TN, February 6, 1913, Poteat Papers, box 9, folder 1021.

101. Poteat, "Putting the Kingdom First," 12.

102. Poteat, "Putting the Kingdom First," 15. He said, "The call of the Kingdom is a call from the endless logo machines which have absorbed too much of Christian energy these centuries. It is a call from the battle of Christian sect against Christian sect."

103. Poteat, "Putting the Kingdom First," 17–18.

104. See Matt. 3:2, 4:17; Mark 1:15.

105. Poteat, "Putting the Kingdom First," 19.

106. William L. Poteat, "The Coming Kingdom," *Biblical Recorder*, November 12, 1930, 3.

107. Matthew Avery Sutton has argued that American evangelicals grew to make premillennial eschatology the center of their theology and single-mindedly stressed an otherworldly kingdom theology. Although he overlooked some of the nuances of evangelical eschatology he rightly identified evangelicals' focus on the kingdom's future realization and their preoccupation with the second coming of Christ for the kingdom's consummation. See Matthew A. Sutton, *American Apocalypse: A History of Modern Evangelicalism* (Harvard University Press, 2014).

108. For a concise survey of Christian eschatology since the Protestant Reformation see Michael Horton, "Eschatology," in *Mapping Modern Theology: A Thematic and Historical Introduction*, ed. Kelly M. Kapic, and Bruce L. McCormick (Baker, 2012), 377–403. Randal Hall concluded similarly and described Poteat's "post-millennial theological declaration that contrasted with the argument of many religious conservatives who believed that the transformation of earthly society would come only after a physical second coming of Jesus." Hall, *William Louis Poteat*, 65.

109. John W. Phillips, "The Kingdom." Sermon, Southern Baptist Convention, May 13, 1931, Mobile, AL, Southern Baptist Convention Sermon Collection, Southern Baptist Historical Library and Archives, Nashville, TN.

110. Phillips, "The Kingdom," 1.

111. Phillips, "The Kingdom," 2. He added, "Churchmen can be as parochial and exclusive as were the Pharisees, but kingdom men must be all-inclusive as the uttermost reach of the finger tips of God's love."

112. Phillips, "The Kingdom," 3. The Old Testament cultic system met his displeasure, but free spirit of the prophets as he perceived of them better fit his vision for religion.

113. Phillips, "The Kingdom," 11. Additionally "as descendants of the priests we may be satisfied by adding numbers to our churches and dollars to its treasury, but as sons of the prophets, we shall be satisfied with nothing less than the personal and social righteousness of the sermon on the mount." Phillips, "The Kingdom," 13.

114. Phillips, "The Kingdom," 5.

115. Phillips, "The Kingdom," 6.

116. Phillips, "The Kingdom," 9.

117. Phillips, "The Kingdom," 11.

118. Phillips was elected vice president of the convention in 1932. See Flynt, *Alabama Baptists*, 262.

119. James Chapman, "Doctor Alfred J. Dickinson," 10–12, Biographical Account. Chapman Papers, Southern Baptist Historical Library and Archives, Nashville, TN. Chapman gathered this account shortly after Dickinson's death from his own personal knowledge of Dickinson and from Dickinson's family.

120. Charles S. Gardner, "Thy Kingdom Come," 1, Sermon, Southern Baptist Convention, May 17, 1911, Jacksonville, FL, Southern Baptist Convention Sermon Collection, Southern Baptist Historical Library and Archives, Nashville, TN. Gardner made several of the same points as Dickinson and Phillips, but he, like Edgar Y. Mullins, was generally more conservative and retained the main contours of Christian orthodoxy.

121. Chapman, "Doctor Alfred J. Dickinson," 16.

122. Chapman, "Doctor Alfred J. Dickinson," 18. Chapman said, "In 1918 he laid down his official toga, and went out to minister to the soldiers as Y.M.C.A. Secretary at Camp Sheridan, Montgomery, Alabama, and afterward to devote his remaining days to a notable service of preaching the gospel of health as platform speaker under the United States Department of Health."

123. Alfred J. Dickinson, "The Religion of the Risen Lord," 12, sermon, Southern Baptist Convention, May 1907, Richmond, VA, Southern Baptist Convention Sermon Collection, Southern Baptist Historical Library and Archives, Nashville, TN.

124. "Social Christianity" is the term commonly used by scholars to describe the more decidedly socially oriented Christianity of late-nineteenth-century and early-twentieth-century America. This is not entirely synonymous with the social gospel movement although social-gospel Christianity was a part of this larger movement in American Protestantism toward a more energetic social activism. See John L. Eighmy, *Churches in Cultural Captivity: A History of Social Attitudes of Southern Baptists*, 2nd ed. (University of Tennessee Press, 1987); and Keith Harper, *Quality of Mercy: Southern Baptists and Social Christianity, 1890–1920* (University of Alabama Press, 1996). For a work that explores the role of Southern Baptist women in this movement see Carol C. Holcomb, *Home Without Walls: Southern Baptist Women and Social Reform in the Progressive Era* (University of Alabama

Press, 2020). For a broader survey of social Christianity see Paul T. Phillips, *A Kingdom on Earth: Anglo-American Social Christianity, 1880–1940* (Pennsylvania State University Press, 1995). Phillips rightly argued that the movement primarily advanced over the sixty-year period from 1880 to 1940.

125. Poteat, *The Way of Victory*, 29.

126. Poteat, *The Way of Victory*, 36.

127. Poteat, *The Way of Victory*, 33.

128. Poteat, *The Way of Victory*, 39.

129. Poteat, *Can a Man Be a Christian To-day?*, 107–8.

130. Poteat, *The Way of Victory*, 40.

131. Poteat, *The Way of Victory*, 41. He clarified, "I am not saying that this great social ideal was wholly misconceived or forgotten by our predecessors but that modern conditions have released it in unwonted clearness and power."

132. Poteat, *The Way of Victory*, 44.

133. Poteat, *The Way of Victory*, 45. Poteat cited Luke 4:18–21, in which Jesus read Isaiah 61:1–2 and declared himself its fulfillment as a deliverer. Poteat seemed to apply the theme of deliverance to the Christian mission to redeem society.

134. Poteat, *The Way of Victory*, 60–81.

135. Poteat, *The Way of Victory*, 81–82.

136. Hall, *William Louis Poteat*, 102.

137. Gary Dorrien argued that Ritschl's theology provided a theological foundation for America's social gospel movement. Dorrien, *Kantian Reason and Hegelian Spirit*, 320. Roger Olson contended: "The American social gospel movement represented the most practical and concrete expression of classical liberal theology. Most of its underlying theological methods and themes go back to Ritschl, but it combined them with an evangelical fervor for social reform absent in most European liberal theology." Olson, *The Journey of Modern Theology*, 166. Although not the first figure in the movement the Baptist Walter Rauschenbusch became the movement's leading figure. For a secondary source on Rauschenbusch see Christopher H. Evans, *The Kingdom is Always but Coming: A Life of Walter Rauschenbusch* (Eerdmans, 2004). For Rauschenbusch's key works see *Christianity and Social Crisis* and *A Theology for the Social Gospel*. For a source on the history of the social gospel see Christopher H. Evans, *The Social Gospel in American Religion: A History* (New York University Press, 2017). See also Christopher H. Evans, "Walter Rauschenbusch and the Second Coming: The Social Gospel as Baptist History," in *Through a Glass Darkly: Contested Notions of Baptist Identity*, ed. Keith Harper (University of Alabama Press, 2012), 145–71. Evans argued that Rauschenbusch's social theology was not incidental to his Baptist heritage but rather inspired by it, particularly Baptists' emphasis on liberty and the democratic spirit.

138. For sources on the social gospel among Southern Baptists see Paul Harvey, "Southern Baptists and the Social Gospel: White Religious Progressivism in the South, 1900–1925," *Fides Et Historia* (January 1995): 59–77; and Wayne Flynt, "Not an Island Unto Itself: Southern Baptists and the New Theological Trends (Liberalism, Ecumenism, and the Social Gospel, 1890–1940)," *American Baptist Quarterly* (June 2003): 158–79. In *Alabama Baptists* Wayne Flynt rightly challenged C. Vann Woodward's argument in *Origins of the New South* that the major trends of American religion—modernism, ecumenism, and the social gospel—bypassed the South: "Despite Woodward's standing as the most influential American historian of the twentieth century, on this judgment he was incorrect." Flynt, *Alabama Baptists*, 251. Flynt concluded that "the almost total lack of support for organic

church union [ecumenism] among Alabama Baptists provided the single most compelling support for C. Vann Woodward's thesis that the three major trends of early twentieth-century American Christianity passed by the South. Strong support for the application of Christian principles to social problems constituted the greatest exception to his argument." Although ecumenism had little to no constituency in a Deep South state like Alabama, the social gospel did.

139. Thomas S. Kidd and Barry Hankins, *Baptists in America: A History* (Oxford University Press, 2015), 171. For the best source on the New South see Ayers, *The Promise of the New South*. See also C. Vann Woodward's classic work, *Origins of the New South*.

140. Kidd and Hankins, *Baptists in America*, 171. James Thompson agreed and argued that Gwaltney "took stances similar to those of the Northern Social Gospelers." Thompson, *Tried As By Fire*, 33. Wayne Flynt examined the background of Gwaltney's theology: "Gwaltney came to the social gospel through his own pastoral experiences. His first pastorate in Alabama was at Prattville Baptist Church, a congregation consisting of businesspeople, farmers, and workers from Continental Gin Company and the city's cotton mills." Flynt, *Alabama Baptists*, 276.

141. William L. Poteat, Diary, October 11, 1896, Poteat Papers, box 4, folder 475. Gwaltney remained on the more conservative side of the spectrum of theological liberalism, but he did embrace the modernist framework for revising Christianity in light of modernity, for instance by embracing the social gospel. For Gwaltney's autobiography see Gwaltney, *Forty of the Twentieth*. See also a collection of his sermons, Leslie L. Gwaltney, *Christ and Our Liberties* (Birmingham Printing Company, 1937).

142. Sources on Gaines are few and mainly the minutes of the Georgia Social Service Commission and other minutes from the Georgia Baptist Convention from 1911 to 1937. He was an attorney in Atlanta, Georgia, and member of Capitol Avenue Baptist Church. For a secondary source see Eighmy, *Churches in Cultural Captivity*, 95, 111, 117–19, 122. William Link called Atlanta the "cradle of the New South" and noted its place as a leading city of the New South. See William A. Link, *Atlanta: Cradle of the New South* (University of North Carolina Press, 2013).

143. Eighmy, *Churches in Cultural Captivity*, 111.

144. For a work that examines the influence of the social gospel at Southern Baptist Theological Seminary see Walters, "Though the Heavens Fall": Liberal Theology and the Southern Baptist Theological Seminary, 1894–1925."

145. Edwin C. Dargan, *Society, Kingdom, and Church* (American Baptist Publication Society, 1907).

146. Edwin C. Dargan to Charles S. Gardner, January 26, 1921.

147. Dargan to Gardner, January 26, 1921.

148. See Hall, *William Louis Poteat*, 60–102.

149. Eighmy, *Churches in Cultural Captivity*, 156.

150. For a clear articulation of his views see Edwin M. Poteat Jr., *Jesus and the Liberal Mind* (Judson Press, 1934). He was a two-time graduate of South Carolina Baptists' Furman University (1912 and 1913), where his father was president for a time, and of Southern Baptists Theological Seminary in Louisville, Kentucky (1916).

151. Eighmy, *Churches in Cultural Captivity*, 155. See Das K. Barnett, "The New Theological Frontiers for Southern Baptists," *Review and Expositor* 38 (July 1941): 264–76. His magazine *Christian Frontiers* was a relatively brief example of the more aggressive form of theological liberalism that developed in the years immediately after William Poteat.

Eighmy rightly noted, "Its causes were too far advanced to develop strong support from a basically conservative denomination. The journal's circulation was never very large, and financial difficulty forced the suspension of publication after three years." Eighmy, *Churches in Cultural Captivity*, 156.

152. Randal Hall rightly observed the relative freedom that existed but also the great care that was required of liberal leaders: "In this era of unsettling social and economic conflict, new ideas such as evolution and critical biblical study could be offered as options for a time. Liberal thought gained relatively few followers, but the comparative freedom with which intellectual ideas were presented reveals at least a moment of possibility when somewhat more cosmopolitan theological and scientific beliefs were options for southern Victorians." Hall, *William Louis Poteat*, 22.

153. For a substantial treatment of Poteat's social activity see Hall, *William Louis Poteat*, 60–102. See also Suzanne C. Linder, *William Louis Poteat: Prophet of Progress* (University of North Carolina Press, 1966), 78–103.

154. Henry D. Baker to William L. Poteat, February 10, 1934.

155. J. W. Beaton to William L. Poteat, May 24, 1928, Poteat Papers, box 1.

156. See correspondence with Arthur J. Barton of the Social Service Commission, Poteat Papers, box 1, folder 20. See, especially, Arthur J. Barton to William L. Poteat, March 10, 1932. See also Minutes of the Social Service Commission, August 18, 1937. It was signed by W. W. Gaines, secretary. See Poteat Papers, box 2, folder 125.

157. The orphanage published a paper called *Charity and Children*, edited by Archibald Johnson. See Poteat Papers, box 2, folder 202.

158. See correspondence with Charles G. Rose in Poteat Papers, box 3, folder 357.

159. For the best source on the commission see Ann Wells Ellis, *The Commission on Interracial Cooperation, 1919–1944: Its Activities and Results* (PhD diss., Georgia State University, 1975).

160. See his manifesto for temperance, William L. Poteat, *Stop-Light* (Broadman Press, 1935). He was a member of the Anti-Saloon League of America, based in Westerville, OH. See William L. Poteat, personal receipts from Anti-Saloon League, Poteat Papers, box 1.

161. Hall, *William Louis Poteat*, 60. Hall argued that Poteat's social Christianity was limited, apparently due to Poteat's emphasis on individuals as the agents for social change. However Poteat's lifetime of energetic service demonstrated this was anything but an excuse for lethargy. Hall seemed strangely underappreciative of Poteat's contribution to social reform. Also Poteat's commitment to eugenics demonstrated that he did not always place the individual before the larger social good as he perceived of it. See Hall, *William Louis Poteat*, 80–81.

162. Mims, *The Advancing South*, 280.

CHAPTER FOUR: THE MODERN CULTURE OF REFINEMENT AND PIOUS RESPECTABILITY

1. Gary Dorrien, *Kantian Reason and Hegelian Spirit: The Idealistic Logic of Modern Theology* (Wiley-Blackwell, 2012), 5.

2. See Friedrich Schleiermacher, *On Religion: Speeches to Its Cultured Despisers*, trans. Richard Crouter (1988; repr., Cambridge University Press, 2003).

3. Dorrien, *Kantian Reason and Hegelian Spirit*, 5.

4. The South's new middle class had a formative influence on the modern South. For sources on the history of professionalization and the middle class in America see

Bruce A. Kimball, *The "True Professional Ideal" in America: A History* (1992; repr., Rowman & Littlefield Publishers, 1995); and Burton J. Bledstein, *The Culture of Professionalism: The Middle Class and the Development of Higher Education in America* (W. W. Norton & Co., 1978). Between the two main subgroups within the middle class, the professionals and businesspeople, Bledstein argued that "the most emphatically middle-class man was the professional." See Bledstein, *The Culture of Professionalism*, ix. See also Bernard Lightman and Bennett Zon, eds. *Victorian Culture and the Origin of Disciplines* (Routledge, 2019). For the best source on the history of a Southern middle class see Daniel Wells and Jennifer R. Green, eds. *The Southern Middle Class in the Long Nineteenth Century* (Louisiana State University Press, 2011). For a carefully nuanced essay about defining the middle class and the relative diversity within the South's middle class see Martin Ruef, "The Human and Financial Capital of the Southern Middle Class, 1850–1900," in *The Southern Middle Class in the Long Nineteenth Century*, 202–24.

5. Burton Bledstein's analysis of the American middle class largely held true for the emerging middle class of the New South. He defined it as a culture that was grounded in a set of values, tastes, and habits of thought. See Bledstein, *The Culture of Professionalism.* Don Doyle similarly argued that the new class was "identifiable not simply by the wealth of its members but also by the emblems of a common culture and style of life." He explained, "In its homes and suburban neighborhoods, in its exclusive clubs and social rituals, and in its cultural institutions, the New South's urban upper class assumed its modern form for the first time." See Don H. Doyle, *New Men, New Cities, New South: Atlanta, Nashville, Charleston, Mobile, 1860–1910* (University of North Carolina Press, 1990), 225.

6. For an exploration of Victorian culture in American life see Thomas J. Schlereth, *Victorian America: Transformations in Everyday Life* (Harper Collins, 1991).

7. For an insightful work on the place of the "bourgeoisie" in modern society and in modern thought see Steven B. Smith, *Modernity and Its Discontents: Making and Unmaking the Bourgeois from Machiavelli to Bellow* (Yale University Press, 2016). See especially Smith, *Modernity and Its Discontents*, 16–20. Smith argued that modern "civilization had produced a new kind of human being, the bourgeois, who was polite, civil, and refined but also craven, false, and insincere." Smith, *Modernity and Its Discontents*, 16.

8. Edwin Mims, *The Advancing South: Stories of Progress and Reaction* (Doubleday, Page, and Co., 1926), vii–viii.

9. Mims, *The Advancing South*, 315.

10. Mims, *The Advancing South*, 316.

11. Michael O'Brien, *The Idea of the American South, 1920–1941* (Johns Hopkins University, 1979), 9. O'Brien characterized Mims's work as a study of the liberalizing forces that were driven by the South's middle class. O'Brien argued that Virginius Dabney's work aimed for the same end. See O'Brien, *The Idea of the American South*, 8–9. For Dabney's work, which arrived a few years after Mims's see Virginius Dabney, *Liberalism in the South* (University of North Carolina Press, 1932).

12. For the significance of cities in the New South see Doyle, *New Men, New Cities, New South.* For bourgeois culture in New South cities see Doyle, *New Men, New Cities, New South*, 189–225.

13. Doyle, *New Men, New Cities, New South*, 222.

14. Mims, *The Advancing South*, 144.

15. Mims, *The Advancing South*, 114–15.

16. Mims, *The Advancing South*, 141. Mims was referencing Robert Winston who was an 1879 graduate of the University of North Carolina. He became a lawyer, judge, and well-respected author. For a source on Winston see Samuel A. Ashe, ed., *Biographical History of North Carolina: From Colonial Times to the Present*, vol. 2 (Charles Van Noppen, 1905).

17. Alfred J. Dickinson, *Alabama Baptist*, September 6, 1916, 11. See also John H. Burrows, "The Great Disturber: The Social Philosophy and Theology of Alfred James Dickinson." (MA thesis, Samford University, 1970), 53–54.

18. Randal L. Hall, *William Louis Poteat: A Leader of the Progressive-Era South* (University of Kentucky Press, 2000), 4.

19. See Wilbur J. Cash, "The Mind of the South," *The American Mercury*, October 1929, in Joseph L. Morrison, *W. J. Cash: Southern Prophet, A Biography and Reader* (Alfred A. Knopf, 1967), 197. Cash expanded this article into his well-known book, *The Mind of the South,* in 1941. Cash's later biographer, Bruce Clayton, recognized Poteat's vision, "In President Poteat Wake Forest had a courageous exemplar of New South liberalism—that idealistic, perhaps even sentimental notion that social change could be effected by modern middle-class reformers." See Bruce Clayton, *W. J. Cash: A Life* (Louisiana State University Press, 1991), 27.

20. Dabney, *Liberalism in the South*, 301.

21. For the original "four great traditional professions" of theology, law, medicine, and education that had defined Western civilization since the Middle Ages and American society since the seventeenth century see Kimball, *The "True Professional Ideal" in America*, 6–9, 99, 187. For the development of education as a notable profession in the United States and science as a respected profession see Kimball, *The "True Professional Ideal" in America*, 198–300. Education and science were closely related because educational institutions became the means of transmission of scientific knowledge. Kimball argued that schools, especially colleges and universities, became the institutional loci for science just as churches were the institutional loci of religion. See Kimball, *The "True Professional Ideal" in America*, 213–15. For a source on the history of science see Bernard Lightman, ed. *A Companion to the History of Science* (Wiley-Blackwell, 2019). For the role of Darwin's theory of evolution in the rise of modern science see Peter J. Bowler, *Evolution: The History of an Idea,* 25th anniversary ed. (University of California Press, 2009).

22. For the general development of science in American life see Kimball, *The "True Professional Ideal" in America*, 211–12. Kimball argued in reference to American life in general, "Science thus gained authority over other domains of intellectual life in the second half of the nineteenth century." See also Hall, *William Louis Poteat*, 39.

23. For the new authority given to the "man of science" see Kimball, *The "True Professional Ideal" in America*, 203.

24. Poteat kept a busy schedule of speaking engagements. For a record of an address at Duke University see Frederick Archer to William L. Poteat, February 13, 1928, Poteat Papers, box 1, Z. Smith Reynolds Library Archives, Wake Forest University, Winston-Salem, NC. For Stetson University in Deland, Florida see W. S. Allen to William L. Poteat, April 8, 1937, Poteat Papers, box 1. For an invitation to give the opening address for convocation as the University of North Carolina see Western Union message from Francis F. Bradshaw to William L. Poteat, no date, Poteat Papers, box 1, folder 15. For an invitation to give a commencement address at the Clemson Agricultural College see E. W. Sikes to William L.

Poteat, November 26, 1928, Poteat Papers, box 1. For one of several addresses at Tuskegee Normal and Industrial Institute in Alabama see Robert R. Morton to William L. Poteat, January 2, 1929, Poteat Papers. For an example of an address at a church see Pamphlet, Alameda Baptist Church, Sunday, January 21, 1934, Poteat Papers, box 1. For an address on race see William L. Poteat, *Christ and Race*, Baptist State Convention of North Carolina, Raleigh, NC, 1938, Poteat Papers, box 7, folder 774. See the recording on cassette tape in Poteat Papers, box 7, folder 794. For his work on temperance see William L. Poteat, *Stop-Light* (Broadman Press, 1935). He was also a member of the Anti-Saloon League of America, based in Westerville, OH. See William L. Poteat, personal receipts from Anti-Saloon League, Poteat Papers, box 1. For Poteat's activity in social issues see Hall, *William Louis Poteat*, 60–102; and Suzanne C. Linder, *William Louis Poteat: Prophet of Progress* (University of North Carolina Press, 1966), 78–103.

25. For Poteat's personal library see William L. Poteat, Manuscript, "List of Books from the Library of Dr. William Louis Poteat Given to Wake Forest College," Poteat Papers, box 7, folder 727. For a sample of his reading regimen see William L. Poteat, Diary, May 6, 1896–February 16, 1897, Poteat Papers, box 4, folder 475. He read the Greek and Roman classics, philosophical works, ethics, modern critical theological works, the Bible, and poetry. For Poteat's affection for poetry and literature see Hall, *William Louis Poteat*, 45–46.

26. His honorary doctorate degrees included: LLD, Baylor University, 1905; LLD, University of North Carolina, 1906; LLD, Brown University, 1927; LLD, Duke University, 1932; LittD., Mercer University, 1933. Poteat's doctoral hoods are preserved in his collection at the Z. Smith Reynolds Library Archives, Wake Forest University, Winston-Salem, NC.

27. England's Queen Victoria reigned from 1837 to 1901, and this roughly defined the Victorian era. For Victorian culture in American life see Schlereth, *Victorian America: Transformations in Everyday Life, 1876–1915*. For a work on the Victorian influence on Southern culture, particularly evidenced by the new Southern literature see Daniel J. Singal, *The War Within: From Victorian to Modernist Thought in the South, 1919–1945* (University of North Carolina Press, 1982).

28. For an insightful exploration of the influence of Victorian culture on Christian theology see Timothy Larsen, *Contested Christianity: The Political and Social Contexts of Victorian Theology* (Baylor University Press, 2004); and Timothy Larson, *Crisis of Doubt: Honest Faith in Nineteenth-Century England* (Oxford University Press, 2006). Larson challenged the argument that the Victorian era was largely characterized by religious apostasy.

29. Hall, *William Louis Poteat*, 39.

30. For information on Poteat's domestic life with his family see Poteat, Diary, May 6, 1896–February 16, 1897. See also the large collection of correspondence with his wife and children, Poteat Papers, box 1.

31. Hall, *William Louis Poteat*, 41.

32. See Hall, *William Louis Poteat*, 23–24. For the best source on the history of American higher education see John R. Thelin, *A History of American Higher Education*, 3rd ed. (Johns Hopkins University Press, 2019).

33. William L. Poteat, "Christianity and Enlightenment," Pamphlet, Address to Baptist State Convention of North Carolina, December 1922, Winston-Salem, NC, James P. Boyce Library and Archives, Southern Baptist Theological Seminary, Louisville, KY.

34. See William L. Poteat, *The New Peace: Lectures on Science and Religion* (Gorman Press, 1915), 43.

35. For a work that explores scientific advancement in the Victorian era see Bernard Lightman, *Victorian Science in Context* (University of Chicago Press, 1997).

36. In chapter 7 I explore Poteat's advocacy of Darwinian evolution and the religious controversies that arose in the 1920s as well as his role in the defeat of North Carolina's Poole bill, which forged a path for North Carolina that contrasted with its neighboring state of Tennessee, known for its anti-evolution legislation and the Scopes trial that challenged it.

37. Gary Dorrien, *The Making of American Liberal Theology: Imagining Progressive Religion, 1805–1900* (Westminster John Knox, 2001), 401.

38. Doyle, *New Men, New Cities, New South*, 96.

39. Doyle, *New Men, New Cities, New South*, 96–98.

40. See Gerald W. Johnson, "'The Future and Dr. Poteat': Memorial Address at the Wake Forest College Commencement," *Biblical Recorder*, June 29, 1938, Clipping, Poteat Papers, box 4. For the best source on Johnson see Vincent Fitzpatrick, *Gerald W. Johnson: From Southern Liberal to National Conscience* (Louisiana State University Press, 2002).

41. Johnson, "'The Future and Dr. Poteat': Memorial Address at the Wake Forest College Commencement." *Biblical Recorder*, June 29, 1938.

42. Thomas T. Martin, *Three Fatal Teachings* (n.p., 1920), 13.

43. George W. Paschal, "The Case for Dr. Poteat," in Martin, *Three Fatal Teachings*, 8. He said, "I am certain that in one point I am representing practically everybody in North Carolina and especially those who are or have been in any way connected with Wake Forest College."

44. Paschal, "The Case for Dr. Poteat," in Martin, *Three Fatal Teachings*, 9.

45. Martin, *Three Fatal Teachings*, 15. For a source on Crawford Toy, a pioneering Southern Baptist liberal, see Michael C. Parsons, *Crawford Howell Toy: The Man, the Scholar, the Teacher* (Mercer University Press, 2019). For Bushnell see Robert B. Mullin, *The Puritan as Yankee: A Life of Horace Bushnell* (Eerdmans, 2002).

46. O. T. Binkley to William L. Poteat, November 8, 1937, Poteat Papers. For a source on Binkley see George W. Paschal, *History of Wake Forest College* (Edwards & Broughton, 1943), 3:77–79.

47. T. A. Avera to William L. Poteat, April 16, 1935, Poteat Papers.

48. George W. Blount to William L. Poteat, July 9, 1932, Poteat Papers, box 1.

49. See Clayton, *W. J. Cash*, 71.

50. Fitzpatrick, *Gerald W. Johnson*, xii, 14, 20–21. Fitzpatrick argued, "In the end, his religion was his art, and his devotion his utter dedication to this craft." For Johnson's veneration of Poteat see Johnson, "'The Future and Dr. Poteat': Memorial Address at the Wake Forest College Commencement." *Biblical Recorder*, June 29, 1938.

51. A broad movement to "liberalize" Southern society gained traction in the early twentieth century, particularly in regions where New South ideology had the greatest influence. The elite of Southern society used this terminology to refer to a personal sense of enlightenment in the context of progressive movements in education, politics, society, and religion. In religion it referred especially to freedom from theological orthodoxy or doctrinal dogma. Poteat called one of his study trips "liberalizing," meaning it was intellectually stimulating and enlightening. See William L. Poteat to Stantford Martin, December 16, 1927, Poteat Papers, box 2, folder 258, Z. Smith Reynolds Library Archives, Wake Forest University, Winston-Salem, NC. Poteat praised Edwin Mims's *The Advancing South* as a history of "the liberal movements in the South." Virginius Dabney turned to Poteat for help when he wrote his classic *Liberalism in the South* in the early 1930s. In these letters,

Poteat summarized the history of liberal movements in the South as well as his own sense of his contribution. See Letter, Virginius Dabney to William L. Poteat, May 19, 1931; Letter, William L. Poteat to Virginius Dabney, June 15, 1931; and Letter, Virginius Dabney to William L. Poteat, June 22, 1931, Poteat Papers, box 1, folder 83. Wilbur J. Cash's *The Mind of the South* also surveyed the liberal movements in the South, of which Cash himself was a significant part as an author and newspaper editor at the *Charlotte Observer*. See Wilbur J. Cash, *The Mind of the South* (Alfred A. Knopf, 1941). For a biography of Cash see Clayton, *W. J. Cash*. For a source on the New South see Edward Ayers, *The Promise of the New South: Life After Reconstruction*, 15th anniversary ed. (Oxford University Press, 2007). For the classic source see C. Vann Woodward, *Origins of the New South, 1877–1913* (1951; repr., Louisiana State University Press, 1971). For the central role of the Bible in the liberal-conservative divide in evangelicalism see David W. Bebbington, *Evangelicalism in Modern Britain: A History from the 1730s to the 1980s* (Routledge, 1989), 14: "Attitudes to the Bible drew apart until, in the wake of the First World War, the Evangelical world divided into conservatives and liberals primarily on that issue. The importance attributed by Evangelicals to the Bible eventually led to something approaching schism in their ranks."

52. Alfred J. Dickinson, "The Problem of Modernism among Baptists," *Alabama Baptist*, February 5, 1913. For a conservative response to Dickinson's article see *Alabama Baptist*, February 19, 1913, 3. Dickinson fired back in the *Alabama Baptist*, February 26, 1913. That Dickinson had the liberty to express and defend his views suggests the level of relative freedom that theological liberals enjoyed, even in a stereotypically conservative state like Alabama. For a secondary source on Dickinson see John H. Burrows, "The Great Disturber: The Social Philosophy and Theology of Alfred James Dickinson." (MA thesis, Samford University, 1970).

53. Eugene Lankford to William L. Poteat, January 14, 1929, Poteat Papers, box 2, folder 225. Lankford said about Poteat's liberal view of religion, "I believe our views on this subject run closely together." And Lankford assured Poteat of his "high esteem."

54. Eugene Lankford to William L. Poteat, April 1929, Poteat Papers, box 2, folder 225.

55. Eugene Lankford to William L. Poteat, April 1929, Poteat Papers, box 2, folder 225.

56. William L. Poteat to Eugene Lankford, April 2, 1929, Poteat Papers, box 2, folder 225. The two seemed to exchange at least one other letter, but it is missing from the collection.

57. David Morgan to William L. Poteat, July 26, 1937, Poteat Papers, box 3, folder 272.

58. Rimmer was an itinerate Presbyterian fundamentalist preacher. Roger Schultz explained that Rimmer dedicated himself to challenging evolution and defending the traditional conception of the Bible. See Roger D. Schultz, "All Things Made New: The Evolving Fundamentalism of Harry Rimmer, 1890–1952" (PhD diss., University of Arkansas Press, 1989).

59. David Morgan to William L. Poteat, July 26, 1937, Poteat Papers, box 3, folder 272.

60. William L. Poteat to David Morgan, July 28, 1937, Poteat Papers, box 3, folder 272.

61. William L. Poteat, *Can a Man Be a Christian To-day?* (Oxford University Press and University of North Carolina Press, 1925), 69–70. Poteat had already lent Morgan his

personal copy of Harry Emerson Fosdick's *Modern Use of the Bible*, which Morgan had found helpful. See William L. Poteat to David Morgan, July 28, 1937, Poteat Papers, box 3, folder 272.

62. David Morgan to William L. Poteat, July 31, 1937, Poteat Papers, box 3, folder 272.

63. William L. Poteat to Walter Lippmann, May 13, 1929, Poteat Papers, box 2, folder 244. By "essentials and incidentals" he referred to what was essential to Christianity and those elements of organized Christianity that were incidental, having developed over the centuries as appendages to Christianity. Christian doctrines, for instance the Trinity and atonement, were incidentals, but Jesus and his kingdom message were essentials. Poteat stressed that theological modernism did not jeopardize the essentials of the faith. For Poteat's full treatment of this question see *Can a Man Be a Christian To-day?* For a source on Walter Lippmann see Ronald Steel, *Walter Lippmann and the American Century* (Routledge, 1999).

64. William L. Poteat to Walter Lippmann, May 13, 1929, Poteat Papers, box 2, folder 244. The two men seemed to be friends, not merely professional acquaintances. For a more intimate letter see William L. Poteat to Walter Lippmann, October 21, 1936, Poteat Papers, box 2, folder 244.

65. 2 Pet. 1:21. All references to the Bible are from the English Standard Version unless otherwise noted.

66. 1 Thess. 2:13.

67. Charles E. Hill rightly argued, "The Christian church did not so much construct a doctrine of Scripture as inherit one. It succeeded to its conception of the divinity and authority of Holy Scripture, one might say, bequeathed to it from the broad Jewish heritage in general." See Charles E. Hill, "The Truth Above Demonstration," in *The Enduring Authority of the Christian Scriptures*, ed. D. A. Carson (Eerdmans, 2016), 44.

68. See Hill, "The Truth Above Demonstration," in Carson, *The Enduring Authority*, 44–46. On the self-authenticating nature of Scripture, Hill surveyed early figures like Justin Martyr, whose introduction to the Hebrew Scriptures led him to believe in Christianity; Clement of Alexandria; Origen; and Eusebius. He clarified, "None of the Christian writers treated above found that faith in the teachings of Scripture impeded the robust and exacting employment of logic, historical study, philosophy, or any other tool of human erudition. For them, this view of Scripture provided the only sure foundation for intellectual endeavors of any kind. From Justin and his unnamed Christian teacher, to Clement, Origen, Gregory, and Augustine in our period, through the intellectual achievements of the Middle Ages, right up to Reformed Epistemology in the present, a Scripture-based Christianity has not avoided the encounter with non-Christian philosophies nor has it shirked a responsibility to 'lead every thought captive to Christ' (2 Cor 10:5) and to do the positive labor of ordering human thought in accordance with Scripture." Hill, "The Truth Above Demonstration," in Carson, ed. *The Enduring Authority*, 54.

69. For a work on Christians' views in the Middle Ages see Woodbridge, *Biblical Authority*, 45–48. Gerald Bray declared, "The authority of Scripture as divine revelation was uncontested during the Middle Ages." See Gerald Bray, *Biblical Interpretation: Past & Present* (InterVarsity, 1996), 145.

70. See also Robert Kolb, "The Bible in the Reformation and Protestant Orthodoxy," in Carson, ed. *The Enduring Authority*, 89–114.

71. Poteat, *Laboratory and Pulpit*, 45.

72. Before the modern era, Christians assumed biblical inspiration. By the late nineteenth century, the Enlightenment, biblical criticism, and the rise of theological liberalism challenged the idea that the very words of the Bible were revealed by supernatural means. For background see Daniel J. Treier, "Scripture and Hermeneutics," in *Mapping Modern Theology: A Thematic and Historical Introduction*, ed. Kelly M. Kapic and Bruce L. McCormick (Baker, 2012), 67–68; Olson, *The Journey of Modern Theology*; Michael C. Legaspi, *The Death of Scripture and the Rise of Biblical Studies* (Oxford, 2011); and Gertrude Himmelfarb, *The Roads to Modernity: The British, French, and American Enlightenments* (Vintage, 2004).

73. See Gregory A. Wills, *Southern Baptist Theological Seminary: 1859–2009* (Oxford University Press, 2009), 108–49. As Wills notes, Charles Briggs, Toy's contemporary, rightly identified him as the first professor in America to be fired over embracing liberal theology. However scholars have widely overlooked Toy's significance, just as they overlooked liberalism in the South generally. For Wills's statement see Wills, *Southern Baptist Theological Seminary,* 108. For Briggs see Charles A. Briggs, *General Introduction to the Study of Holy Scripture,* Scribner's 1899), 286. Poteat was a student at Wake Forest College when concerns were first raised over Toy's views. Poteat graduated the same month that James P. Boyce, Southern Seminary's president, asked Toy to give a full account of his position on the doctrine of inspiration in June 1877. Poteat did not comment on the Toy affair, but he likely viewed it in similar terms to the "Whitsitt incident," which he called a "heresy trial," likened to Servetus's condemnation at the hands of Calvin's Geneva. See William L. Poteat, Diary, May 10, 1896, Poteat Papers, box 4, folder 475; and Poteat, Diary, May 10, 1896. For Poteat's time in college see Charles F. Hudson, "The Authorized Personal Interview of Dr. W. L. Poteat," Poteat Papers, box 4, folder 532. For another perspective on Toy and his dismissal from Southern Seminary see Parsons, *Crawford Howell Toy*. For the Whitsitt controversy at Southern Baptist Theological Seminary see James H. Slatton, *W. H. Whitsitt: The Man and the Controversy* (Mercer University Press, 2009).

74. Manly was one of the four founding professors of Southern Baptist Theological Seminary but left in 1871 to become the president of Georgetown College, in Georgetown, Kentucky. Manly returned to Southern in 1879 to fill the vacancy created by Toy's departure. See Wills, *Southern Baptist Theological Seminary, 1859–2009*.

75. Basil Manly Jr., *The Bible Doctrine of Inspiration Explained and Vindicated* (1888; repr., Sprinkle Publications, 1985), 13.

76. Manly, *The Bible Doctrine of Inspiration Explained and Vindicated,* 26–28.

77. Manly, *The Bible Doctrine of Inspiration Explained and Vindicated,* 30.

78. Manly, *The Bible Doctrine of Inspiration Explained and Vindicated,* 116–21.

79. Manly, *The Bible Doctrine of Inspiration Explained and Vindicated,* 98–103.

80. Manly, *The Bible Doctrine of Inspiration Explained and Vindicated,* 113.

81. Benjamin B. Warfield, *The Inspiration and Authority of the Bible* (1948; repr., SBTS Press, 2014), 72. For a secondary source on the Old Princeton tradition see Gary Steward, *Princeton Seminary: 1812–1929* (P & R, 2014); Warfield, *The Inspiration and Authority of the Bible,* 107.

82. Warfield, *The Inspiration and Authority of the Bible,* 107. He argued, "This attitude of entire truth in every word of the Scriptures has been characteristic of the people of God from the very foundation of the church." He was aware of Enlightenment rationalism that had challenged the traditional view, as well as forms of mysticism, but the

formal teaching of the church had consistently held the Bible to be "an oracular book, in all its parts and elements, alike, of God, trustworthy in all its affirmations of every kind." Warfield, *The Inspiration and Authority of the Bible,* 112–14.

83. Warfield, *The Inspiration and Authority of the Bible,* 150.

84. Warfield, *The Inspiration and Authority of the Bible,* 150.

85. Warfield, *The Inspiration and Authority of the Bible,* 157–58.

86. Dagg's *Manual of Theology* was published in 1857, when Poteat was one year old. It was the first comprehensive systematic theology published by a Baptist in the United States.

87. John L. Dagg, *Manual of Theology and Church Order* (1857–1858; repr., Gano Books, 1982), 22. For Dagg's autobiography see *Autobiography of Rev. John L. Dagg,* in Dagg, *Manual of Theology and Church Order*, 1–53.

88. Dagg, *Manual of Theology and Church Order*, 22.

89. Dagg, *Manual of Theology and Church Order*, 23.

90. Dagg, *Manual of Theology and Church Order*, 23.

91. Dagg, *Manual of Theology and Church Order*, 24. Dagg sketched the history of the Bible's preservation and the science of textual criticism: Dagg, *Manual of Theology and Church Order*, 24–25. Basil Manly similarly argued, "We have no assurance, nor the slightest reason to suppose, that the supernatural guardianship which insured the correctness of the original record was continued and renewed every time anybody undertook to make a copy of it." Therein lies the importance of the science of textual criticism. See Manly, *The Bible Doctrine of Inspiration Explained and Vindicated,* 82.

92. Dagg, *Manual of Theology and Church Order*, 24–25. See also Dagg's "Origin and Authority of the Bible," given as an appendix in Dagg, *Manual of Theology and Church Order*, 26–42.

93. Poteat did not have these works in his personal library. He did however own two copies of Basil Manly Jr.'s *Approved Hymns for Baptist Churches,* 1892. See Manuscript, "List of Books from the Library of Dr. William Louis Poteat Given to Wake Forest College," Poteat Papers, box 7, folder 727, number 790.

94. Carl F. H. Henry, *God, Revelation, and Authority* (1976; repr., Crossway, 1999), 1:44.

95. Poteat, *Laboratory and Pulpit,* 46–47.

96. Manly, *The Bible Doctrine of Inspiration Explained and Vindicated,* 23–24. Poteat and his fellow Baptist liberals tended not to deny the biblical miracles outright. Instead they emphasized the spiritual or moral meaning of accounts that recorded miracles.

97. See George Burman Foster, *The Finality of the Christian Religion* (University of Chicago Press, 1906). See also Dorrien, *The Making of Modern Theology, 1900–1950,* 161–63. For an in-depth study of Foster see W. Creighton Peden, *From Authority Religion to Spirit Religion: An Intellectual Biography of George Burman Foster, 1857–1918* (University of Cambridge Press, 2013). William Newton Clarke came to a similar conclusion although with a less aggressive posture than did Foster. See Straub, *The Making of a Battle Royal*, 100–123. Clarke wrote the first systematic theology from the liberal perspective, originally published in 1894 for his students, but subsequently as William Newton Clarke, *An Outline of Christian Theology* (Charles Scribner's Sons, 1898). For his religious journey see William Newton Clarke, *Sixty Years with the Bible: A Record of Experience* (Charles Scribner's Sons, 1909).

98. Poteat, *Laboratory and Pulpit*, 61.

99. Poteat, *Laboratory and Pulpit*, 61–62. He argued that the Westminster Confession and London Confession represented this practice of forcing the Bible into polemics.

100. Poteat, *Laboratory and Pulpit*, 62.

101. Poteat, *Laboratory and Pulpit*, 62–63. In addition to being embarrassing, it was a waste of Christian energy. He said, "I know not how many more vagaries will spring out of this same hotbed to distress us and dissipate in endless controversy the Christian energy which ought to be saving the world."

102. Poteat, *Laboratory and Pulpit*, 63.

103. Poteat, *Laboratory and Pulpit*, 63.

104. Poteat, *Laboratory and Pulpit*, 64–65.

105. Poteat, *Laboratory and Pulpit*, 65. Poteat clarified that this revelation was experience based and not verbal or propositional.

106. See W. R. L. Smith, "Prof. W. L. Poteat and the Gay Lectures," *Baptist Argus,* May 3, 1900; S. C. Mitchell, "Gratitude to the Founder of the Gay Lectures," *Baptist Argus,* April, 5, 1900; Article, "Laboratory and Pulpit," *Baptist Argus,* May 30, 1901, Clipping, Poteat Papers, box 8. In addition to the *Baptist Argus* South Carolina's *Baptist Courier* called the lectures "wise and judicious." See Article, "Prof. Poteat and Theistic Evolution," *Baptist Courier,* April 26, 1900, 4, Clipping, Poteat Papers, box 8. North Carolina's *Biblical Recorder* also gave a positive review. New York Baptists' *Examiner* praised the lectures. See Article, "The Gay Lectures," *The Examiner,* April 5, 1900, 27, Clipping, Poteat Papers, box 8.

107. Smith, "Prof. W. L. Poteat and the Gay Lectures," *Baptist Argus,* May 3, 1900, Clipping, Poteat Papers, box 8.

108. Smith, "Prof. W. L. Poteat and the Gay Lectures," *Baptist Argus,* May 3, 1900, Clipping, Poteat Papers, box 8.

109. Poteat, *Laboratory and Pulpit*, 66.

110. Poteat, *Laboratory and Pulpit*, 67. Poteat revered Thomas Henry Huxley, who was his favorite source on evolutionary theory. Poteat had five volumes by Huxley in his personal library: *Introductory*, *Science and Christian Tradition*, *The Advance of Science in the Last Half-Century*, *Evolution and Ethics*, and *Hume*, as well as one by Thomas H. Huxley's grandson, Julian Huxley, *Essays in Popular Science*. See List of Books from the Library of Dr. William Louis Poteat Given to Wake Forest College. Poteat Papers, box 7, folder 727. For a secondary source on Huxley see Paul White, *Thomas Huxley: Making the "Man of Science"* (Cambridge University, 2003).

111. "Are Preachers, as a Class, Mossbacks?," *Word and Way,* May 3, 1900, Clipping, Poteat Papers, box 8.

112. Poteat, *Can a Man Be a Christian To-day?*, 34.

113. For a source on the John Calvin McNair Lectures see Hall, *William Louis Poteat*, 149–56.

114. Poteat, *Can a Man Be a Christian To-day?*, 34.

115. Poteat, *Can a Man Be a Christian To-day?*, 34–35. Poteat would have agreed and likely seen himself in a statement by Edgar Y. Mullins, who said, "Weary of the controversies over ritual and doctrine, of heresy trials and strife among the religious denominations, many men of fine moral character, especially in college and university life, eschew all church relations and insist upon the sufficiency of the individual in the culture of the spiritual life."

See Edgar Y. Mullins, *Axioms of Religion*, ed. C. Douglas Weaver (1908; repr., Mercer University Press, 2010), 177.

116. Poteat, *Can a Man Be a Christian To-day?*, 35. He said, "And now that certain Christian teachers are reviving the dictation theory of the origin of the Bible and endeavoring by its use to recover a small area of the scientific territory, namely, the method of creation, we are again in the morass out of which we struggled painfully nearly a half century ago." See Poteat, *Can a Man Be a Christian To-day?*, 60.

117. Poteat, *Can a Man Be a Christian To-day?*, 35.

118. Poteat, *Can a Man Be a Christian To-day?*, 36. He called it "amazing and disheartening."

119. Poteat, *Can a Man Be a Christian To-day?*, 56.

120. Manly, *The Bible Doctrine of Inspiration Explained and Vindicated*, 44.

121. Poteat, *Can a Man Be a Christian To-day?*, 58.

122. Treier, "Scripture and Hermeneutics," in *Mapping Modern Theology*, 86.

123. See Poteat, *Can a Man Be a Christian To-day?*, 58, 69.

124. For Dickinson's citation see Jer. 1:9 (KJV). Alfred J. Dickinson, Notebook on the Book of Jeremiah, chapters 1–11, Dickinson Collection, Samford University Library Archives, Birmingham, AL. A note in the front of the notebook claimed it was found in the basement of First Baptist Church (Birmingham?) in May 1925.

125. Dickinson, Notebook on the Book of Jeremiah, chapters 1–11.

126. Dickinson, Notebook on the Book of Jeremiah, chapters 1–11.

127. Edgar Y. Mullins, *The Christian Religion in Its Doctrinal Expression* (Sunday School Board of the Southern Baptist Convention, 1917), 24. For Mullins's growing concern about the more advanced form of theological modernism and his defense of religion's place in modern society see Edgar Y. Mullins, *Christianity at the Cross Roads* (Southern Baptist Sunday School Board, 1924).

128. Poteat might have resented that Mullins called theology a science. During the same period but evidently apart from meaningful attention from Southern Baptists, theologians at Princeton Seminary were also grappling with these questions about theology's status as a science and its ability to produce "facts." Historian Bradley Gundlach explores the evolving challenge for those at Princeton who witnessed the ascension of modern science during the nineteenth century and into the twentieth. See Bradley J. Gundlach, *Process and Providence: The Evolution Question at Princeton, 1845–1929* (Eerdmans, 2013), 63–73.

129. Mullins, *The Christian Religion in Its Doctrinal Expression*, 25.

130. Mullins, *The Christian Religion in Its Doctrinal Expression*, 47. For Mullins's larger discussion see Mullins, *The Christian Religion in Its Doctrinal Expression*, 41–48.

131. Mullins, *The Christian Religion in Its Doctrinal Expression*, 144. For Mullins's larger discussion on revelation see Mullins, *The Christian Religion in Its Doctrinal Expression*, 137–53. Virginius Dabney, in *Liberalism in the South*, considered Mullins to have surrendered to conservative forces in his denomination. Mullins was progressive but not liberal enough for Dabney, who considered Poteat a hero of Southern liberalism. For Dabney's evaluation of Mullins see Virginius Dabney, *Liberalism in the South* (University of North Carolina Press, 1932), 301–02. For his praise of Poteat see Dabney, *Liberalism in the South*, 300–301.

132. Warfield preferred natural and supernatural revelation instead of general and special: "The one is communicated through the media of natural phenomena, occurring in

the course of Nature or of history; the other implies an intervention in the natural course of things and is not merely in source but in mode supernatural." Warfield, *The Inspiration and Authority of the Bible,* 74.

133. William L. Poteat, "Wherein Lies the Efficacy of Jesus' Work in the Reconciliation?," *Proceedings of the Baptist Congress: Eighteenth Annual Session* (Baptist Congress, 1900), 94–102. Poteat would likely have argued that men like Irenaeus, Anselm, and Calvin were not getting their rationalism from the Bible. Poteat argued that it initially came from the intrusion of Greek philosophy into Christianity. The influence of Harnack's hellenization thesis is clear, most notably found in Adolf von Harnack's *History of Dogma,* published between 1886 and 1889. See also Treier, "Scripture and Hermeneutics," *Mapping Modern Theology,* 70. For a more recent assessment of Harnack's theory see Paul L. Gavrilyuk, *The Suffering of the Impassible God: The Dialectics of Patristic Thought* (Oxford University Press, 2006).

134. Poteat, "Wherein Lies the Efficacy of Jesus' Work in the Reconciliation?," 99.

135. Poteat, *Laboratory and Pulpit,* 99. Romanticism had a deep influence on Poteat. For a source on Romanticism see Michael Ferber, *Romanticism: A Very Short Introduction* (Oxford University, 2010). Samuel Taylor Coleridge and Robert Browning were Poteat's favorite poets. For the influence of Romanticism in liberal theology see Olson, *The Journey of Modern Theology*, 109–14.

136. Poteat, *Laboratory and Pulpit,* 100.

137. Poteat, *Can a Man Be a Christian To-day?*, 99. For the best secondary source on Schleiermacher see Jacqueline Marina, ed., *The Cambridge Companion to Friedrich Schleiermacher* (Cambridge University Press, 2005).

138. Poteat, *Can a Man Be a Christian To-day?*, 33. By fundamentalists Poteat sometimes referred to the militant evangelical Protestants who actively opposed liberal theology. But at other times he seemed to envision a broader category of conservative theologians who were devoted to doctrinal clarity and a standard of theological orthodoxy. Here he seems to envision the latter.

139. Phillips's rejection of traditional Protestant Christianity is discernible in his sermon before the Southern Baptist Convention in 1931. For instance he supplanted the supernatural nature of salvation for one's own efforts for a moral life. To be a Christian was to live according to the principles of Jesus for the good of mankind. He said, "Salvation is neither mystical nor magical, but the practical application of the principles of Christ and of Galilee and Calvary to the motives and methods of men." Christ's death on the cross did not have an objective power but was an encouragement to righteousness. See Sermon, "The Kingdom," Annual Convention Sermon of the Southern Baptist Convention, Mobile, AL, May 13, 1931, Southern Baptist Historical Library and Archives, Nashville, TN.

140. Wayne Flynt, *Alabama Baptists: Southern Baptists in the Heart of Dixie* (University of Alabama, 1998), 262.

141. John H. Chapman, Biographical sketch of John W. Phillips, John H. Chapman Papers, box 2, Samford University Library Archives, Birmingham, AL. Chapman, who was a professor at Birmingham's Howard College, collected an impressive assortment of records on key Baptist leaders in Alabama, especially progressives, such as Leslie L. Gwaltney, Alfred J. Dickinson, and John W. Phillips. See John H. Chapman Papers, Samford University Library Archives, Birmingham, AL. See also Flynt, *Alabama Baptists*, 262–63.

142. Chapman, Biographical sketch of John W. Phillips, John H. Chapman Papers, box 2.

143. William L. Poteat to Amzi C. Dixon, January 19, 1923, Amzi C. Dixon Papers, Southern Baptist Historical Library and Archives, Nashville, TN. Dixon was himself a graduate of Wake Forest College and had attended at the same time as Poteat. The two men could hardly have taken more divergent paths: Poteat embraced liberal theology while Dixon became a militant fundamentalist. See Amzi C. Dixon Papers, Southern Baptist Historical Library and Archives, Nashville, TN. For a secondary source see Jeffrey Mayfield, "Striving for Souls by the Power of God: The Light of Amzi Clarence Dixon" (PhD diss., Southern Baptist Theological Seminary, 2010). Randal Hall rightly identified Dixon as a sharp contrast to Poteat. While together at Wake Forest, they both participated in the school's Euzelian Society. Dixon had declined the presidency of Wake Forest in 1882 and became a famous Baptist minister, serving in New York, Boston, Chicago, and London. Hall summarized their relationship well: "Poteat and Dixon chose quite different paths, and their viewpoints clashed in the twenties." Hall, *William Louis Poteat*, 131.

144. It was subsequently published as a pamphlet, which is held by the James P. Boyce Library Archives, Southern Baptist Theological Seminary, Louisville, KY.

145. William L. Poteat to Amzi C. Dixon, January 19, 1923.

146. Poteat to Dixon, January 19, 1923. There is no record of a response from Dixon.

147. Poteat, *Laboratory and Pulpit*, 100.

148. Poteat, *The New Peace*, 100.

149. Poteat, *The New Peace*, 104.

150. For Poteat's larger discussion see Poteat, *The New Peace*, 96–116.

151. Manly, *The Bible Doctrine of Inspiration Explained and Vindicated*, 35.

152. Manly, *The Bible Doctrine of Inspiration Explained and Vindicated*, 37.

153. Manly, *The Bible Doctrine of Inspiration Explained and Vindicated*, 96.

154. Article, "Midsummer Musings: Jesus the Beautiful," by William L. Poteat, Clipping, no source, no date, Poteat Papers, box 9. Poteat was interested in historical Jesus studies and engaged in some such work himself. For one example see William L. Poteat, Manuscript, "Christian Origins, Lecture II. Jesus of Nazareth," Poteat Papers, box 7, folder 803; and William L. Poteat, Manuscript, "The Thirty Silent Years," by William L. Poteat, Poteat Papers, box 10, folder 1097. However religious experience remained supreme for Poteat.

155. Dorrien argued that this mediation was central to the very nature of liberalism. See Dorrien, *The Making of American Liberal Theology, 1805–1900*, xiii-xxv.

156. Poteat, *Can a Man Be a Christian To-day?*, 68.

157. Poteat, *Can a Man Be a Christian To-day?*, 71.

158. Poteat, *Can a Man Be a Christian To-day?*, 77. James Thompson rightly noted, "After a period of confusion and distress, [Poteat] adjusted the discrepancies between science and scripture by concluding that biblical 'science' represented the primitive attempts of an unscientific people to understand the mystery of life's origin." Thompson, *Tried as by Fire*, 66.

159. Poteat, *Can a Man Be a Christian To-day?*, 72–73.

160. Poteat, *Can a Man Be a Christian To-day?*, 79.

161. Treier, "Scripture and Hermeneutics," in Kapic and McCormick, *Mapping Modern Theology*, 69.

162. Article, "Doctor Chase," *Hamlet News-Messenger,* February 18, 1926, Clipping, Poteat Papers, box 6. For a secondary source on Chase see William D. Snider, *Light on the Hill: A History of the University of North Carolina at Chapel Hill* (University of North Carolina Press, 1992), 169–93.

163. Anonymous, Clipping, Poteat Papers, box 6.

CHAPTER FIVE: THE RISE OF CONSERVATIVE OPPOSITION

1. For Randal Hall's account of the rise of conservative opposition against Poteat see Hall, *William Louis Poteat*, 127–56.

2. For the doctrinal history of Baptists see James Leo Garrett, *Baptist Theology: A Four-Century Study* (Mercer University Press, 2009). See also L. Russ Bush and Thomas J. Nettles, *Baptists and the Bible,* rev. ed. (B&H, 1999). For the use of the term "biblicism" I am drawing from David Bebbington's definition of evangelicalism—the Bebbington quadrilateral, which in addition to biblicism included conversionism, activism, and crucicentrism, all of which accurately described Baptists in the South. See Bebbington, *Evangelicalism in Modern Britain*, 1–17.

3. For the still standard source on fundamentalism see George M. Marsden, *Fundamentalism and American Culture,* 3rd ed. (Oxford University Press, 2022). See also Andrew Atherstone and David C. Jones, eds. *The Oxford Handbook of Christian Fundamentalism* (Oxford University Press, 2023). For another work that explores fundamentalism's relationship to American culture see Madison Trammel, *Fundamentalists in the Public Square: Evolution, Alcohol, and Culture Wars after the Scopes Trial* (Lexham Academic, 2023). For fundamentalism among Baptists in the South see James J. Thompson, Jr., *Tried as by Fire: Southern Baptists and the Religious Controversies of the 1920s* (Mercer University Press, 1982). For North Carolina in particular see Willard Gatewood, *Preachers, Pedagogues, & Politicians: The Evolution Controversy in North Carolina, 1920–1927* (University of North Carolina Press, 1966).

4. Randal L. Hall, *William Louis Poteat: A Leader of the Progressive-Era South* (University of Kentucky, 2000), 22. Historian H. Leon McBeth also noted the "relative quiet" that had prevailed during the period leading up to the 1920s. See H. Leon McBeth, *The Baptist Heritage: Four Centuries of Baptist Witness* (Broadman Press, 1987), 679.

5. To see this dynamic among Presbyterians see Bradley J. Longfield, *The Presbyterian Controversy: Fundamentalists, Modernists, & Moderates* (Oxford University Press, 1991). To see this dynamic among Baptists see Jeffrey Paul Straub, *The Making of a Battle Royal: The Rise of Liberalism in Northern Baptist Life, 1870–1920* (Pickwick, 2018). For the best overview of the rise of liberal Protestantism in America see Gary Dorrien, *The Making of American Liberal Theology, 1805–1900* (Westminster John Knox, 2001); and Gary Dorrien, *The Making of American Liberal Theology, 1900–1950* (Westminster John Knox, 2003). Roger Olson has rightly observed that in the late nineteenth and early twentieth centuries conservatives put liberals on trial, but by "the 1920s, however, things had turned around in the so-called mainline Protestant denominations and trials were going against conservatives." Roger Olson, *The Journey of Modern Theology: From Reconstruction to Deconstruction* (InterVarsity, 2013), 213. Olson argued, "If liberal theology was maximal acknowledgement of modernity, fundamentalism was maximal conservatism—intentionally and sometimes militantly preserving and defending the perceived heritage of

Protestant orthodoxy that had reigned within Protestantism from the Reformers until the rise of liberal theology." Olson, *The Journey of Modern Theology*, 215.

6. In addition to the controversy in North Carolina, J. Frank Norris, pastor of the First Baptist Church of Fort Worth, Texas, led assaults against liberal Southern Baptist leaders and eventually the Southern Baptist Convention itself. For the best work on Norris see Barry Hankins, *God's Rascal: J. Frank Norris and the Beginnings of Southern Fundamentalism* (University of Kentucky Press, 1996). For works on Southern fundamentalism see William R. Glass, *Strangers in Zion: Fundamentalists in the South, 1900–1950* (Mercer University Press, 2001); and Andrew C. Smith, *Fundamentalism, Fundraising, and the Transformation of the Southern Baptist Convention, 1919–1925* (University of Tennessee Press, 2016). Glass argued that fundamentalism was decidedly Northern in formation and character, which made for an awkward fit within Southern Protestantism. Smith followed Glass's basic argument but also contended that the anti-evolution debate represented a somewhat separate historical phenomenon from the main fight waged by the fundamentalists. Smith's distinction does not seem to be helpful. Both Glass and Smith seem to overlook the presence of theological liberalism among educated Southern Baptists, which created a situation similar to what occurred the North. Particularly in North Carolina, Baptists experienced a controversy that resembled the fundamentalist-modernist controversy in the North, both in its character and in its outcome. Historian James Thompson rightly argued that the fundamentalist-modernist controversy did indeed reach the South. See James J. Thompson Jr., *Tried as by Fire: Southern Baptists and Religious Controversies of the 1920s* (Mercer University Press, 1982).

7. For secondary sources see Willard B. Gatewood, *Preachers, Pedagogues, & Politicians: The Evolution Controversy in North Carolina, 1920–1927* (University of North Carolina Press, 1966); Thompson, *Tried as by Fire*; and Hall, *William Louis Poteat*. See also David Stricklin, *A Genealogy of Dissent: Southern Baptist Protest in the Twentieth Century* (University of Kentucky Press, 1999). Baptist papers like the *Western Recorder* of Kentucky and the *Biblical Recorder* of North Carolina became the primary vehicles for the debate between fundamentalists and liberals.

8. One notable exception was Amzi C. Dixon, who attended Wake Forest College with Poteat but remained decidedly traditional in his theology. Dixon became a leading critic of evolution, higher criticism, and liberal theology. He and R. A. Torrey edited *The Fundamentals: A Testimony to the Truth*, which served as a basis for the name "fundamentalist." See Amzi C. Dixon and R. A. Torrey, eds., *The Fundamentals: A Testimony to the Truth*, vol. 1–12 (Testimony, 1910–15).

9. For early examples of Poteat's evolutionary thought see William L. Poteat, "The Effect on the College Curriculum of the Introduction of the Natural Sciences," *Science* 21 (March 31, 1893), 170–72; and William L. Poteat, "Lucretius and the Evolution Idea," *Popular Science Monthly* 60 (December 1901), 166–72. Wake Forest alumnus Wilbur J. Cash outlined Poteat's role as an early prophet of evolution: "In the early 1900's William Louis Poteat . . . had begun to teach biology without equivocation, to set forth the theory of evolution frankly and fully, as having, as he said, more evidence behind it than Copernican theory—certainly the first wholly honest and competent instruction of the sort in a Southern evangelical school, and the first in Southern schools of any sort save such exceptional ones as I have before noted." Wilbur J. Cash, *The Mind of the South* (1941; repr., Alfred A. Knopf, 1978), 321.

10. Richard T. Vann, "What Have Baptist Colleges to do with Fundamentalism and

Modernism," Address to Southern Baptist Education Conference, Memphis, Tennessee, February 4, 1925, 5, James P. Boyce Library Archives, Southern Baptist Theological Seminary, Louisville, KY.

11. Tom P. Jimison, "Fundamentalists Making World Safe for Orthodoxy," *Tar Heel*, October 22, 1925, Clipping, Poteat Papers, box 6.

12. Mims, *The Advancing South*, 12.

13. See Smith, *Fundamentalism, Fundraising, and the Transformation of the Southern Baptist Convention*; and Glass, *Strangers in Zion*. Smith and Glass both argue that fundamentalism was stronger in the North, which might be explained by the greater presence of Northern liberalism. But fundamentalism, like liberalism, was not merely a Northern phenomenon. The South was a part of the larger movements that affected American Protestantism in the early twentieth century.

14. William L. Poteat, *The New Peace: Lectures on Science and Religion* (Gorham Press, 1915), 15–16. He gave these lectures at Hamilton Theological Seminary of Colgate University in May 1905, then in October and November 1905 at Crozer Theological Seminary, Newton Theological Institution, Rochester Theological Institution, and the Divinity School of the University of Chicago. See "Prefatory Note" in *The New Peace*. William Newton Clarke encouraged their publication. For theological liberalism among Baptists in the North see Straub, *The Making of a Battle Royal: The Rise of Liberalism in Northern Baptist Life, 1870–1920*.

15. Poteat, *The New Peace*, 96.

16. Gary Dorrien has argued that the rejection of external authority was central to theological liberalism. He defined liberalism as "the idea that Christian theology can be genuinely Christian without being based upon external authority. Since the eighteenth century, liberal Christian thinkers have argued that religion should be modern and progressive and that the meaning of Christianity should be interpreted from the standpoint of modern knowledge and experience." Dorrien, *The Making of American Liberal Theology: Imagining Progressive Religion, 1805–1900*, xiii.

17. William L. Poteat, "The Bible Says," *Biblical Recorder*, January 27, 1938, Clipping, Poteat Papers, box 7, folder 761.

18. Poteat, "The Bible Says," *Biblical Recorder*, January 27, 1938, Clipping, Poteat Papers, box 7, folder 761.

19. Although he worked with theological subjects his entire career, preached regularly, and was widely recognized as a religious leader, Poteat stressed that he was a layperson. He was a biologist, educator, and church member but objected to being called a minister or theologian. For an example of his denial that he was a theologian see William L. Poteat to Amzi C. Dixon, January 19, 1923, Amzi C. Dixon Papers, Southern Baptist Historical Library and Archives, Nashville, TN. For a denial that he was preacher see William L. Poteat to Vardry McBee, November 5, 1930, Poteat Papers. Archibald T. Robertson of Southern Baptist Theological Seminary wrote to Poteat in 1930 to express his great satisfaction with Poteat's ability as a preacher: "Maybe you ought to have been a preacher instead of a scientist!" Archibald T. Robertson to William L. Poteat, September 1, 1930, Poteat Papers, box 3, folder 354.

20. William O. Carver to Edwin C. Dargan, September 3, 1921, Dargan Papers, Southern Baptist Historical Library and Archives, Nashville, TN.

21. Dabney, *Liberalism in the South*, 288, 290.

22. For a source on the honor culture of the South, which was based in the Old South

but undeniably continued into the New see Bertram Wyatt-Brown, *Southern Honor: Ethics & Behavior in the Old South,* 25th anniversary ed. (Oxford University Press, 2007). For honor as part of Southern personhood see Ted Ownby, *Subduing Satan: Religion, Recreation, & Manhood in the Rural South, 1865–1920* (University of North Carolina Press, 1990). Honor culture is evident in works like Virginius Dabney's *Liberalism in the South,* which intended to demonstrate the South's cultural progress to the outside world.

23. Article, "Baptists, 1200 Strong, Are Expected at Convention Here," *Charlotte Observer,* October 12, 1925, Poteat Papers, box 6.

24. Article, "Baptists, 1200 Strong, Are Expected at Convention Here," *Charlotte Observer,* October 12, 1925, Poteat Papers, box 6.

25. For additional sources see Article, "Did the Anti-Evolution Forces Win or Lose in the Action of the Baptist Convention?," by S. F Conrad, *Charlotte Observer*, November 21, 1925; Article, "Evolution and Naming of Trustees to be Discussed By Baptists in Charlotte," *Charlotte Observer,* November 17, 1925; Article, "Baptist Convention Dodged Issues," *The Times,* Raleigh, NC, November 1925; and Article, "Barrett Resolution," by W. C. Barrett, *Biblical Recorder,* November 11, 1925, Clipping, Poteat Papers, box 6. For secondary sources see Randall L. Hall, *William Louis Poteat: A Leader of the Progressive-Era South* (University of Kentucky Press, 2000); and Gatewood, *Preachers, Pedagogues, & Politicians.*

26. See Gatewood, *Preachers, Pedagogues, & Politicians*; and Thompson, *Tried as by Fire.* I explore these events in detail in chapter 6.

27. For the best secondary sources on the Seventy-Five Million Campaign and the subsequent development of the Cooperative Program see Robert A. Baker, *The Southern Baptist Convention and Its People, 1607–1972* (Broadman Press, 1974), 392–94, 402–4; and McBeth, *The Baptist Heritage*, 616–23, 678–80. See also Smith, *Fundamentalism, Fundraising, and the Transformation of the Southern Baptist Convention, 1919–1925.* For the campaign see H. Leon McBeth, ed. *A Sourcebook for Baptist Heritage* (Broadman Press, 1990), 447–53. State conventions like those in North Carolina held the vision of the Seventy-Five Million Campaign before the people. The campaign was featured prominently at the 1922 Baptist State Convention in North Carolina. For the lengthy special report see *Annual of the Baptist State Convention of North Carolina, 1922*, 36–38, James P. Boyce Library Archives, Southern Baptist Theological Seminary, Louisville, KY. This became the Cooperative Program in 1925. For the Cooperative Program report in 1925 see *Annual of the Baptist State Convention of North Carolina, 1925*, 40, James P. Boyce Library Archives, Southern Baptist Theological Seminary, Louisville, KY.

28. Suzanne C. Linder, "Poteat and the Evolution Controversy," *The North Carolina Review* 40, no. 2 (April 1963): 139.

29. Vann, "What Have Baptist Colleges to Do with Fundamentalism and Modernism." Vann demonstrated a robust understanding of the theological differences represented by traditional Protestants and theological modernists. See Vann, "What Have Baptist Colleges to do with Fundamentalism and Modernism," 1–5.

30. Vann, "What Have Baptist Colleges to do with Fundamentalism and Modernism," 3–7. Vann cited both Edgar Y. Mullins and Shailer Mathews on this point.

31. Vann, "What Have Baptist Colleges to do with Fundamentalism and Modernism," 4. Vann cited Harry E. Fosdick as an example.

32. Vann, "What Have Baptist Colleges to do with Fundamentalism and Modernism," 7.

33. Vann, "What Have Baptist Colleges to do with Fundamentalism and Modernism," 14–15.

34. Vann, "What Have Baptist Colleges to do with Fundamentalism and Modernism," 8. Vann was correct in recognizing that there were two relatively small coalitions of fundamentalists and liberals who were clashing. But most Southern Baptists held an orthodox theology shaped by evangelical Protestantism, while many held it in simple terms. A larger number of these however did not share the militant spirit of the fundamentalists. Liberal Baptists were represented almost exclusively among educated leaders in Baptist life.

35. Vann, "What Have Baptist Colleges to do with Fundamentalism and Modernism," 14.

36. Mims, *The Advancing South*, 21.

37. Mims, *The Advancing South*, 21–22. Mims seemed to be referring particularly to Poteat's address before the North Carolina Baptist Convention in 1922.

38. Gerald W. Johnson, "Billy with a Red Necktie," 6.

39. Dorrien, *Kantian Reason and Hegelian Spirit*, 5. The language of "cultured despisers of religion" originated with Friedrich Schleiermacher in his first major work, *On Religion: Speeches to Its Cultured Despisers*, first published in 1799.

40. Dorrien, *Kantian Reason and Hegelian Spirit*, 5.

41. Evans, *The Kingdom Is Always But Coming*, 22.

42. Olson argued that "liberal theology aims at reconstructing Christian doctrines to balance contemporary cultural relevance with faithfulness to Christian sources. Usually, and this is probably the *sine qua non* of liberal theology, relevance to contemporary culture is given equal if not great weight than faithfulness to traditional Christian sources." Olson, *The Journey of Modern Theology*, 128.

43. In the standard history of liberalism in America, Gary Dorrien completely overlooked liberalism in the South. See Dorrien, *The Making of American Liberal Theology: Imagining Progressive Religion, 1805–1900*; and Dorrien, *The Making of American Liberal Theology: Idealism, Realism, & Modernity, 1900–1950*. Roger Olson likewise ignored the Southern scene in *The Journey of Modern Theology*. Older works likewise missed Southern liberalism. For instance C. Vann Woodward argued that "one searches vainly" for liberal religion in the early-twentieth-century South. See C. Vann Woodward's classic work, *Origins of the New South, 1877–1913* (1951; repr., Louisiana State University Press, 1971), 450. Randal Hall, Poteat's most recent biographer, concluded that Poteat was only moderately liberal, and he largely overlooked the broader movement of liberalism in the region. Hall captured well the pervasive influence that Poteat had as a public intellectual and social activist, but he underestimated the maturity of Poteat's liberalism and that of other liberals in the South. For Hall's assessment of Poteat's "somewhat muddled half-acceptance of liberal theology" see Hall, *William Louis Poteat*, 47–59. Wayne Flynt, however, has accurately observed that liberalism took root in the South. See Flynt, *Alabama Baptists;* and Wayne Flynt, "Not an Island Unto Itself: The New Theological Trends (Liberalism, Ecumenism, and the Social Gospel), 1890–1940," *American Baptist Quarterly* (June 2003): 158–79. Historian Paul Harvey has also observed that liberalism existed in the South. See Paul Harvey, "Southern Baptists and the Social Gospel: White Religious Progressivism in the South, 1900–1925," *Fides et Historia* (January 1995): 59–77. For sources by Poteat's contemporaries who recognized and welcomed liberalism in the South see Virginius Dabney, *Liberalism in the South* (University of North Carolina Press, 1932); and Edwin Mims, *The Advancing South* (Doubleday, Page & Co., 1926).

44. Chapman, "Doctor Alfred J. Dickinson, 21.

45. Chapman, "Doctor Alfred J. Dickinson, 23.

46. Chapman, "Doctor Alfred J. Dickinson, 19.

47. Johnson, "Billy with a Red Necktie," 9.

48. Dorrien rightly defined the third-way nature of liberalism as it began in Germany: "In Germany, the liberal movement called itself 'mediating theology' because it took seriously the challenge of a rising culture of aggressive deism and atheism. Liberal religious thinkers, unavoidably, had to battle with conservatives for the right to liberalize Christian doctrine." Dorrien, *Kantian Reason and Hegelian Spirit*, 4–5. Likewise in America, liberalism was a third option "between the authority-based orthodoxies of traditional Christianity and the spiritless materialism of modern atheism or deism." Dorrien, *The Making of American Liberal Theology*, 1805–1900, xiii.

49. Poteat stressed the limits of science: that science could not deliver a holistic system. He argued that "[science]. is impotent before [the] central mysteries of nature & life & that its instruments (clock, foot-rule, balance) & method are inappropriate in those spheres of reality where religion functions." Poteat, "My Approach to Religion," 4. See also Poteat, *An Intellectual Adventure,* 284–86.

50. William L. Poteat, *The Way of Victory* (University of North Carolina, 1929), 34.

51. Poteat's *Youth and Culture* provides a superb example of Poteat's apologetic mission, particularly for the younger, more educated, generation of Southerners. It comprises several of his addresses to Wake Forest students. He made this point summarily: "The new world rapidly forming about us belongs of right to the young—its inheritance of dissolving traditions, the new types of freedom into which they will be recomposed, the control of the transition, the leadership of the new order. The very marks and traits of youth impose upon it these responsibilities. Its memory is too short to be preoccupied with the past. Its mind is not set, but adjustable and receptive." Poteat, *Youth and Culture*, 7.

52. George M. Bryan, "Billy Poteat and the 'Watchmen on the Wall,'" *News and Observer,* June 18, 1961, Clipping, Poteat Papers, box 1, folder 1.

53. For the best secondary source on the Scopes trial see Edward J. Larson, *Summer for the Gods: The Scopes Trial and America's Continuing Debate over Science and Religion*, 2nd ed. (Basic Books, 2006). For a contemporary account see Charles M. Puckette, "The Evolution Arena at Dayton," *New York Times*, Sunday July 5, 1925, Clipping, Poteat Papers, box 6. The article summarized: "Circus sideshows and curious visitors descend upon Tennessee mountain town, but legal struggle will involve Christian faith, science, free speech, and the constitution."

54. These lectures were published as *Can a Man be a Christian To-day?*

55. I explore Poteat's controversies and opposition in subsequent chapters. For Poteat's role in the evolutionary controversies in North Carolina see Gatewood, *Preachers, Pedagogues, & Politicians;* and Powell, *Encyclopedia of North Carolina*, 404–5.

56. Bryan, "Billy Poteat and the 'Watchmen on the Wall,'" *News and Observer.* North Carolina did develop a more progressive image in comparison to other Southern states. See Milton Ready, *The Tar Heel State: A History of North Carolina* (University of South Carolina Press, 2005), 301–22; and Link, *North Carolina*, 353–55. For a contemporary account see Mencken, "The Sahara of the Bozart."

57. Bryan, "Billy Poteat and the 'Watchmen on the Wall,'" *News and Observer.*

58. For the theology of conversion in early evangelicalism see David Bebbington, *Evangelicalism in Modern Britain: A History from the 1730s to the 1980s* (Routledge

1989), 8–10. For sources on evangelicalism in the South see John B. Boles, *The Great Revival: Beginnings of the Bible Belt* (University of Kentucky Press, 1996); and Donald G. Mathews, *Religion in the Old South* (University of Chicago Press, 1977). For background on early American Evangelicalism more broadly see Mark A. Noll, *The Rise of Evangelicalism: The Age of Edwards, Whitefield, and the Wesleys* (InterVarsity, 2003); and Thomas S. Kidd, *The Great Awakening: The Roots of Evangelical Christianity in Colonial America* (Yale University Press, 2007).

59. Diary, July 17, 1896, box 4, folder 475, Z. Smith Reynolds Library Archives, Wake Forest University, Winston-Salem, NC. Poteat was reflecting on John 10:10 "The thief comes only to steal and kill and destroy. I came that they may have life and have it abundantly."

60. William L. Poteat to Eugene Lankford, April 2, 1929, Poteat Papers, box 2, folder 225. See also Lankford's letter, Eugene Lankford to William L. Poteat, April 1929, Poteat Papers, box 2, folder 225.

61. Poteat and Gwaltney were close friends. Poteat frequently mentioned Gwaltney in his private diary from the middle 1890s. Poteat preached at Gwaltney's church several times, and the Poteats hosted Gwaltney and his wife in their home. See William L. Poteat, Diary, May 6, 1896–February 16, 1897. For Gwaltney's autobiography see Leslie L. Gwaltney, *Forty of the Twentieth or the First Forty Years of the Twentieth Century* (Birmingham Printing Company, 1940).

62. Diary, July 26, 1896, Poteat Papers, box 4, folder 475. Poteat did not indicate whether or not he believed that the incarnation was a historic reality. In this case it was unimportant for his point about achieving the abundant life.

63. William L. Poteat, *The Way of Victory* (University of North Carolina Press, 1929), 29. He delivered the lectures October 16 through 18, 1928, at the Chapel Hill School of Religion, which was an independent institution from the University of North Carolina.

64. Poteat, *The Way of Victory*, 29. Poteat argued that "the community is composed of individuals, and it cannot be redeemed apart from the redemption of its constituent units."

65. Poteat, *The Way of Victory*, 35. Poteat argued that this led to personal fulfillment: "Another name for [self-renunciation] is self-realization."

66. Poteat, *The Way of Victory*, 31.

67. Acts 2:38.

68. Mark 1:15.

69. Poteat, *The Way of Victory*, 30–31.

70. Poteat, *The Way of Victory*, 32.

71. Poteat, *The Way of Victory*, 33.

72. William L. Poteat, "Wherein Lies the Efficacy of Jesus' Work in the Reconciliation?," in *Proceedings of the Baptist Congress: Eighteenth Annual Session* (Baptist Congress, 1900), 101.

73. Diary, 1925–1926, no date, Poteat Papers, box 4, folder 475. Poteat's original read, "Children are naughty bec. adults are stupid." This was one of many favorite quotations and personal insights that he recorded in the back of his diary. This quotation came from a collegiate magazine: *The Teke*, October-November 1925.

74. Diary, September 23, 1896, box 4, folder 475. Poteat seemed to have settled on these ideas in the early years of his career. No significant development in his thought on sin and salvation is discernible later.

75. Diary, December 17, 1896, Poteat Papers, box 4, folder 475. Poteat placed "plan of salvation" in quotation marks, presumably with a sense of derision.

76. Diary, December 17, 1896, Poteat Papers, box 4, folder 475.

77. On the mystical nature of salvation Poteat said, "In this crisis of the inner life processes go forward so mystical, so profound, so charged with destiny that I make no pretense of understanding them." Poteat, *The Way of Victory*, 30.

78. Wayne Flynt, *Alabama Baptists: Southern Baptists in the Heart of Dixie* (University of Alabama Press, 1998), 253. This was particularly true in the latter years of his pastorate.

79. James H. Chapman, "Doctor Alfred J. Dickinson," Southern Baptist Historical Library and Archives, Nashville, TN. See also John H. Burrows, "The Great Disturber: The Social Philosophy and Theology of Alfred James Dickinson" (MA thesis, Samford University, 1970), 101–6.

80. Chapman, "Doctor Alfred J. Dickinson." See also Flynt, *Alabama Baptists*, 253.

81. For a survey of Poteat's social activism see Randal L. Hall, *William Louis Poteat: A Leader in the Progressive-Era South* (University of Kentucky Press, 2000), 60–102. For sources on social ministry among Southern Baptists see John L. Eighmy, *Churches in Cultural Captivity: A History of the Social Attitudes of Southern Baptists*, 2nd ed. (University of Tennessee Press, 1987); and Keith Harper, *Quality of Mercy: Southern Baptists and Social Christianity, 1890–1920* (University of Alabama Press, 1996). Although Eighmy gave reasonable attention to Poteat, surprisingly he made no reference to Dickinson.

82. Diary, October 6, 1896, Poteat Papers, box 4, folder 475. This entry is lengthy and candid. He recorded deep questions and thoughts that consumed him during this episode.

83. Diary, October 6, 1896, Poteat Papers, box 4, folder 475.

84. This record stemmed from a relatively early period, but by this point, the midpoint of his career, his thought in these fundamental areas was generally mature and remained consistent throughout his subsequent life.

85. Poteat, "Wherein Lies the Efficacy of Jesus' Work in the Reconciliation?," 99.

86. Poteat, *Can a Man Be a Christian To-day?*, 107. Poteat also argued that Jesus revealed "the divine requirement summarized in love" and that Jesus "came not to limit life but to give life, to heighten its quality and enlarge its volume." Similarly at the Baptist Congress of 1910 Poteat contended that Jesus revealed God's universal fatherhood and tender approval for all of humanity: "The significance of Jesus lies in the personal revelation which he made of the abstract Universal Intelligence as being in sympathetic neighborhood to human need, and in His clearing the way for freer commerce with the Unseen." William L. Poteat, "The Place of Prayer in the Modern Worldview," in *Proceedings of the Baptist Congress: Twenty-Eighth Annual Session* (University of Chicago Press, 1911), 38–39.

87. Poteat, *Can a Man Be a Christian To-day?*, 107. Poteat's theology of religious experience also broadly supports the point that nothing separated mankind from God. God held no grudge against sin but beckoned his children to encounter him.

88. Edwin M. Poteat Sr., *The Scandal of the Cross: Studies in the Death of Jesus* (Harper & Brothers, 1928), 81. Edwin Poteat made a case for the moral influence / subjective theory of the atonement and rejected penal substitution. He considered the idea reprehensible that God "punished His Son on the cross."

89. For a survey of Ritschl's theology and legacy see Olson, *The Journey of Modern Theology*, 147–67. For Ritschl's most significant theological work see Albrecht Ritschl, *The*

Christian Doctrine of Justification and Reconciliation, trans. H. R. Mackintosh and A. B. Macaulay (T & T Clark, 1900).

90. Roger Olson referred to the American theologian Horace Bushnell when he said "similarity is not always evidence of influence, but it seems fairly obvious that Bushnell's influence, however indirect, is reappearing in twenty-first century theology." Roger Olson, *The Journey of Modern Theology: From Reconstruction to Deconstruction* (InterVarsity, 2013), 293. There is no direct evidence that Poteat read Ritschl, but Ritschl's influence was by then clearly in the atmosphere of American Protestant liberalism, and it went well with Poteat's redefinition of Christianity.

91. Frame, *A History of Western Philosophy and Theology*, 302. Emphasis in original. See also Olson's discussion of Ritschl's redefinition of sin and salvation. Olson, *The Journey of Modern Theology*, 153–54.

92. Theologian Kirk MacGregor summarized Ritschl well: "Ritschl began by defining Christianity as an ellipse with two foci—Jesus, who reveals God's love for us and reconciles us, and the church, which is the spiritual and ethical community Jesus founded that aims to transform human society into the kingdom of God." Kirk R. MacGregor, *Contemporary Theology: An Introduction: Classical, Evangelical, Philosophical, and Global Perspectives* (Zondervan, 2019), 103.

93. For Poteat's "baggage" argument see Poteat, *Can a Man Be a Christian To-day?*, 45–79.

94. Friedrich Schleiermacher famously relegated the doctrine of the Trinity to an appendix in *The Christian Faith*, and by the twentieth century most liberals had abandoned trinitarian theology altogether. Scholars have credited Georg W. F. Hegel as a leading influence in the rejection of the trinitarian doctrine. Hegel himself redefined trinitarian theology in pantheistic terms. Gary Dorrien argued that the rejection of trinitarian theology became standard for liberal theologians in America. See Gary Dorrien, *The Making of American Liberal Theology: Imagining Progressive Religion, 1805–1900* (Westminster John Knox, 2001), 399–400. For a more in-depth survey of the doctrine of the Trinity in modern theology see Fred Sanders, "The Trinity," in *Mapping Modern Theology: A Thematic and Historical Introduction*, ed. Kelly M. Kapic and Bruce L. McCormick (Baker Academic, 2012), 21–45.

95. I have appropriated the language of "verging on pantheism" from Roger Olson's related argument for Albrecht Ritschl. See Olson, *The Journey of Modern Theology*, 153. Olson concluded, "Overall, partly because of Ritschl, liberal theology's emphasis in the doctrine of God fell on the divine immanence within history rather than God's transcendence over it." Poteat lacked sufficient depth or clarity on this point to determine whether he might more rightly be characterized as pantheist or panentheist, both of which denied divine transcendence.

96. Edward Grace, "The Place of Prayer in the Modern World-View," in *Proceedings of the Baptist Congress: Twenty-Eighth Annual Session* (University of Chicago Press, 1911), 15–16. Edgar Mullins recognized the movement toward pantheism in modern theology. He challenged this tendency that he recognized in more advanced forms of liberalism in *Christianity at the Cross Roads*. See Edgar Y. Mullins, *Christianity at the Cross Roads* (Southern Baptist Sunday School Board, 1924), 113–37.

97. Poteat, "Wherein Lies the Efficacy of Jesus' Work in the Reconciliation?," 98.

98. Poteat, "Wherein Lies the Efficacy of Jesus' Work in the Reconciliation?," 98–99.

99. Poteat followed a daily reading plan for his evenings after returning home from his office at the college. He recorded many of the books that he read. For references to Hegel see Diary, February 4, 1897, Poteat Papers, box 4, folder 475.

100. See Josiah Royce's *The Religious Aspect of Philosophy*, 1897 listed as number 479, and *The Sources of Religious Insight* as 345, in William L. Poteat, "List of books from the library of Dr. William Louis Poteat given to Wake Forest College." Poteat Papers, box 7, folder 727. Poteat cited Royce in William L. Poteat, *Laboratory and Pulpit: The Relation of Biology to the Preacher and His Message; the Gay Lectures, 1900* (Griffith & Rowland, 1901), 49, 68, 91. For a source of Royce's Hegelian thought see Gary Dorrien, *Kantian Reason and Hegelian Spirit: The Idealistic Logic of Modern Theology* (Wiley Blackwell, 2012), 17. Dorrien argued that Royce was "the greatest Anglo-American interpreter of German idealism."

101. I have drawn this insight from Poteat's contemporary, the Dutch Reformed theologian Herman Bavinck. See Herman Bavinck, *Philosophy of Revelation: A New Annotated Edition*, ed. Cory Brock and Nathaniel G. Sutanto (Hendrickson, 2018), 15–17.

102. This view was based in biblical texts that suggested a special affection that God had for his redeemed people, whom he made a family and thus made his children, set apart from humanity more generally. See, for example, John 1:12–14: "But to all who did receive him, who believed in his name, he gave the right to become children of God, who were born, not of blood nor of the will of the flesh nor of the will of man, but of God," and 1 John 3:1–2: "See what kind of love the Father has given to us, that we should be called children of God; and so we are. The reason why the world does not know us is that it did not know him. Beloved, we are God's children now, and what we will be has not yet appeared; but we know that when he appears we shall be like him, because we shall see him as he is." Poteat's opponent, Thomas T. Martin, essentially made this argument in Thomas T. Martin, *Three Fatal Teachings* (n.p., 1920), 13–14.

103. The titles of "brother" and "sister" were honored among Baptists and other evangelicals. For Baptists in the South see Gregory A. Wills, *Democratic Religion: Freedom, Authority, and Church Discipline in the Baptist South, 1785–1900* (Oxford University Press, 1997), 44–45. Evangelicals drew the language of "household of faith" from Galatians 6:10, which exhorted the Galatian church to "do good to everyone" but especially "to those who are of the household of faith."

104. Olson, *The Journey of Modern Theology*, 154.

105. Kevin Vanhoozer offered a helpful summary of objective versus subjective views of the atonement in Kevin J. Vanhoozer, "Atonement," in Kelly M. Kapic and Bruce L. McCormick, *Mapping Modern Theology: A Thematic and Historical Introduction* (Baker, 2012), 177–79. Vanhoozer identified the general movement among modern theologians and argued that progressive theologians gravitated toward subjective theories of the atonement: "The nineteenth-century concern with human consciousness and experience, coupled with the tendency to reject divine retributive justice and affirm God's love, led to a second coming as it were of [Peter] Abelard's moral influence theory." Twentieth-century theologian Gustaf Aulen coined the language of objective versus subjective theories of the atonement. See Gustaf Aulen, *Christus Victor: An Historical Study of the Three Main Types of the Idea of the Atonement* (MacMillan, 1969).

106. In the first two-thirds of the nineteenth century the moral government theory of the atonement influenced a generation of Southern Baptists leaders. But the influence of

James P. Boyce and the seminary that he founded, Southern Baptist Theological Seminary, reasserted the older, pre-Edwardsean confessional Calvinism, including an emphasis on the penal substitutionary view of the atonement, which had remained prominent among grassroots Baptists in the South. Not until the rise of liberal theology was there a substantial challenge to the consensus on the atonement among Southern Baptists. For the Edwardsean influence and moral government theology among early Southern Baptists see Obbie Todd, "An Edwardsean Evolution: The Rise and Decline of Moral Government Theory in the Southern Baptist Convention," *Journal of the Evangelical Theological Society* 62, no. 4 (December 2019): 789–802. For the doctrine of the atonement among Baptists in America see E. Brooks Holifield, *Theology in America: Christian Thought from the Age of the Puritans to the Civil War* (Yale University Press), 278–90.

107. Gary Dorrien, *The Making of American Liberal Theology: Imagining Progressive Religion, 1805–1900* (Westminster John Knox, 2001), 400.

108. Hall, *William Louis Poteat*, 156. Hall rightly argued, "Liberals such as Poteat were vital in introducing new ideas, but the extent to which those ideas were adopted was limited."

109. By the early twentieth century, Southern Baptist leaders had grown to have a general distaste for public challenges of theology. They embraced a normative posture that considered interpersonal criticism to be distasteful. Previously theological accountability had a substantial place in Southern Baptist life. See Wills, *Democratic Religion*; and Robert Elder, *The Sacred Mirror: Evangelicalism, Honor, and Identity in the Deep South, 1790–1860* (University of North Carolina Press, 2016). See the collection of articles in Martin's *Three Fatal Teachings* for examples of the dismay expressed toward Martin by Baptist leaders like Livingston Johnson of the *Biblical Recorder* and George W. Paschal of Wake Forest College. Martin pushed against the grain when he said, "Woe to Southern Baptists when state editors shall shut off discussion of denominational and doctrinal affairs and then lampoon any outside discussion." See Martin, *Three Fatal Teachings*, 8. Willard Gatewood agreed and noted that educated North Carolinians were disgusted by Martin's attacks. See Willard B. Gatewood, *Preachers, Pedagogues, & Politicians: The Evolution Controversy in North Carolina, 1920–1927* (University of North Carolina Press, 1966), 36. For additional background see Hall, *William Louis Poteat*, 130–45.

110. Martin became a leading fundamentalist in the South and led the charge against the teaching of evolution in North Carolina. For his classic text on evolution see Thomas T. Martin, *Hell and the High Schools* (Western Baptist Publishing, 1923). For secondary sources on Martin see Thomas J. Nettles, *The Baptists* (Christian Focus, 2007), 3:181–87; and Willard B. Gatewood Jr., *Preachers, Pedagogues, & Politicians: The Evolution Controversy in North Carolina: 1920–1927* (University of North Carolina Press, 1966), 30–37, 189–196. For Martin's articles against Poteat see Thomas T. Martin, "The Three Fatal Teachings of President Poteat of Wake Forest College," *Western Recorder*, January 22, 1920; February 5, 1920; February 12, 1920. They were later published together with a few external responses to his articles as Martin, *Three Fatal Teachings*. The first two "fatal teachings" that Martin addressed related to the atonement, and the third addressed evolution. For secondary sources see Gatewood, *Preachers, Pedagogues, & Politicians*, 27–38, and Hall, *William Louis Poteat*, 129–140. Gatewood called this the beginning of the fundamentalist-modernist controversy in North Carolina. Gatewood, *Preachers, Pedagogues, & Politicians*, 30.

111. The address set forth a broadly liberal view of soteriology and corresponding doctrines, but Martin took aim at the atonement and evolution. See Martin, *Three Fatal Teachings*, 18–31.

112. One North Carolinian from Asheville, Inez J. Woodall, said in 1920, "I came into the state at about the time of Dr. Poteat's declaration at Richmond and have heard the rumblings of discontent in the camp ever since, but never have I heard any one express any adverse criticism of him personally." This level of restraint generally characterized denominational life in this period. Progressive leaders had substantial leeway during these years until the 1920s and the rise of the fundamentalist-modernist controversy, which affected the South much the same as it did the North. For the fundamentalist-modernist controversy among Northern Baptists see Jeffrey P. Straub, *The Making of a Battle Royal: The Rise of Liberalism in Northern Baptist Life, 1870–1920* (Pickwick, 2018). For the controversy in the South see James J. Thompson Jr., *Tried as by Fire: Southern Baptists and the Religious Controversies of the 1920s* (Mercer University Press, 1982). For a broader survey see Martin Marty, *Modern American Religion*, vol. 2, *The Noise of Conflict, 1919–1941* (University of Chicago Press, 1991), 155–205.

113. King's role receded into the background as Martin led the public challenge. In fact King's early role became largely unknown as the controversy advanced. For instance George Paschal seemed unaware that it was King who initially printed and circulated Poteat's address. See Paschal's response to Martin's articles: *Three Fatal Teachings*, 8–9.

114. Martin, *Three Fatal Teachings*, 18.

115. Martin, *Three Fatal Teachings*, 19–20. See also Poteat, "Wherein Lies the Efficacy of Jesus' Work in the Reconciliation?," 102–3.

116. Martin, *Three Fatal Teachings*, 7. Willard Gatewood argued that Poteat "drew heavily from the theology of Horace Bushnell," which is likely but not entirely clear. See Gatewood, *Preachers, Pedagogues, & Politicians*, 32. For sources on Bushnell see Robert B. Mullin, *The Puritan as Yankee: A Life of Horace Bushnell* (Eerdmans, 2002); and Dorrien, *The Making of American Liberal Theology: Reimagining Progressive Religion, 1805–1900*, 143–48.

117. Martin, *Three Fatal Teachings*, 20. Martin contended, "Everybody knows that these views do come from Chicago University." Martin, *Three Fatal Teachings*, 13. Martin concluded, "Chicago University is the hope of German evolution. Germanizing American education and theology and Wake Forest through President Poteat, is the hope of Chicago University ever permeating the South with the same teachings." Martin, *Three Fatal Teachings*, 30.

118. Martin, *Three Fatal Teachings*, 13.

119. Martin, *Three Fatal Teachings*, 14. Martin cited John 8:42 and John 1:12.

120. Poteat, "Wherein Lies the Efficacy of Jesus' Work in the Reconciliation?," 97. Poteat argued that the only matter of urgency was revising Christianity for the modern world: "There is urgent need of a 'revised version,' which will in no wise modify the content of Christian truth, or relax the strenuousness of the Christian demand, but set forth both in terms intelligible to our day."

121. Gatewood, *Preachers, Pedagogues, & Politicians*, 33.

122. Martin, *Three Fatal Teachings*, 5. For the letter's original publication see William L. Poteat, Letter, *Biblical Recorder* 85 (February 11, 1920), 6.

123. Martin, *Three Fatal Teachings*, 5.

124. Poteat argued that religious experience, spirituality, and morality were the essentials of the Christian religion and not a body of doctrines.

125. When Martin first wrote in January of 1920 he could say, "It has been the hope of some that [Poteat] would repudiate the teachings of that document, but during these years there has never been one word of repudiation." Furthermore Martin noted that within the last five years, Poteat had advanced the same theology in an address at Southwestern Baptist Theological Seminary and to the extent that "President Scarborough of the seminary felt compelled to repudiate [Poteat's views]." See Martin, *Three Fatal Teachings*, 12, 18. For defenses of Poteat see Martin, *Three Fatal Teachings*, 3–5, 8–12. After claims that Poteat no longer held such views Martin said, "Its teachings are what I have written about, not about President Poteat's present views." Martin, *Three Fatal Teachings*, 13. However neither Johnson nor Paschal offered any evidence that Poteat had indeed changed his views, and evidently he had not.

126. Poteat, *Can a Man Be a Christian To-day?*, 55–56.

127. Dorrien noted that after Horace Bushnell liberal theologians widely rejected objective theories of the atonement for the subject moral influence theory. Gary Dorrien, *The Making of American Liberal Theology: Imagining Progressive Religion, 1805–1900*, 400.

128. Poteat, *The Way of Victory*, 32.

129. Poteat, *The Way of Victory*, 34.

130. Nettles, *The Baptists*, 3:147–148.

131. Nettles, *The Baptists*, 3:188. Nettles cited William L. Poteat, *Laboratory and Pulpit: The Relation of Biology to the Preacher and His Message; The Gay Lectures, 1900* (Griffith and Rowland Press, 1901), 44.

132. For a secondary source on Albrecht Ritschl's Christology and atonement theology see Olson's *Journey of Modern Theology*,154–57. For the key primary source see Ritschl, *The Christian Doctrine of Justification and Reconciliation*. See for instance Ritschl, *The Christian Doctrine of Justification and Reconciliation*, 13.

133. Vanhoozer, "Atonement," *Mapping Modern Theology*, 179.

134. Gary Dorrien, *The Making of American Liberal Theology: Imagining Progressive Religion, 1805–1900* (Westminster John Knox, 2001), 399. Dorrien explained that liberals "began with the Calvinist doctrines of human nature, atonement, and divine predestination, which for them failed the moral test."

CHAPTER 6: AN IMPREGNABLE LEADERSHIP

1. Edwin Mims, *The Advancing South: Stories of Progress and Reaction* (Doubleday, Page, and Co., 1926), vii–viii.

2. Gerald Johnson in the foreword to Suzanne C. Linder, *William Louis Poteat: Prophet of Progress* (University of North Carolina Press, 1966), viii.

3. King's and Martin's attacks were initially based on an article from 1900 in which Poteat advocated the moral theory of the atonement. See William L. Poteat, "Wherein Lies the Efficacy of Jesus' Work in the Reconciliation?," in *Proceedings of the Baptist Congress: Eighteenth Annual Session* (Baptist Congress, 1900), 101. For Martin's articles against Poteat see Thomas T. Martin, "The Three Fatal Teachings of President Poteat of Wake Forest College," *Western Recorder*, January 22, 1920; February 5, 1920; February 12, 1920. They were later published together along with a few external responses to his articles as Martin, *Three Fatal Teachings*. The first two "fatal teachings" that Martin addressed related

to the atonement, and the third addressed evolution. For secondary sources see Gatewood, *Preachers, Pedagogues, & Politicians*, 27–38, and Hall, *William Louis Poteat*, 129–40.

4. For sources that demonstrate Poteat's longtime advocacy of evolution see Poteat, "The Effect on the College Curriculum of the Introduction of the Natural Sciences," *Science* 21 (March 31, 1893), 170–72; and Poteat, "Lucretius and the Evolution Idea," *Popular Science Monthly* 60 (December 1901), 166–72. Poteat became convinced of evolutionary science in the 1880s as a young professor at Wake Forest. See William L. Poteat, "An Intellectual Adventure: A Human Document," *American Scholar* 5, no. 3 (Summer 1936): 280–86. For a secondary source see Gatewood, *Preachers, Pedagogues, & Politicians*, 33.

5. This article was originally published in New York's *Watchman-Examiner.* It was reprinted by Livingston Johnson, editor of the *Biblical Recorder*. See William L. Poteat, "Was Paul an Evolutionist?" *Biblical Recorder*, March 8, 1922.

6. Poteat, "Was Paul an Evolutionist?" *Biblical Recorder*, March 8, 1922.

7. J. J. Taylor, "Was Paul and Evolutionist?" *Biblical Recorder*, April 5, 1922.

8. Hall, *William Louis Poteat*, 140.

9. Taylor, "Was Paul an Evolutionist?" *Biblical Recorder*, April 5, 1922.

10. See Gatewood, *Preachers, Pedagogues, & Politicians*, 61–63.

11. Robert H. Spiro, "Can the Evolutionist Be a Christian?" *Biblical Recorder*, May 10, 1922.

12. Thompson, *Tried as By Fire*, 106–9.

13. W. J. Berryman, "Was Paul an Evolutionist?" *Biblical Recorder*, April 19, 1922.

14. William L. Poteat, "Evolution," *Biblical Recorder*, April 19, 1922.

15. Poteat, "Evolution," *Biblical Recorder*, April 19, 1922. Poteat did acknowledge that scientists continued to debate the precise details of exactly how evolution occurred, but they were overwhelmingly in agreement that the general ideas of the theory were sound.

16. William L. Poteat, "May a Christian Be an Evolutionist?" *Biblical Recorder*, April 26, 1922.

17. For a source on the question of evolution at Princeton University and the cautious but open spirit of Charles Hodge and other professors see Bradley J. Gundlach, *Process and Providence: The Evolution Question at Princeton, 1845–1929* (Eerdmans, 2013).

18. For sources that explore Strong's careerlong wrestling with modern questions while aiming to remain orthodox see Grant Wacker, *Augustus H. Strong and the Dilemma of Historical Consciousness* (1985; repr., Baylor University, 2018); and John Aloisi, *Augustus Hopkins Strong and the Struggle to Reconcile Christian Theology with Modern Thought* (University of Rochester Press, 2021).

19. Poteat, "Evolution," *Biblical Recorder*, April 26, 1922.

20. Randal Hall rightly drew out the theme of democratic localism and leadership by the elite in this controversy: "The worldviews of democratic localism and specialized professionalism clashed repeatedly as the fight to end liberal heresy among Baptist educators continued." Hall, *William Louis Poteat*, 141.

21. D. F. King, "Will North Carolina Baptists Stand for the Teaching of Evolution at Wake Forest College?" *Biblical Recorder*, May 17, 1922.

22. King, "Will North Carolina Baptists Stand for Teaching of Evolution at Wake Forest College?" *Biblical Recorder*, May 17, 1922.

23. For the activity of the conservative movement leading up to the convention see Hall, *William Louis Poteat*, 143–44.

24. Bernard W. Spilman, "Dr. Poteat and His Teaching," *Biblical Recorder*, May 10, 1922. Spilman later presided over the convention in December 1922 and also submitted the Spilman resolution at the 1925 convention.

25. "Intolerance," *Old Gold and Black*, April 21, 1922.

26. "A Fight Which Must Be Made in the Open," *Raleigh Times*, April 25, 1922.

27. "Wake Forest True to Fundamentals," *Biblical Recorder*, May 31, 1922. For a secondary source on Poteat's meeting with Wake Forest trustees see Hall, *William Louis Poteat*, 143.

28. *Annual of the Baptist State Convention of North Carolina, 1922*, 12. The convention met at Winston-Salem, December 12 through 15.

29. Poteat, "Christianity and Enlightenment," 1.

30. Poteat, "Christianity and Enlightenment," 8.

31. *Annual of the Baptist State Convention of North Carolina, 1922*, 32. Richard T. Vann made a motion that the convention publish his address, and the motion carried.

32. Hall, *William Louis Poteat*, 144–45.

33. Hall, *William Louis Poteat*, 145.

34. Edwin M. Poteat to William L. Poteat, March 4, 1923, Poteat Papers, box 10, folder 1163, Z. Smith Reynolds Library Archives, Wake Forest University, Winston-Salem, NC.

35. Hall, *William Louis Poteat*, 149. I explore the political battles related to the teaching of evolution in North Carolina in chapter 7.

36. Charles H. Bluske to William L. Poteat, September 17, 1925, Poteat Papers, box 6. Bluske said, "This must be taken up within 30 days, or I will publish this letter and show you up as a 'bluffer.'" In addition to his challenge, Bluske spent five pages to critique the theory of evolution with an argument based on the laws of nature.

37. See Gerald W. Johnson, "Men Are Fighting Over Baggage," *Alumni Review*, June 1925, Clipping, Poteat Papers, box 5. For the best secondary source on Johnson see Vincent Fitzpatrick, *Gerald W. Johnson: From Southern Liberal to National Conscience* (Louisiana State University Press, 2002).

38. Johnson, "Men Are Fighting Over Baggage."

39. Johnson, "Men Are Fighting Over Baggage." For Poteat's statements see Poteat, *Can a Man Be a Christian To-day?*, 35–36, 59–62.

40. Editorial, "Dr. Poteat Retains Leadership," *Winston-Salem Journal*, June 5, 1925, Clipping, Poteat Papers, box 6. For an article on Poteat's resolve to withstand his opposition see "Poteat Declares He'll Not Resign," *Savannah Morning News*, Savannah, GA, November 19, 1925, Clipping, Poteat Papers, box 6.

41. "Evolution and Naming of Trustees to Be Discussed by Baptists in Charlotte," *Charlotte Observer*, November 17, 1925, Clipping, Poteat Papers, box 6. Barrett said, "It will bring or tend to bring the institutions closer to the people; it will make it impossible for these institutions to ever get out of the hands of the Baptists of North Carolina."

42. W. C. Barrett, "Barrett Resolution," *Biblical Recorder*, November 11, 1925. In his article Barrett was exploring the current state of Baptist ownership of its institutions and directing a way forward.

43. "Baptists 1200 Strong Are Expected at Convention Here," *Charlotte Observer*, October 12, 1925.

44. "Baptists, 1200, Strong Are Expected at Convention Here," *Charlotte Observer*, October 12, 1925. See also "Barrett Resolution Would Oust Wake Forest President,"

Charlotte Observer, October 17, 1925, Clipping, Poteat Papers, box 6. If Poteat did not resign immediately conservatives hoped that gradual changes within the board over time would lead to conservative leadership.

45. "Baptists, 1200, Strong Are Expected at Convention Here," *Charlotte Observer*, October 12, 1925, Clipping, Poteat Papers, box 6.

46. Although the convention did not reach the 1200 to 1500 members predicted in the *Charlotte Observer*, the one thousand messengers who did attend broke all previous records. See *Annual of the Baptist State Convention of North Carolina, 1925*, 47, James P. Boyce Library Archives, Southern Baptist Theological Seminary, Louisville, KY.

47. See Rom. 5:12–21 and 1 Cor. 15:22, 45.

48. Theologians have emphasized the interrelatedness of the various doctrinal loci. One theologian has used the analogy of theology as a fabric with many interwoven parts. See Richard Lints, *The Fabric of Theology: A Prolegomenon to Evangelical Theology* (Eerdmans, 1993).

49. *Annual of the Baptist State Convention of North Carolina, 1925*. The convention met from November 17 to 19. For the Bateman resolution see *Annual of the Baptist State Convention of North Carolina, 1925*, 28–30.

50. William L. Poteat, "Alumni Banquet Address," November 18, 1925, Manuscript, Poteat Papers, box 7, folder 746.

51. *Annual of the Baptist State Convention of North Carolina, 1925*, 31.

52. "Baptist Convention Adopts Barrett Resolution without Debate," *Charlotte News and Observer*, November 19, 1925, Clipping, Poteat Papers, box 6.

53. *Annual of the Baptist State Convention of North Carolina, 1925*, 31–32.

54. S. F. Conrad, "Did the Anti-Evolution Forces Win or Lose in the Action of the Baptist Convention?," Editorial, *Charlotte Observer*, November 23, 1925, Clipping, Poteat Papers, box 6. The author concluded that the convention was a complete victory for conservatives.

55. Hall, *William Louis Poteat*, 154.

56. The *Raleigh Times* declared that the convention was not nearly as exciting as many had expected, but the editor claimed that he had predicted that this would be the case. See "Baptists Convention Dodged Issues," *Raleigh Times*, December 1, 1925, Clipping, Poteat Papers, box 6.

57. "Baptists Convention Dodged Issues," *Raleigh Times*, December 1, 1925. The editorial also appeared in the *Greensboro Daily News*. See Jno. W. Kurfrees, "Baptist Convention Retrospect," December 1, 1925, Clipping, Poteat Papers, box 6.

58. S. F. Conrad, "Did the Anti-Evolution Forces Win or Lose in the Action of the Baptist Convention?" Editorial, *Charlotte Observer*, November 23, 1925.

59. Hall, *William Louis Poteat*, 156.

60. Mims, *The Advancing South*, 16.

61. Editorial, "Dr. Poteat Retains Leadership," *Winston-Salem Journal*, June 5, 1925, Clipping, Poteat Papers, box 6.

62. Gerald W. Johnson, "Carolina's 'Fort Douaumont,'" *Greensboro Daily News*, May 16, 1926. For Johnson's praise of Poteat's leadership and influence see Gerald W. Johnson, "Billy with the Red Necktie," *Virginia Quarterly Review*, 19 (Autumn 1943); and Gerald W. Johnson, "'The Future and Dr. Poteat': Memorial Address at the Wake Forest College Commencement," *Biblical Recorder*, June 29, 1938.

63. Hall, *William Louis Poteat*, 130.

64. Article, "Dr. Poteat Retires as Head of Wake Forest College," *Twin City Sentinel,* Winston-Salem, NC, June 2, 1927, Clipping, Poteat Papers, box 6. See also "Dr. W. L. Poteat, Scientist and Christian," *The Record*, Greensboro, NC, June 2, 1927, Clipping, Poteat Papers, box 6. The *New York Times* also noted Poteat's retirement. See "Liberal Advance," *New York Times*, June 6, 1927, Clipping, Poteat Papers, box 6.

65. For Poteat's social work in the years after his retirement see Hall, *William Louis Poteat*, 157–94. For the impact of Progressivism in the South see Dewey W. Grantham, *Southern Progressivism: The Reconciliation of Progress and Tradition* (University of Tennessee Press, 1983), and William A. Link, *The Paradox of Southern Progressivism, 1880–1930* (University of North Carolina Press, 1992).

66. *Annual of the Baptist State Convention of North Carolina, 1936–1937*, James P. Boyce Library Archives, Southern Baptist Theological Seminary, Louisville, KY.

CHAPTER SEVEN: A SOUTHERN PROPHET OF EVOLUTION

1. By 1900 paternalistic elitism was a Southern tradition. For the best source on this history see C. Vann Woodward, *The Origins of the New South, 1877–1913* (1951; reprint, 1971). For the elite's lack of trust for broad democracy see Woodward, *The Origins of the New South,* 51–55. For the redeemers' efforts toward oligarchy see Woodward, *The Origins of the New South,* 55–59. Woodward argued that the redeemers established the political foundations of the modern South. Woodward, *The Origins of the New South,* 22. For the same impulse in Southern Progressivism see William A. Link, *The Paradox of Southern Progressivism* (University of North Carolina Press, 1992). Link argued, "Most reformers expressed what can be described as, at best, uneasiness with majoritarian democracy" Link, *The Paradox of Southern Progressivism,* 58–59. Southern Populism was a related but somewhat separated movement that historians have largely confined to 1880 to 1900. Essentially political it consisted of an alternative vision to that of the New South boosters like Henry Grady. For sources on Southern Populism see James M. Beeby, ed. *Populism in the South Revisited* (University of Mississippi Press, 2012). For Populism in North Carolina see James M. Beeby, "'Equal Rights to All and Special Privileges to None': Grassroots Populism in North Carolina," *North Carolina Historical Review* 78, no. 2 (April 2001): 156–86. For a broader history of Populism in America see Charles Postel, *The Populist Vision* (Oxford University Press, 2009).

2. Randal L. Hall, *William Louis Poteat: A Leader of the Progressive-Era South* (University of Kentucky, 2000), 4.

3. Hall, *William Louis Poteat,* 155–56.

4. J. P. Huskins, "America Is Nation of Eighth Graders, Dr. Poteat Asserts," *Greensboro Daily News*, May 28, 1932, Clipping, Poteat Papers, box 7, Z. Smith Reynolds Library Archives, Wake Forest University, Winston-Salem, NC.

5. Huskins, "America Is Nation of Eighth Graders, Dr. Poteat Asserts," *Greensboro Daily News*, May 28, 1932.

6. William L. Poteat, "Liberty and Restraint," March 4, 1927, Manuscript, Poteat Papers, box 8, folder 925.

7. Willard B. Gatewood, *Preachers, Pedagogues, & Politicians: The Evolution Controversy in North Carolina, 1920–1927* (University of North Carolina Press, 1966), 169.

8. Gerald W. Johnson, "Billy with the Red Necktie," *Virginia Quarterly Review* 19, no. 4 (Autumn 1943).

9. Hall, *William Louis Poteat*, 155.

10. William L. Poteat to Edwin M. Poteat, April 7, 1931, Poteat Papers, box 10, folder 1165.

11. For Cash's magnus opus in which he articulated his low estimation of the Southern mind see Wilbur J. Cash, *The Mind of the South* (Alfred A. Knopf, 1941). See also Bruce Clayton, *W. J. Cash: A Life* (Louisiana State University Press, 1991), 90.

12. Poteat used the analogy of tradition as accumulated baggage. A fresh analysis of Christianity by modern men like Poteat demonstrated that it had accumulated unnecessary and increasingly burdensome baggage around itself that had to be removed for Christianity to maintain relevance in the modern world. See William L. Poteat, *Can a Man Be a Christian To-day?* (University of North Carolina Press, 1925). For an example of another liberal see Alfred J. Dickinson of Alabama, who shared Poteat's liberal views and elitist mind-set. See Wayne Flynt, *Alabama Baptists: Southern Baptists in the Heart of Dixie* (University of Alabama Press, 1998), 250–54, 260–62. Dickinson became so removed from the common people that he struggled to relate to them. See John H. Burrows, "The Great Disturber: The Social Philosophy and Theology of Alfred James Dickinson," (MA thesis, Samford University, 1970), 97–98.

13. Gerald W. Johnson, "Billy with the Red Necktie." Woelfkin and Faunce were quintessential members of America's religious class of elites. Cornelius Woelfkin was pastor of the prominent Fifth Avenue Baptist Church in New York City. See Cornelius Woelfkin, *Religion, Thirteen Sermons* (Doubleday, 1928). William Herbert Perry Faunce was Woelfkin's predecessor at Fifth Avenue Baptist before becoming president of Brown University from 1899 to 1929, as well as a lecturer at Yale and the University of Chicago. See Brown University Office of the President, "William Herbert Perry Faunce, 1899–1929," Brown University, https://www.brown.edu/about/administration/president/people/past-presidents/william-herbert-perry-faunce-1899–1929 [accessed July 8, 2023].

14. "The Struggle for Truth," *Durham Morning Herald*, no date, Clipping, Poteat Papers, box 6. Although the article is not dated, it was likely published in 1922 or 1925, when Poteat was under the most pressure from conservative members of his denomination.

15. "The Struggle for Truth," *Durham Morning Herald*, no date, Clipping, Poteat Papers, box 6.

16. Dabney, *Liberalism in the South*, 190.

17. Mims, *The Advancing South*, 279.

18. Poteat, Diary, June 8, 1896, Poteat Papers, box 4, folder 475.

19. William L. Poteat to William P. McCorkle, November 23, 1931, Poteat Papers, box 3.

20. William L. Poteat, *Youth and Culture* (Wake Forest College, 1938), 150.

21. Mims, *The Advancing South*, 309–10. Mims was particularly referring to the concluding section of Poteat's work, in which Poteat exhorted his listeners to hold onto spirituality and faith. He said, "Dare to look into the any dark recess, to walk on any far-looking crest in God's universe, for you will find Him everywhere in proportion to the penetration and range of your vision. If a ray of the infinite effulgence dazzles you into confusion and fear lest the light be darkness, hold fast your confidence, and you will come to see it melt in a white peace into the enveloping sea of light." William L. Poteat, *Can a Man Be a Christian To-day?* (University of North Carolina Press, 1925), 110.

22. Mims, *The Advancing South*, 313.

23. Poteat, "Christianity and Enlightenment," 2.

24. Hall, *William Louis Poteat*, 102.

25. On education in the South see Joseph M. Stetar, "In Search of a Direction: Southern Higher Education after the Civil War," *History of Education Quarterly* 25, no. 3 (Autumn 1985): 341–67. For American education broadly see Thelin, *A History of American Higher Education.*

26. Stetar, "In Search of a Direction: Southern Higher Education after the Civil War," 348.

27. Poteat, *Youth and Culture*, 139. For an example of the character values that Poteat advocated see Poteat, "Culture and Restraint," in *Youth and Culture*, 140–41.

28. Hall, *William Louis Poteat*, 70.

29. Poteat, Diary, June 8, 1896, Poteat Papers, box 4, folders 475. Kerfoot was also a kind of rival to the seminary's president William H. Whitsitt, whom Poteat supported during a controversy that eventually led to Whitsitt's resignation from the seminary. For Kerfoot's rivalry with Whitsitt see Gregory A. Wills, *Southern Baptist Theological Seminary, 1859–2009* (Oxford University Press, 2009), 190–92. For Poteat's support of Whitsitt see Poteat, Diary, May 10, 1896, Poteat Papers, box 4, folder 475, and Poteat, Diary, May 23, 1896. For background on Kerfoot see Wills, *Southern Baptist Theological Seminary, 1859–2009*, 165–66, 220–21.

30. Poteat, Diary, June 8, 1896, Poteat Papers, box 4, folders 475.

31. See Hall, *William Louis Poteat*, 31. Poteat opposed the election of James C. Blasingame to Meredith College in 1899. Hall cited a diary that is in the private possession of the Poteat family. The entry was from March 18, 1899. Blasingame was elected, but he served for less than a year. See Mary L. Johnson, *A History of Meredith College*, 2nd ed. (Meredith College, 1972), 53.

32. Poteat, *Youth and Culture*, 150. Poteat cited one of his favorite verses, John 10:10, when Jesus said, "I came that they may have life and may have it abundantly."

33. Poteat, *Youth and Culture*, 147. Poteat said this at the commencement address for the class of 1927.

34. Poteat, *Youth and Culture*, 148–49.

35. Poteat, *Youth and Culture*, 139.

36. Poteat, *The New Peace*, 16.

37. Poteat, *The New Peace*, 96.

38. Mims, *The Advancing South*, 316.

39. Randal Hall argued that one "hallmark of the modern mind is a critical spirit, the willingness to test sacred assumptions." Hall, *William Louis Poteat*, 2.

40. Mims, *The Advancing South*, 307.

41. Mims, *The Advancing South*, x. Mims did not consider this a problem. He defined theological liberalism as "the liberal interpretation of religion in light of modern science and criticism."

42. Mims, *The Advancing South*, 124. Mims included a helpful biographical introduction to Johnson as a prominent editor, author, and professor. He highlighted Johnson's "alertness of mind [and his] singular insight into contemporary Southern problems, and a style that marks him as the most promising essayist of the present generation of Southern writers."

43. Poteat, *Youth and Culture*, 131.

44. Johnson, "'The Future and Dr. Poteat': Memorial Address at the Wake Forest College Commencement," *Biblical Recorder*, June 28, 1938.

45. Johnson, "'The Future and Dr. Poteat': Memorial Address at the Wake Forest College Commencement," *Biblical Recorder*, June 28, 1938.

46. Mims, *The Advancing South*, 314.

47. For early examples of Poteat's advocacy of evolution see William L. Poteat, "The Effect on the College Curriculum of the Introduction of the Natural Sciences," *Science* 21 (March 31, 1893): 170–72; and William L. Poteat, "Lucretius and the Evolution Idea," *Popular Science Monthly* 60 (December 1901): 166–72.

48. Wilbur J. Cash, *The Mind of the South* (1941; repr., Alfred A. Knopf, 1978), 321.

49. "Teaching in Southern Baptist Schools," *Biblical Recorder*, February 22, 1922. The paper included a statement from Poteat dated January 23, 1922.

50. Cash, *The Mind of the South*, 321.

51. Poteat, "The Effect on the College Curriculum of the Introduction of the Natural Sciences," *Science* 21 (March 31, 1893): 170.

52. Poteat, "The Effect on the College Curriculum of the Introduction of the Natural Sciences," *Science* 21 (March 31, 1893): 172.

53. Poteat, "Lucretius and the Evolution Idea," *Popular Science Monthly* 60 (December 1901): 166–72.

54. Poteat, "Lucretius and the Evolution Idea," *Popular Science Monthly* 60 (December 1901). Poteat quoted a large section of Lucretius's work *De Rerum Atura*, which indeed contains ideas that are reminiscent of Darwinian natural selection.

55. Poteat, "Lucretius and the Evolution Idea," *Popular Science Monthly* 60 (December 1901). Although as Poteat indicates some ancients theorized in ways that resemble aspects of modern evolutionary theory Poteat seemed to minimize the originality of Darwin's ideas and that of modern biology. For a source on the history of evolution see Peter J. Bowler, *Evolution: The History of an Idea*, new ed. (University of California Press, 2009).

56. Richard T. Vann, "What Have Baptist Colleges to Do with Fundamentalism and Modernism?," Address to Southern Baptist Educational Conference, Memphis, TN, February 4, 1925, 15, James P. Boyce Library and Archives, Southern Baptist Theological Seminary, Louisville, KY.

57. Vann, "What Have Baptist Colleges to do with Fundamentalism and Modernism?, 15.

58. Vann, "What Have Baptist Colleges to do with Fundamentalism and Modernism?," 16–17.

59. Poteat, *The New Peace*, 160.

60. Poteat frequently cited Huxley. See, for example, William L. Poteat, *The New Peace: Lectures on Science and Religion* (Gorham, 1915), as well as Poteat, "The Effect on the College Curriculum of the Introduction of the Natural Sciences," *Science* 21 (March 31, 1893): 171; Poteat, "Lucretius and the Evolution Idea," *Popular Science Monthly* 60 (December 1901); and William L. Poteat, *Laboratory and Pulpit: The Relation of Biology to the Preacher and His Message* (Griffith & Rowland, 1901), 67.

61. For a secondary source see Paul White, *Thomas Huxley: Making the "Man of Science"* (Cambridge University Press, 2003). White demonstrated that Huxley was reluctant to use the term "scientist" because of its utilitarian connotations and preferred to call himself a "man of science," which envisioned a person of "broad learning and moral gravity, capable of pronouncing on matters of general interest." See White, *Thomas Huxley: Making*

the "Man of Science," 1–2. White demonstrated the great influence that Huxley had on the scientific profession as he led away from the older model of the gentleman scientist and "fundamentally [reshaped] the social world of Victorian natural history even within the scientific community itself." Huxley employed Charles Darwin as the model man of science, and he promoted an image of Darwin as an industrious, objective researcher and man of genius who also personified the ideal of Victorian domesticity. See White, *Thomas Huxley: Making the "Man of Science,"* 32–66.

62. See White, *Thomas Huxley: Making the "Man of Science,"* 67–81. For the best sources on the movement to popularize Darwinism as a part the broader movement for advancing science see Bernard Lightman, *Victorian Popularizers of Science: Designing Nature for New Audiences* (University of Chicago Press, 2007); and Gowan Dawson and Bernard Lightman, ed. *Victorian Scientific Naturalism: Community, Identity, Continuity* (University of Chicago Press, 2014).

63. Poteat, *Laboratory and Pulpit*, 67.

64. The 1925 John Calvin McNair Lectures at the University of North Carolina were published as *Can a Man Be a Christian To-day?*.

65. Poteat, *Can a Man Be a Christian To-day?*, 73.

66. Poteat, *Can a Man Be a Christian To-day?*, 75.

67. "Pastor Believers Science Has Found God's Process," *Evening Tribune-Times*, Uniontown, PA, July 22, 1925. Clark was pastor of First Baptist Church, Uniontown, Pennsylvania, near the border with West Virginia.

68. Poteat, *Can a Man Be a Christian To-day?*, 76.

69. Poteat, *Can a Man Be a Christian To-day?*, 76.

70. Gary Dorrien, *The Making of American Liberal Theology: Imagining Progressive Religion, 1805–1900* (Westminster John Knox, 2001), 402.

71. Poteat, *Can a Man Be a Christian To-day?*, 77–79.

72. "The Poole Bill," *Biblical Recorder*, Feb 25, 1925.

73. For sources on the political debates related to evolution see Michael Liensch, *In the Beginning: Fundamentalism, The Scopes Trial, and the Making of the Antievolution Movement* (University of North Carolina Press, 2007); Edward J. Larson, *Trial and Error: The American Controversy over Creation and Evolution*, 3rd ed. (Oxford University Press, 2003); Edward J. Larson, *Summer for the Gods: The Scopes Trial and America's Continuing Debate over Science and Religion* (Basic Books, 1997); and George E. Webb, *The Evolution Controversy in America* (University of Kentucky Press, 1994).

74. Gatewood, *Preachers, Pedagogues, & Politicians*, 124–25.

75. Suzanne C. Linder, "William Louis Poteat and the Evolution Controversy," *North Carolina Historical Review* 40, no. 2 (Spring 1963): 142.

76. Hall, *William Louis Poteat*, 147–48.

77. For secondary sources see Hall, *William Louis Poteat*, 148; and Gatewood, *Preachers, Pedagogues, & Politicians*, 125. For the Poole bill see *The North Carolina Manual, 1927* (North Carolina Historical Commission). For D. Scott Poole see *The North Carolina Manual, 1927*, 547–48; and "D. S. Poole Dies at 96," *News and Observer*, Raleigh, NC, April 21, 1955.

78. North Carolina General Assembly, "Joint Resolution Restricting the Teaching of Darwinism in the Public Schools of North Carolina," 1925, in William A. Link, *North Carolina: Change and Tradition in a Southern State*, 2nd ed. (Wiley Blackwell, 2018), 400–401. Poole was a committed Presbyterian church member, and Southern Presbyterians became

key proponents of Poole's bill. They also became leaders in the anti-evolution movement in North Carolina. For Poole's religious commitments see D. Scott Poole, "Why the Opposition," *Carolina Magazine* 57 (October 1926):19–20. See also "D. S. Poole Dies at 96," *News and Observer*, Raleigh, NC, April 21, 1955, and Gatewood, *Preachers, Pedagogues, & Politicians*, 124–26. For Southern Presbyterianism in this period see Sean M. Lucas, *For a Continuing Church: The Roots of the Presbyterian Church in America* (P&R Publishing, 2015), 1–65.

79. North Carolina General Assembly, "Joint Resolution Restricting the Teaching of Darwinism in the Public Schools of North Carolina," 1925.

80. North Carolina General Assembly, "Joint Resolution Restricting the Teaching of Darwinism in the Public Schools of North Carolina," 1925.

81. D. Scott Poole, "Why the Opposition," *Carolina Magazine* 57 (October 1926):19–20.

82. D. Scott Poole, "Why the Opposition," *Carolina Magazine* 57 (October 1926):19–20.

83. For a history of the University of North Carolina see William D. Snider, *Light on the Hill: A History of the University of North Carolina at Chapel Hill* (University of North Carolina Press, 1992).

84. Link, *North Carolina: Change and Tradition in a Southern State*, 361.

85. North Carolina State College also sent representatives to the House Committee on Education debate in 1925, namely two members of the science faculty. But other schools like North Carolina College for Women and smaller state-supported schools in Boone and Greenville did not address the bill publicly. At Wake Forest, a private institution, Poteat declined any active role in the debates. See Gatewood, *Preachers, Pedagogues, & Politicians*, 128–29.

86. For the university's efforts against the Poole bill see Gatewood, *Preachers, Pedagogues, & Politicians*, 132–47. For a contemporary account of Chase's leadership at the University of North Carolina and his role in the anti-evolution conflict see Mims, *The Advancing South*, 135–39.

87. "Anti-Evolution Bills Fails of Committee O.K.," *Charlotte Observer*, February 11, 1925.

88. The tale of Galileo's persecution at the hands of Roman Catholics is legendary. The claim that Galileo was condemned, tortured, and imprisoned by the Roman Church has been disproved by historians. For the best source on this and other myths about the conflict between science and religion see Ronald L. Numbers, ed., *Galileo Goes to Jail and Other Myths about Science and Religion* (Harvard University Press, 2009), 68–78. Maurice A. Finocchiaro concluded, "The myths of Galileo's torture and imprisonment are thus genuine myths: ideas that are in fact false but once seemed true—and continue to be accepted as true by poorly educated persons and careless scholars." Numbers, ed., *Galileo Goes to Jail and Other Myths about Science and Religion*, 78. John Draper and Andrew D. White were important purveyors of this myth. For another source that demonstrates its discrediting see John H. Brooke, *Science and Religion* (Cambridge University Press, 1991).

89. "Anti-Evolution Bills Fails of Committee O.K.," *Charlotte Observer*, February 11, 1925.

90. James R. Pentuff, "Dr. Pentuff on Poole Bill," *Biblical Recorder*, March 4, 1925. Pentuff also challenged the science behind evolution, particularly singling out the "missing links." See Linder, *William Louis Poteat*, 132.

91. For the argument in the context of Christian education see Thomas T. Martin and D. F. King, in Thomas T. Martin, *Three Fatal Teachings* (n.p., 1920).

92. Harry W. Chase to William L. Poteat, February 16, 1925, Harry Woodburn Chase Papers, 1911–1956, Southern Historical Collection, Louis Round Wilson Special Collections Library, University of North Carolina, Chapel Hill. See also Gatewood, *Preachers, Pedagogues, & Politicians,* 129–30. Gatewood explained that Chase "assumed Poteat's mantle at a critical moment."

93. Mims, *The Advancing South,* 139.

94. Frank P. Graham, "Evolution, the University and the People," *Alumni Review* 13 (1924–25): 205–7. For the best secondary source on Graham see Warren Ashby, *Frank Porter Graham: A Southern Liberal* (John F. Blair Publishing, 1980).

95. Graham, "Evolution, the University and the People," *Alumni Review* 13 (1924–25): 205–7.

96. The committee initially voted seventeen to seventeen before Connor's tie-breaking vote against it. See "The Pool [*sic*] Bill" *Biblical Recorder*, February 18, 1925; and "Poole Bill Up in House Tonight," *News and Observer*, February 17, 1925, Clipping, Poteat Papers, box 6. For detailed coverage of the proceedings see Gatewood, *Preachers, Pedagogues, & Politicians,* 124–47.

97. "The Poole Bill," *Biblical Recorder*, February 25, 1925. Willard Gatewood rightly noted that Vann was "former president of Meredith College and a Baptist leader whose influence in North Carolina was probably second only to that of Poteat himself." See Gatewood, *Preachers, Pedagogues, & Politicians*, 69.

98. "The Poole Bill," *Biblical Recorder*, February 25, 1925.

99. Some of the more aggressive opponents of the Poole bill likewise opposed the Connor bill. Harry Chase opposed it because of what he considered vague language that could potentially play into the hands of anti-evolutionists. See Gatewood, *Preachers, Pedagogues, & Politicians*, 144.

100. Link, *North Carolina: Change and Tradition in a Southern State*, 361.

101. Gatewood, *Preachers, Pedagogues, & Politicians*, 134–36, 146–47. Gatewood demonstrated that all of the seven most influential newspapers in North Carolina except the *Charlotte Observer* had opposed the Poole bill and welcomed its defeat.

102. Mims, *The Advancing South*, 139.

103. For the best detailed account of events after the first Poole bill see Gatewood, *Preachers, Pedagogues, & Politicians*, 148–78. Gatewood argued that the "failure of the anti-evolution bill in the legislature of 1925 only served to enhance the drive for some means of thwarting the spread of 'infidelity' on the University campus." See Gatewood, *Preachers, Pedagogues, & Politicians*, 180.

104. North Carolina General Assembly, "A Bill to be Entitled an Act to Prohibit the Teaching of Evolution in Certain Schools and Colleges in the State of North Carolina," 1927, in William A. Link, *North Carolina: Change and Tradition in a Southern State*, 2nd ed. (Wiley Blackwell, 2018), 406–7.

105. Gatewood, *Preachers, Pedagogues, & Politicians*, 158–61, 201.

106. Link, *North Carolina: Change and Tradition in a Southern State*, 361.

107. For the role of Martin and other outside organizers see Gatewood, *Preachers, Pedagogues, & Politicians*, 184–201. Martin was heavily involved in the religious debates among Baptists while also actively organizing against evolution within North Carolina politics. And his aggressive style and sensationalism, along with that of other traveling

evangelists, seemed to have alienated some common North Carolinians over time. Gatewood insightfully noted that after 1925 Martin made no direct attacks on Poteat and for good reason: "The irony of Martin's decision lay in the fact that he waged war on Poteat from afar for six years, only to abandon it when he arrived in Poteat's own domain. But, undoubtedly, Martin had come to appreciate Poteat's strength in North Carolina and preferred not to jeopardize the success of his new crusade by further entanglements with the Baptist biologist." Gatewood, *Preachers, Pedagogues, & Politicians*, 190.

108. Unknown author, "A Man Who Made It Easier to Think in the South." [1929?], Clipping, Poteat Papers, box 3. Although the article is not dated, internal evidence suggests that it was published in the latter part of the 1920s, shortly after the cessation of these conflicts and after Poteat's 1927 retirement from the presidency of Wake Forest College.

109. George M. Bryan, "Billy Poteat and the 'Watchmen on the Wall,'" *News and Observer*, June 18, 1961, Clipping, Poteat Papers, box 1, folder 1.

110. Bryan, "Billy Poteat and the 'Watchmen on the Wall,'" *News and Observer*, June 18, 1961.

111. Linder, *William Louis Poteat*, 132. Richard T. Vann likewise declined to speak.

112. Hall, *William Louis Poteat*, 148–49.

113. Linder, *William Louis Poteat*, 136.

114. Mims, *The Advancing South*, 308.

CHAPTER EIGHT: RACE AND EUGENICS

1. Social Darwinism was a system of thought that developed in the nineteenth century by drawing social implications from Darwinian evolution. It took the concept of natural selection and human biological evolution and applied social strategies to advance human evolution or to forestall devolution of the human race. Social polices like eugenics and forced institutionalization were strongly informed by social Darwinism. For a source on social Darwinism see Mike Hawkins, *Social Darwinism in European and American Thought* (Cambridge University Press, 1997).

2. For a work that explores Southern paternalism in the Progressive Era see Paul Harvey's "'The Right-Minded Members of That Race': Southern Religious Progressives Confront Race, 1880–1930," *Perspectives in Religious Studies* (Fall 2012). See especially 240–42.

3. For Poteat's detailed account of life at Forest Home see William L. Poteat, "Memories," Diary, 1928, 3, Poteat Papers, box 3, Z. Smith Reynolds Library Archives, Wake Forest University, Winston-Salem, NC.

4. Poteat, "Memories," 7–9, 12. Poteat recalled that Morris's favorite Bible passage was John 3.

5. Poteat, "Memories," 3–4.

6. Poteat, "Memories," 18.

7. William L. Poteat, "Characteristics and Functions of the Educated Person," handwritten notes for commencement address, Poteat Papers, box 8, folder 853. The notes are not dated, but internal evidence suggests that they were for the graduating class of 1896.

8. Poteat, "Memories," 12.

9. For his statement that he saw the abolition of slavery as a result of Christians' application of the kingdom of God to social ethics see William L. Poteat, *The Way of Victory* (University of North Carolina Press, 1929), 47.

10. Poteat, "Memories," 7.

11. Poteat, "Memories," 20. Poteat recorded this visit in a later entry dated June 24, 1930.

12. On the development of the legal tradition of segregation in the 1890s, popularly called Jim Crow see Henry L. Gates, Jr., *Stony the Road: Reconstruction, White Supremacy, and the Rise of Jim Crow* (Penguin Books, 2019).

13. Michael McGerr, *A Fierce Discontent: The Rise and Fall of the Progressive Movement in America, 1870–1920* (Oxford University Press, 2003), 185–87.

14. William A. Link, *The Paradox of Southern Progressivism: 1880–1930* (University of North Carolina Press, 1992), 58–67. See also Link, *The Paradox of Southern Progressivism*, 68–91, 239–67. Link argued, "Few [reformers] favored equality in any sense of the word." See Link, *The Paradox of Southern Progressivism*, 67. For further background on race relations and paternalism in the New South see Don Doyle, *New Men, New Cities, New South*, 260–312. Doyle helpfully defined racial paternalism: "Paternalism, at bottom, operated as an informal agreement between patron and client to fulfill a set of mutual obligations that went beyond the rational, contractual exchanges of the marketplace." See Doyle, *New Men, New Cities, New South*, 295. See also W. E. B. Du Bois, *Black Reconstruction in America: 1860–1880* (1935; repr., The Free Press, 1998), and Eric Foner, *Reconstruction: America's Unfinished Revolution, 1863–1877* (Harper & Row, 1988).

15. William L. Poteat, "Christ and Race," Pamphlet, Address to Baptist State Convention of North Carolina, 1938, Poteat Papers, box 7, folder 742. The address was to the Baptist State Convention, Wilmington, NC, November 17, 1937. See also William L. Poteat, "Christ and Race," audio recording, cassette tape, Poteat Papers, box 7, folder 794.

16. Poteat, "Christ and Race," 1–5.

17. For the best comprehensive history on the Commission on Interracial Cooperation see Ann W. Ellis, "The Commission on Interracial Cooperation, 1919–1944: Its Activities and Results" (PhD diss., Georgia State University, 1975). For Poteat's work with the organization see Hall, *William Louis Poteat*, 91–95, 190–91. For the movement for interracial cooperation see C. Chilton Pearson, "Race Relations in North Carolina: A Field Study in Moderate Opinion," *The South Atlantic Quarterly* 23, no. 1 (January 1924): 1–9.

18. Robert B. Eleazer, "An Adventure in Faith: A Brief History of the Interracial Movement in the South," pamphlet, Commission on Interracial Cooperation, Atlanta, GA, Poteat Papers, box 2.

19. Eleazer claimed that they had conducted courses in hundreds of colleges. Edwin Mims put the amount at sixty when he wrote in 1926. See Mims, *The Advancing South*, 261, and Eleazer, "An Adventure in Faith," 2.

20. Eleazer, "An Adventure in Faith," 3. Mims, *The Advancing South*, 259.

21. Eleazer, "An Adventure in Faith," 1–3. See also "An Announcement by the Commission on Interracial Cooperation Incorporated," 1–5, manuscript, December 1929, Poteat Papers, box 2; and Mims, *The Advancing South*, 258–67.

22. W. C. Jackson to William L. Poteat, October 16, 1928, Poteat Papers, box 2. Jackson was the chair of the organization, based in Greensboro, North Carolina.

23. For Poteat's opposition to the Klan see Hall, *William Louis Poteat*, 95.

24. Randal L. Hall, *William Louis Poteat: A Leader of the Progressive-Era South* (University of Kentucky Press, 2000), 95.

25. Poteat, "Christianity and Enlightenment," 5, pamphlet, Address to North Carolina Baptist State Convention, Winston-Salem, NC, December 13, 1922, James P. Boyce Library Archives, Southern Baptist Theological Seminary, Louisville, KY.

26. Wilbur J. Cash, *The Mind of the South*, (1941; repr., Alfred A. Knopf, 1978), 327.

27. Bruce Clayton, *W. J. Cash: A Life* (University of Louisiana Press, 1991), 136.

28. Harvey, "The Right-Minded Members of that Race," 235.

29. Clayton, *W. J. Cash*, 38.

30. William L. Poteat, "The Negro in the South," notebook entry February 27, 1927, Poteat Papers, box 9, folder 967.

31. Hall, *William Louis Poteat*, 92.

32. For segregation as a means of keeping the peace see McGerr, *A Fierce Discontent*, 183. McGerr rightly argued that "the progressives turned to segregation as a way to halt dangerous social conflict that could not otherwise be stopped. True to their sense of compassion the progressives turned to segregation as a way to preserve weaker groups, such as African-Americans and Native Americans, facing brutality and even annihilation."

33. Poteat, "Christ and Race," 5. See also Eleazer, "An Adventure in Faith," 1.

34. The new Klan's membership swelled into the millions making it one of the most powerful political organizations of the 1920s. Although it began in the South it quickly spread into the Midwest, Western states, and beyond to become a national organization. The Klan employed terror to achieve its political and social ends. For works on the second Klan see William Rawlings, *The Second Coming of the Invisible Empire* (Mercer University Press, 2016); and Nancy MacLean, *Behind the Mask of Chivalry: The Making of the Second Ku Klux Klan* (Oxford University Press, 1995).

35. See Hall, *William Louis Poteat*, 29.

36. William L. Poteat, Diary, November 3–8, 1896, Poteat Papers, box 4, folder 475. For their correspondence see Poteat Papers, box 4. For the best secondary source on Dixon, who was the brother of the fundamentalist minister and Wake Forest alumnus Amzi C. Dixon see Michele K. Gillespie and Randal L. Hall, eds., *Thomas Dixon Jr. and the Birth of Modern America* (Louisiana State University Press, 2006). For Dixon's autobiography see Thomas Dixon Jr., *Southern Horizons: The Autobiography of Thomas Dixon* (IWV Publishing, 1984).

37. For the best source on eugenics see Alison Bashford and Philippa Levine, eds., *The Oxford Handbook of the History of Eugenics* (Oxford University Press, 2010). For sources on the role of liberal Protestants in the eugenics movement see Dennis L. Durst, *Eugenics and Protestant Social Reform: Hereditary Science and Religion in America, 1860–1940* (Pickwick Publications, 2017); and Christine Rosen, *Preaching Eugenics: Religious Leaders and the American Eugenics Movement* (Oxford University Press, 2004). For the American Progressive movement and the spirit of reform see McGerr, *A Fierce Discontent*.

38. Eugene S. Talbot, *Degeneracy: Its Causes, Signs, and Results* (Walter Scott Publishing, 1912), 36. For a secondary source see Durst, *Eugenics and Protestant Social Reform*, 6–17. This reading of evolution favored the pre-Darwinian theory of Jean Baptiste Lamarck over Darwinian natural selection. For a source that explores the role of biological evolution in eugenics see Diane B. Paul and James Moore, "The Darwinian Context: Evolution and Inheritance," in *The Oxford Handbook of the History of Eugenics*, 27–42.

39. Durst argued that eugenics-minded reformers held that both heredity and environment were factors in the progress of degeneration, but they increasingly tended toward greater emphasis upon heredity. See Durst, *Eugenics and Protestant Social Reform*, 4, 12–13.

40. Durst, *Eugenics and Protestant Social Reform*, 16–17.

41. Durst, *Eugenics and Protestant Social Reform,* 3. Durst called Morel "a pioneer in integrating biological explanation of human defectiveness with psychiatry." Durst, *Eugenics and Protestant Social Reform,* 12.

42. Rosen, *Preaching Eugenics*, 7.

43. For a discussion of racist and ethnocentric themes of the eugenics movement see Francis Galton, *Inquiries into Human Faculty and Its Development* (E. P. Dutton, 1908). See also the original version of this work from 1883 in which Galton originally coined the term eugenics: Francis Galton, *Inquiries into Human Faculty and Its Development* (MacMillan, 1883). Poteat twice cited Galton's 1883 work in an address to the Southern Baptist Educational Association. He did so with approval and recognized Galton as the originator of the term eugenics, "the science of race improvement." See William L. Poteat, "The Standard Man: Presidential Address to the Southern Baptist Education Association," *Baptist Education Bulletin,* Birmingham, AL, December 3–5, 1921, Clipping, Poteat Papers, box 9, folder 1085.

44. For the contribution of evolution see Edward D. Cope, *The Origins of the Fittest: Essays on Evolution* (D. Appleton & Co., 1887). See also David Orebaugh, who argued that the rising crime rate in America was due to a degeneration of the purer American stock by mass immigration of inferior races: David A. Orebaugh, *Crime, Degeneracy, and Immigration: Their Interrelations and Interreactions* (Richard G. Badger, 1929). See also William H. Tucker, *The Science and Politics of Racial Research* (University of Illinois Press, 1994), 54–111.

45. Durst, *Eugenics and Protestant Social Reform,* 134–39.

46. Dan R. Frost, *Thinking Confederates: Academia and the Idea of Progress in the New South* (University of Tennessee Press, 2000), 58–59. Many White Southerners believed that after the end of slavery African Americans might eventually disappear. See also Paul M. Gaston, *The New South Creed: A Study in Mythmaking,* new ed. (NewSouth Books, 2002), 124–25.

47. Mims, *The Advancing South*, 243–44.

48. For the best source on the social gospel see Christopher H. Evans, *The Social Gospel in American Religion: A History* (New York University Press, 2017).

49. For the best sources on the interplay of religion in the eugenics movement see Rosen, *Preaching Eugenic;* and Durst, *Eugenics and Protestant Social Reform.* For theologians' appropriation of the foundational ideas of eugenics see Durst, *Eugenics and Protestant Social Reform* 1–2, 157–80. Christine Rosen argued that liberal ministers were predisposed to embrace eugenics. She argued that the loosely defined theology of liberalism seemed almost to be a prerequisite for eugenics advocacy among religious adherents. And Darwinian evolution, a mainstay for liberal thinkers, "made the science of eugenics conceivable." Rosen, *Preaching Eugenics*, 5, 12–15. For a source that explores the connection of Darwinism to eugenics see Paul and Moore, "The Darwinian Context: Evolution and Inheritance," in *The Oxford Handbook of the History of Eugenics*, 27–42. For a source that weaves theological themes with the idea of human degeneration see Augustus H. Strong, "Degeneration," in *Miscellanies,* vol. 2 (Griffith & Rowland, 1912), 110–28. For an example of a scientist using religious themes for eugenics see Charles B. Davenport, *Eugenics as a Religion* (Eugenics Record Office, 1916).

50. Durst, *Eugenics and Protestant Social Reform,* 15–16.

51. Thomas C. Leonard, *Illiberal Reformers: Race, Eugenics, & American Economics in the Progressive Era* (Princeton University Press, 2016), 124.

52. See Durst, *Eugenics and Protestant Social Reform,* 7–10; and Rosen, *Preaching Eugenics*, 8–13.

53. Rosen, *Preaching Eugenics*, 13.

54. Durst, *Eugenics and Protestant Social Reform,* 8.

55. Indiana became the first of the United States to pass legislation for involuntary sterilization in 1907, eventually followed by more than thirty other states. See Paul A. Lombardo, *From the Indiana Experiment to the Human Genome Era* (Indiana University Press, 2011). In 1927 with *Buck v. Bell* the question of eugenics went before the United States Supreme Court. In this case the court considered whether or not Carrie Buck had the right to procreate despite being deemed feebleminded. The court decided against Buck and upheld the state's right of compulsory sterilization. See Paul A. Lombardo, *Three Generations, No Imbeciles: Eugenics, the Supreme Court and Buck v. Bell* (Johns Hopkins University, 2010). See also Randall Hansen and Desmond King, *Sterilized by the State: Eugenics, Race, and the Population Scare in Twentieth-Century North America* (Cambridge University Press, 2013). For eugenics in North Carolina see William A. Link, *North Carolina: Change and Tradition in a Southern State*, 2nd ed. (Wiley-Blackwell, 2018), 355–57.

56. For his most substantial treatments of eugenics see William L. Poteat, "The Influence of Public Health and Education upon the Development of the Human Race," *Southern Medicine and Surgery* 92 (June 1930): 396–99; and William L. Poteat, "The Standard Man: Presidential Address to the Southern Baptist Education Association," *Baptist Education Bulletin,* Birmingham, AL, December 3–5, 1921, Clipping, Poteat Papers, box 9, folder 1085. For the quotation see Poteat, "The Standard Man: Presidential Address to the Southern Baptist Education Association," 7.

57. Hall, *William Louis Poteat*, 99.

58. Link, *North Carolina: Change and Tradition in a Southern State*, 355–57. Only Virginia performed more involuntary sterilizations than North Carolina. Link cited 6,683 involuntary sterilizations in Virginia and 4,472 in North Carolina. Georgia had the third highest with 2,490. Those sterilized in North Carolina were divided into three categories: the feebleminded (71 percent), mentally ill (24 percent), and epileptics (5 percent).

59. Link, *North Carolina: Change and Tradition in a Southern State*, 355.

60. See "Human Sterilization," Pamphlet, The Human Betterment Foundation, Pasadena, CA, Poteat Papers, box 4. For a secondary source see Hall, *William Louis Poteat*, 188.

61. Ezra S. Gosney to William L. Poteat, December 29, 1931, Poteat Papers, box 2, folder 134. See also Ezra S. Gosney to William L. Poteat, December 10, 1931, Poteat Papers, box 2, folder 134.

62. Ezra S. Gosney to William L. Poteat, October 8, 1936, Poteat Papers, box 2, folder 134.

63. "Human Sterilization," 1.

64. "Human Sterilization," 2–3.

65. "Human Sterilization," 5.

66. "Human Sterilization," 6.

67. Poteat, "The Standard Man: Presidential Address to the Southern Baptist Education Association."

68. Poteat, "The Influence of Public Health and Education upon the Development of the Human Race," 396.

69. Poteat, "The Standard Man: Presidential Address to the Southern Baptist Education Association."

70. Poteat, "The Standard Man: Presidential Address to the Southern Baptist Education Association."

71. William L. Poteat to Frank W. Hanft, February 11, 1933, Poteat Papers, box 2, folder 148. For Hanft's initial letter see Frank W. Hanft to William L. Poteat, January 26, 1933, Poteat Papers, box 2, folder 148.

72. E. D. Jones to William L. Poteat, May 25, 1932, Poteat Papers, box 2, folder 198.

73. William L. Poteat, "Memoranda," Diary, 1926, Poteat Papers, box 4.

74. "Human Sterilization," 12.

75. Temperance was one of Poteat's most consuming social concerns. He was a member of the Anti-Saloon League of America, based in Westerville, Ohio. See receipts and correspondence in Poteat Papers, box 1. See also Poteat's well-received work against beverage alcohol, William L. Poteat, *Stop-Light* (Southern Baptist Sunday School Board, 1935). For secondary sources see Hall, *William Louis Poteat*, 95–97, 178–83, and Suzanne C. Linder, *William Louis Poteat: Prophet of Progress* (University of North Carolina Press, 1966), 170–92.

76. See Durst, *Eugenics and Protestant Social Reform,* 113–16.

77. Poteat, "The Standard Man: Presidential Address to the Southern Baptist Education Association."

78. William L. Poteat, "The New Fates and the Web of Destiny," 1–2, Address, typed manuscript, Wake County public schools commencement, April 3, 1914, Poteat Papers, box 9, folder 969. See also Hall, *William Louis Poteat*, 99–100.

79. Poteat, "The Standard Man: Presidential Address to the Southern Baptist Education Association." Two years later he raised the number to 10 percent of the general population. See William L. Poteat, "The Social Significance of Heredity: Presidential Address to the Southern Baptist Education Association," *Baptist Education Bulletin*, Memphis, TN, February 21, 1923, Clipping, Poteat Papers, box 9, folder 1078. The new number agreed with the statistics in the pamphlet "Human Sterilization."

80. Poteat, "The Standard Man: Presidential Address to the Southern Baptist Education Association."

81. Hall, *William Louis Poteat*, 186.

82. William L. Poteat, "Science and Public Affairs," Address, handwritten notes, October 11, 1933, Poteat Papers, box 9, folder 1059.

83. Durst, *Eugenics and Protestant Social Reform,* 36.

84. Rosen, *Preaching Eugenics*, 23.

85. I am dependent on Hall for this insight. See Hall, *William Louis Poteat*, 99.

86. See Leonard, *Illiberal Reformers.*

CONCLUSION

1. William L. Poteat, *Can a Man Be a Christian To-day?* (University of North Carolina Press, 1925), 79.

2. Christian Rosen, *Preaching Eugenics: Religious Leaders and the American Eugenics Movement* (Oxford University Press, 2004), 13.

Index